Secret Frequencies

AMERICAN LIVES
Series editor: Tobias Wolff

For Harry

Acknowledgments

Acknowledgement is made to: *Colorado Review* 23, no. 1 (1996); *Epoch* 16, no. 1 (1997); *TriQuarterly* 90 (fall 1994); and Kodansha America (*The Smoky Mountain Cage Bird Society and Other Magical Tales from Everyday Life*, 1999) for permission to reprint the portions of this book that they originally published, sometimes in different form.

Permission has been obtained to reprint excerpts from the following copyrighted work: "Where Do You Work-A, John?" Words and Music by Charley Marks, Harry Warren and Mortimer Weinberg. Copyright © 1925, 1952 Shapiro, Bernstein & Co., Inc., New York. Copyright Renewed. International Copyright Secured. All Rights Reserved. Used by Permission

Thanks to my friends Robert Boswell, Stephen Dobyns, Judith Grossman, and Chuck Wachtel, and to the staff at the University of Nebraska Press. A grant from Emerson College was of great help to me in the writing of this book. My deepest gratitude to Emilia Dubicki for her friendship and advice.

In some cases names in this book have been changed.

Secret Frequencies

Close Quarters

Primo stuffed his neighbor's talking crow into a paper bag and rode the F train to Coney Island, where he set it free outside Steeplechase Park. A great aunt threw her yappy Spitz off a cliff in Naples. I heard these stories after school, as I sat across from my mother's ironing board while she sprayed and pressed, surrounded by brass crucifixes and cardboard reproductions of the Blue Grotto and *The Last Supper* that bulged in their frames. She touted the virtue of silence as she rambled on, pausing once in a while to ask a question but answering before I could reply. She repeatedly drew the scene of her brothers and sisters clamoring at dinner, how their hearts stopped when their father raised his finger and shouted "Parola!" The word for *word* shut them up. Enthralled by my mother's steamy, zigzagging sentences, I sat silently, afraid to interrupt, a fear that carried over to the street, where I rarely spoke at all in that scrappy part of Queens, its only park bordered on one side by our church, St. Bartholomew's, a hoary mass of river stone, and on the other by the Masonic Temple's slick white marble, each congregation comprised of immigrants suspicious of newer immigrants.

Taxis and buses interrupted the games of boys swinging broom-sticks at tough rubber balls, and radios thumped from parked cars, their drivers yelling for girls to join them on Judge Street, where I lived with my parents and my aunt Linda. This was the same row house my grandmother moved into when she arrived from Italy and married my grandfather at sixteen, raising eight children alone after he died on his job as a roofer, falling off the peak of the National Sugar Refinery onto a railroad car of pig iron. Families personalized their stoops and yards, because every floor was identical: five rooms in a line, so that to reach either end, you had to go through all of them. This felt like walking through Pullman cars, and so the name, "railroad flats." Our small garden held a half-buried vertical bathtub, a homemade shrine housing a statue of St. Jude, Patron of the Impossible.

The Italian families lived next to each other, a geographical coincidence that Irish neighbors referred to as "Squid Row" in disgust at our fried calamari. My first friends were the three Paretti sisters. One evening we invited the Parettis for drinks, and when my father took their orders, I asked, "Can I have a cocktail too?" Our visitors gasped because I was only five, but my mother laughed, explaining that I had ginger ale with grenadine. The Paretti girls were still shocked. "That's not it," one said. "We didn't know he could talk." I didn't know I could talk either. It was easier to be quiet.

Shortly after that, a cousin brought a huge reel-to-reel tape recorder to my grandmother's birthday party. The apartment shook with the cheer of relatives greeting each other, which my teen-age cousin captured. He returned the next week and replayed the laughter, the toasts, the rustle of wrapping paper. When we were alone, he said, "Want to hear a jerk?" and fast-forwarded to a high voice trying to break into the conversation, saying, "Excuse me, excuse me," over and over. It took me a minute to recognize myself. After that, I lowered my scarce voice to a whisper, having acquired a new fear, the fear of being overheard. And a bigger fear, the fear of being a jerk.

All I wanted was to leave Judge Street for college, not to work for the police force, transit authority, or fire department like most everyone else in the neighborhood. I would have been happy to shelve books in the Elmhurst Public Library, where I read ten volumes on canines when I got Major, my dog, or to file documents near the big oak desk of Max Renpack, the lawyer, who wrote letters and walked to the courthouse each day smoking a pipe. Anything but joining the uniformed men who spat and smoked on our corner, early in the day and again every evening, referring to each other as Ski, Limey, Mick, and—for the newly arrived Basque who always wore a beret—Nipple-Head.

As I began the summer before my last year of high school, I drank chamomile tea with my mother at our dining-room table. I was sixteen, it was hot, and I was helping her stuff polyester sleeping bags for kids headed upstate with the Fresh Air Fund. My father, the sales manager of the Atlantic Paper and Envelope Company, had been away for a month to establish a West Coast office. He called the week before, saying it was going well and that he'd likely be away into the fall. These extended trips were common, and in his absence my mother consumed herself with hobbies such as assembling jigsaw puzzles and sewing bed pads for patients at Elmhurst General. To help her keep this regimen, I took the subway to wholesale houses in Brooklyn, lugging home shopping bags of feathers, cotton, and spools of twine.

My arm was deep inside the nylon bag when the phone rang. It was my Uncle Fred, asking me to meet him at Grand Central, his voice yelling above clanking plates and glasses. He had phoned my mother earlier in the week, saying he'd take me to Yankee Stadium. My mother always wished one of her other brothers, Albert, the milkman, or Louie, a mason, would have volunteered when my father was away, but they had families of their own and lived on Long Island. I told her I was going, and she looked up from the long stretch of cloth, brushing hair off her face. She wore a suede jacket bought in Mexico, fringe dangling from the arms, and her name, *Olga*, stitched in red cursive above her heart. She said that Fred had called her several times recently, that he had just gotten divorced and seemed lonely—the reason for his sudden interest in me.

What I knew of Fred told me he would free me from the piecework, as well as the bedroom where I read Thoreau and Kerouac while I listened to Mantovani. I memorized mockeries of materialism while I twisted the antenna of my transistor radio every few minutes to keep FM 107 floating out easy listening music introduced by a disc jockey with a fake French accent and a fake French name, Charles Duvall.

"Wear a nice white shirt," my mother said. "Even if he's wasted his life in the rackets, Fred has one thing, and that's sophistication. You can learn something about the world from him." She fluttered a raftlike bag toward the ceiling. "This one's almost done." I pushed the

3

hangers around my closet, saying to myself, *the rackets, the rackets*. I liked the sound of it. I had tired of Catholic school uniforms and wore clothes from the American Legion thrift shop, which I combed for dashing, man-about-town accessories. I took off my red smoking jacket with the *js* sketched in blurry magic marker on the breast pocket. My mother and I had worked on the sleeping bag since early morning, our monograms facing each other. I had plenty of the white shirts required at Mater Christi, but the cuffs of the glen-plaid suit bought three years earlier at Macy's basement dangled to my calves, and the sleeves rode up my wrists. I owned three ties and chose the turquoise with its pattern of voluptuous mermaids strumming harps that were dollar-bill signs. I had never worn it. It was my first big change, and I sensed good luck coming as I walked to the subway.

From the moment I saw Fred by the information booth I forgot about Thoreau. Everything about him seemed big: shoulders, ears, bald head, and roman nose. His double-breasted blue suit fit loosely and, although I was approaching six feet, I was skinny and pimply and felt small when he looked me over, surprised by my taut clothes, which pulled tighter as I stretched to full height. Fred grabbed my shoulders, looking into my eyes and smiling an open-mouthed smile. "How's the choir boy?" I jumped at the words, the only thing about me Fred remembered. My other titles in grammar school included president of the Boy Savior, My Captain Club and treasurer of the St. Aloysius Sodality, offices assumed at the urging of my mother, offices achieved by keeping quiet.

Fred said he had to pick up a present for his girl friend, Madeline. I had been in Manhattan only to see the skaters at Rockefeller Plaza at Christmas or buy discounted underwear on Delancey Street. Just walking with Fred, on our way to get a gift for a girl, gave me a feeling of belonging, and I blithely strode next to him until he noticed the paperback sticking out of my jacket.

"It's *On the Road*," I said, and flashed the cover, a handsome young hobo, a lock of hair curling down the center of his forehead, hands in both pockets, shrugging. Fred stopped, opened it, and read aloud from a random page. "A pain stabbed my heart, as it did every time I saw a girl I loved who was going in the opposite direction in this too-

4

big world." He said, "Oh, the sensitive type!" and laughed, slapping me in the stomach with the book as if handing off a football.

With those words, Kerouac began to fade.

It was 1965, and I searched my memory for details about the one man in our family who had made it to Manhattan. He had been arrested at fifteen and, later, spent a year in jail. Yet he seemed the opposite of failure. I clearly remembered his ex-wife, Jeanie, a very young blonde whose tight dresses, sunglasses, and loud laugh brought worried looks from my relatives. She seemed the same age as my high school's older girls, those about to graduate. But she also looked like those who never would, the girls who jumped into revving cars outside school, a blur of makeup and teased hair. She didn't seem like a wife, at least not a wife on my street, where a wife meant a shopping cart and a broom. My mother said their son, Nicky, wasn't Fred's. When I thought of Fred, he was there and not there, and I pictured him the way the movie showed the invisible man after he got wet, dripping footprints on a sidewalk, nothing else.

Everyone we passed on Fifth Avenue seemed beautifully dressed, and I felt Fred stepping back, gazing at my suit. I tried to shrink myself into it by lowering my waist, urging my cuffs to my shoe tops. By the time we turned the corner of Forty-Seventh Street, I walked in a hunched squat. Fred pointed out a string of jewelry stores, and we took a flight of stairs between two display windows. The stencil on the door read: Embassy Gems. Kurt Ret, Proprietor. Fred looked in and called me over. In the center of a room lined with cases of rings, bracelets, and pendants, an old man in a three-piece suit pretended to conduct music we could hear vaguely through the glass. His arms gestured as if he were fluffing pillows in slow motion, and then he turned his wrist suddenly, a corkscrew, to release another section of his imaginary orchestra. His wrinkled gray pants drooped so far over his shoes that only the scuffed toes appeared, and that made me feel better about my suit. Mr. Ret smiled when we walked in and held out two hands.

"Bravo!" Fred said, and then he introduced me. "My nephew," he said, as if it were a title.

"Turn off the radio, Little Fred," Mr. Ret said, pointing to a tall cabinet. I walked across the room, seeing myself in a new light, a part of something, a "little" someone rather than no one at all. I found the right knob and the music stopped. Fred and Mr. Ret went into the back, and I followed them to a room smelling of burned coffee, where Mr. Ret sat in a leather chair studded with brass buttons. A pair of long black socks dangled from the open drawer of a file cabinet, and I stepped on a rubber boot. Fred sank into a couch and crossed his legs near a coffee table. When I looked out the grimy window above Forty-Seventh Street, I saw only my reflection.

"Get us some coffee," Mr. Ret said. I poured the coffee from a fuming pot into three metal cups on top of a banged-up footlocker and settled next to Fred. He and Mr. Ret talked about the price of gold, neither of them touching their mugs. I never drank coffee and swigged mine right down. A white heat seared my lips and tongue.

"The boy burned himself, Fred," Mr. Ret said. I kept the scorching liquid in my mouth, torn between holding it and swallowing.

"Spit it out," Fred said, his handkerchief under my chin. I took one look at the ironed linen square and swallowed.

I got up and shook my head, red and sweaty.

Fred guided me into the showroom, saying, "You'll be okay. Pain's all in the mind." He placed me next to the antique speaker and turned it on. Classical music flowed, and Fred said, "Ever play 'Radio Swami'?" He switched to the all-news station and lowered the volume. He spoke into the brown cloth speaker, "Are good forces or evil forces at work today?" He turned it up. The announcer, caught in midsentence, said, ". . . offers a lot of options . . ." Then Fred shut it off. "See," he said, smiling, "possibilities everywhere. And now for you." He asked the radio, "Will my nephew make it in the Big Apple?" He spun the knob and the voice said, ". . . a dog into space . . ." "That's a hard one," he said. "Anyway, amuse yourself," and he left. I asked the radio if I would live in the city, and it gave a phone number, a Manhattan exchange. I whispered the next question: Would Fred like me? The voice said, "every day." I decided just to think my questions toward the radio. The pain diminished and I joined the back room, slumping into the couch, the cushions so old they felt filled with dust.

"Going to college?" Mr. Ret asked.

"I still have a year of high school," I said, "but I'll probably go after that."

Fred turned. "College? Don't you want to stay in the city? I thought you'd go into business with me."

6

"He's still young, Fred," Mr. Ret said. "There's time." He lit a cigarette with a steamship-shaped table lighter. "Open the top drawer of the file cabinet. Bring me the white box." I rummaged past the socks, a package of salted licorice, and an ashtray of half-finished cigars. Mr. Ret's hands shook badly as he lifted the simple lid with difficulty. He sifted through tissues and layers of cotton batting, producing, at last, a watch.

"This is for you," he said. "It's German, like me." It trembled from his fingertips.

I looked at Fred, who mouthed the words, "Take it."

"Thank you, Mr. Ret," I said, unsure about accepting the gift.

"It's a good one," he said, as he passed the box to Fred. "Madeline's present's there, and a chocolate bar for Nicky."

Fred removed a large Toblerone and then another length of cotton. "Pearls," he said, as the strand slipped out. "Thank you, she'll love them." He held them in the air, picturing them around her neck. I put on the watch and crossed my legs, but my pants rode up so high that I leaned forward, covering my shins with my hands. "I'll pay you next week," Fred said. "I'm a little short."

"Don't worry, Freddie," Mr. Ret said, rubbing his cigarette into the ashtray. He examined the long stub and dropped it into his vest pocket.

Downstairs, Fred said, "Give me the watch. You can get a watch like that anytime. It was a good one, but what you need is a suit." He grabbed the back of my neck and laughed. "You're a good kid," he said. "If we're going to be partners, you've got to look right. Let's walk over to Madison." The coming and going of valuables impressed me. A string of pearls. Cash paid later. The beautiful watch I wore for fifteen minutes, suddenly in the past tense. A new suit. Partners. In Brooks Brothers Fred laid out several blue suits that looked identical.

"Which do you like?" he asked. When I stalled, he showed me the cut of the lapels, the placing and number of buttons, the single and double vents. He chose.

"We'll get it next week, William," he said to the salesman, whom he just met. On the way out he paused by the accessories counter and bought a silver money clip, with penknife and nail file attached. "The suit is from Mr. Ret, but this is from me. Hey, we're later than I thought," he said, as he looked at his wrist, at the watch Mr. Ret had given me an hour before.

We took a table by the window in a Lexington Avenue restaurant called "Close Quarters." With linen tablecloths and napkins, it was the kind of place we never saw in Queens, borough of diners. At Fred's insistence I sat with my back to the window, so I got a full view of the bar. Fred kept his eyes on the street. He ordered two coffees, and when they arrived, he fished an ice cube from his water and dropped it into my cup.

"How's life at home?"

"Okay, but my mother misses Dad."

"He's gone a lot, I know. How long for this time?"

"I'm not sure, at least all summer."

"Good for you to get away too," he said. "That's why I thought we'd go around together." I was glad to hear the future since I had no occasion for the suit without Fred. A woman from the bar joined us as I was picturing myself all dressed up, entering our cramped vestibule, past the wooden milk box and folded aluminum chairs.

"Hello, beautiful," Fred said. He turned to me. "Gail owns the place."

"I'm lunched," she said.

Gail wore a white blouse with a kerchief tied tightly at the collar. A paisley scarf circled her forehead and a pair of glasses hung around her neck, giving an official look. She was so bound by buttons and silks that she reminded me of the man-made clams we had as kids, the kind you dropped into a glass of water so the shell opened after a few seconds, breaking the ribbon that clasped it, releasing a blossom.

Fred said, "You look like a package waiting to be unwrapped," and he yanked the end of her scarf.

"So who's this, your protégé?" She flicked her cigarette toward the ashtray, and a few cinders scattered over the back of my hand.

"This is John, my nephew," he said. She nodded.

"I think you drank too much last weekend," she said to Fred.

He looked startled. "Me? Sorry, Gail. Wrong guy."

"Or else you like me," she said, raising her eyebrows.

"I like you," he said, grinning.

She turned to me. "Fred always smiles," she said, "so you never can tell what he's thinking. He fired a runner last week, right in here, a poor dopey kid with a stutter. Fred was even smiling when he fired him." She stretched her mouth into a mock grin and said through her teeth, "'You're through, Eddie.' That's what he said." She made the frozen face again and repeated it. "'You're through, Eddie.'" She did it so well I wanted to try it.

Fred just sat there, unfolding the *Irish Echo* and the *Amsterdam News*. He boasted earlier that he read about all parts of the city. Unable to rouse him, Gail pushed her chair back and said, "Your uncle fucks 'em and forgets 'em, did you know that?" Then to Fred, "No comment?"

"No comment," Fred said.

"You can really get on someone's nerves," she said.

"If I do, Saboo," he said.

"Sometimes I wonder why I let you hang around in here. You're a real phony."

"If I am, Siam," Fred said, smiling.

Gail made a fake squint toward me. "Haven't I had it from you before?"

This got to him, and Fred crumpled his paper. "Knock it off, Gail," he said.

"See you guys," she said, and returned to the end of the bar.

"I like Gail," Fred said, "but she's a mixed-up girl." I stared into my uncle's face for a hint of irony, for some comment on the nonsense he'd spoken seconds before. He continued focusing on the street over my shoulder and scanning the papers. Occasionally he looked at me. I found myself gazing at him harder since hearing Gail's story about Eddie. Now I feared his smile, the smile that could say, *You're through, Johnny.* I let myself admire him all over again, the soft gray suit, the dark hair on the knuckles of his immaculate hands, his close shave. He looked up from his paper suddenly, and our eyes met. I was embarrassed to be caught staring but, in that moment, he panicked at what he saw behind me. Quietly, but with purpose and speed, he slid his chair away and ducked under the table. My mind surged with the family stories about Fred's Mafia friends, his prison sentence, his having to leave town for months at a time. I figured he had enemies as well, and I imagined a pressure at the back of my skull, my head only a few feet from the café window—the window I felt sure was about to explode. I saw the headline and my own obituary, containing not pig iron but lead, and I twisted and dropped to the floor in a tangle of legs and elbows, bringing my cup and saucer with me.

Fred bent around the table, peering down. "What the hell's with you?" he asked.

"I thought someone might be shooting at us," I said, crawling to my feet.

"What? Where do you get that stuff, from TV?" He grabbed napkins from the next table and sopped up the coffee as I straightened my pants and sleeves.

"I saw you duck," I said.

"Yeah, I ducked," he said. "A cop walked by and I didn't want him to see me."

"You didn't?"

"Hell, no. I'd have to give him twenty dollars." The creased linen tablecloth had wrinkled and stained. My uncle bribed cops just to leave him alone—what was he hiding? Fred looked at the mess and suggested we sit at the bar. Gail flipped through notebooks near the kitchen. The mirror served as a bulletin board, taped with business cards, announcements, and posters. A big green parrot, an amazon, chained by its foot to a perch, squawked and repeated, "Fuck you, half-ass!"

"Ralph!" Fred called, gripping the ledge of the bright bar and rocking into it. "A dry martini with a twist, and a Jack Daniel's neat. And give the bird a cookie so my nephew can watch." His big grin worried me since Gail's story. It could mean bad news or good. Ralph, an old man who had missed shaving several spots on his wiry neck, served us and then held a milk bone to the parrot. Fred laughed out loud when the bird grasped the cookie with one foot and chomped, sending a small landslide of crumbs to the floor. Then he pointed to my drink. "Only the best for you. Here's to our partnership, just the beginning." I brought the glass to my mouth, but even as it made its way from the bar, I could feel it coming, its strong fragrance preceding it like the roar of a train approaching the station. I let the whiskey lap my upper lip, nodding to Fred, who lifted his glass at the same time, winced, and said, "He never makes it dry enough."

A few stools away, a dapper man in a fedora called to the bartender, "Ralph, he doesn't like his drink."

Fred said, "What business is it of yours?" and turned to me, smirking and jerking his thumb toward the man.

"I drink martinis myself," the man said, pointing to his glass. "No offense intended." He put his head to his chest solemnly, and shrugged deeper into his thick herringbone jacket. His pants were heavy corduroy, and I couldn't picture him on the sweltering street.

"Is there a problem?" Ralph asked my uncle.

Fred grinned again. "Not really, Ralph. I should have said very dry, but it's just fine." He cupped his hand protectively around the stem.

"Not at all," Ralph said, and in one motion lifted the glass by the rim and dumped it into the steel sink. He measured more gin, then held a bottle of Noilly Pratt toward Fred with a questioning look.

"Just a little," Fred said, and Ralph poured a small splash. Fred took a sip, saying it was just right, and Ralph slapped the bar lightly, off to another customer.

The man in tweed said, "My friend has an oilcan at home, filled with vermouth. He punches the bottom with his thumb. Two tiny drops jump out."

"Do you think I could have some ice in this, Fred?" I asked.

"No!" he barked. "That's sipping whiskey, John, sipping whiskey. Never diluted." He reached over and took a swig of my drink, diminishing it by half.

The man in tweed continued, "My father used to dip his pinkie into the vermouth and then just jab it into his gin." He made a stabbing motion with his little finger, quick, like pulling it away from a flame. "That's really dry!"

Fred said, "At home I pour the vermouth into the glass and dump it out." Then he called, "Ralph, another martini, and one for my Tyrolean friend here as well." Ralph was bent across the bar, whispering forehead to forehead with a pretty young woman who drank coffee. He picked up her stirrer, shook the drops from it, and walked toward the parrot. A moment later, the bird scratched its head feathers with the slender stick, an expression of pleasure on its thoughtful face. The woman laughed, and Ralph said knowingly, "Using a tool is a sign of intelligence in animals," and he leaned over his work station, juicing a lemon with a wooden spike.

Fred said to me, "And a sign of stupidity in humans." Then he shouted, "Ralph! Did you hear me? Another round!"

"Now you'll see how dry I take it," the man in tweed said. Ralph made a big deal about placing the bottle of vermouth in front of the man while stirring just gin and ice, then pouring the drink. He unscrewed the top as if it were a heroic effort and waved the mouth of the bottle across the icy skin, saying, "Just fumes is all. You'll never see drier!" The man in tweed sipped and nodded, and he and Ralph shared the chuckle.

Fred continued to grin, but I felt his grin could turn to grimace, and I finished my drink, anxious about what Fred would do in the face of this clear challenge. He downed his martini and pushed the glass toward Ralph. "Don't forget my nephew," Fred said, still smiling. "Serve the boy first."

"And a glass of water, please," I said to Ralph.

"You don't need water," Fred said. He turned to the man in tweed. "I never drink water, you know why? Fish fuck in it."

Ralph brought another Jack Daniel's and sneaked a small tumbler of water to the far side of my elbow.

Fred said, "I'd like this one really dry, so let me add the vermouth myself." Ralph poured the gin in front of Fred. Then he brought the bottle of vermouth. Fred said, "And let me have that flashlight next to the cash register, like a good fella." Ralph looked at the man in tweed and wrinkled his eyebrow. The three of us watched as Fred examined the flashlight and spun its beam across the walls and ceiling before shutting it off. He moved the bottle close and lined the cold glass up behind it. Pointing the flashlight at the bottle, just above the label, he flicked the switch, so that the yellow path entered the green glass and exited into my uncle's drink, illuminating it with the glow from the vermouth. He stood the beaming flashlight upright next to the bottle and sipped.

"Dry," he said, lifting the glass so that he toasted himself.

Ralph raised his thick eyebrows and said, "That, I have to say, is very dry, very dry indeed."

The man in tweed slapped his palms onto the bar. "You win," he said to my uncle, and he hoisted his glass, blushing.

I drank all of my water and slid the tumbler down the bar. I continued licking the whiskey off my upper lip. Fred finished his second martini, asked me if I wanted the bourbon, and then tossed it back. On the way out, Fred tapped Gail's left shoulder. When she turned, he whispered into her right ear, surprising her. He kept walking, and she screamed something as he opened the door, a peal of laughter and a shattering glass following us into the air. I wanted to duck again, but I kept myself rigid. There but not there, like Fred.

"I tease Gail," he said. "She can use a laugh, but sometimes she gets hysterical." Then, "I know I promised we'd go to the ball yard tonight, but I just remembered I've got to be somewhere. Suppose we have a quick bite at my place and I see you next week? We'll pick up the suit and you can stay over, okay? You can stay overnight. Ask Olga when you get home."

"All right," I said. I didn't care. I was thinking about Gail's question. *Haven't I had it from you before?* Imitating her squinting eyes made me feel intimate with her.

Reading my mind, Fred said, "Her name's Gail Close. That's how they got the name, 'Close Quarters.'"

We stepped from the cab on Lexington Avenue into a whirl of couples pushing strollers, girls in summer dresses walking trimmed poodles, and shopkeepers arranging fruit and vegetable displays on the sidewalk. The counterman at the deli honored Fred's request, saying, "Thin it is," as he cut the pastrami. Fred ran from aisle to aisle, giving a manly vigor to an activity I had considered entirely effeminate: shopping.

"Real rye bread can't be packaged," he said. "It loses its zest." He pushed a fresh crust under my nose and chortled, throwing the loaf into his basket along with two cylinders of cookies with plaid wrappers. He snatched a box of rice and sneered, "White rice. Pure garbage. All rice is brown, did you know that? They scrape off the outside where the vitamins are. Then they sell the husks back to us in vitamin pills." He inserted the box onto the wrong shelf. "I read we should eat everything raw, even meat. That's what animals do, they don't cook anything. I'll show you my books." On the checkout line Fred inquired about the leg of lamb in the cart of the woman in front of us. "Hear that, Jonathan?" he asked, giving me a new name. "Lamb from New Zealand." He raised his eyebrows as if he just got in on a secret.

Fitz, the doorman, yanked the harness of a mangy terrier, pulling it out of Fred's building as we were about to enter. The dog's owner, Miss

Mahon, elderly and blind, stood on the sidewalk clapping her hands and yelling for her dog. She was dressed in black and wore sunglasses. "I don't know what's wrong with Tippy tonight," she said.

Fred said, "What's wrong with Tippy tonight is what's wrong with Tippy every night—he's not a guide dog."

Miss Mahon asked, "Who's there? Who is it?" and walked up to me. She touched my face, creeping her fingers along my cheek and forehead.

"Don't answer," Fred said, grabbing the edge of my shoulder and pulling me toward the revolving door. "She's a pest. Always hanging around the lobby."

"I'm late for church!" she said. Fitz, having gotten Tippy outside, handed her the leash and rolled his eyes.

"What a kook," Fred said.

"You're right about that, Mr. Bertel," Fitz said. I was surprised at hearing "Bertel." My mother's name was Bertolotti. We took an elevator that went only to Fred's apartment and his neighbor's on the twentieth floor. As he opened the door, Fred said, "This place used to belong to Frank Costello—you know, the gangster? He was big in the forties. These photos were here when I moved in." I passed pictures of Frank Costello surrounded by three New York Yankees; Costello with the winner of a Miss Rheingold Beer Contest; Costello in a restaurant, his arm around a chef; Costello with Abbott and Costello. I wanted my own photo collection. Sitting next to Fred at Close Quarters. Smiling with Gail at the blackboard specials. In front of the brass Brooks Brothers plaque. Mr. Ret presenting me with a watch. My friends would stand around, asking who they were, while I pointed and explained, but suddenly they clashed with the wallpaper my mother and I sloshed up years ago, a pattern of roosters peering over a wire fence.

The dining area looked like a combination conference room and gypsy parlor. Dark beams matched the floor's wood; the walls and ceiling were deep red. I leaned over the long oval table and lifted the lid of a glass jar brimming with matchbooks from Larré's, Pete's Tavern, and Gino. I planned to record my tracks by slipping matchbooks into my pocket.

Fred put the groceries away in a kitchen filled with dead plants. I walked onto the terrace, a square surrounded by a tiled wall. Three wrought-iron tables and chairs stood among flowerpots holding artificial trees. I looked at the cars lining the roads across Central Park. Headlights, taillights, and the medallions of taxis swirled continuously like something on a fairground. "Your sandwich is ready," Fred called. "Hey, we should have a cookout here sometime, a real barbecue." At the table he gave me a giant pastrami on rye and stood while I struggled with the heap of meat. "You'll be home by eight," he said, folding a newspaper. "Game's on TV, just checked."

"Aren't you eating?" I asked.

"Not right now. You know, from what I hear on the radio, and the more I read, the more I think I should correct my diet, maybe go all liquid." He walked across the kitchen and pulled a book from the top of the refrigerator, showing me the cover, *How I Cured My Incurable Ailments*. "Here's some recipes, Pale Moon Cocktail, made of just white and yellow fruits. I'll need a blender. Does your mother still watch the games with you?"

"Most of the time. Do you live here alone?" I asked, and held my breath, afraid to be prying.

"Yes," he said, looking at me earnestly and finally sitting down. "Jeanie and I are divorced, for a few months now. You remember Jeanie, don't you?"

"We met at Christmases."

"And wakes," he said, "but you didn't really know her. She could be a great gal, and she appreciated what I did for her. I met her at a club, Teddy's. She was a teenager, no future, one of those girls who walk around selling stuff from a little tray hanging off their shoulders. All night she said, "Cigars, cigarettes, and almonds," in a high-falutin' voice. We called them, 'Nuts and butts.' But Jeanie was different."

"She was very pretty," I said.

"Still is," he said. "Her face was shaped like a heart and her mouth was shaped like a heart. But she changed, and I changed too. I'm out a lot, so I like to come home. She was in all the time and wanted to go out. And she's a lot younger. That was just one thing. She had Nicky at eighteen, only two years older than you. She's thirty-three now. Toward the end it got bad. She interrupted my sleep. One night, she shoves me, I'm in the middle of a dream. I still remember it. I was coaching the Knicks, yelling on the sideline, and that's when she pushes me, hard. I sit up. 'What's the matter?' I say. She says, 'Your hand was on my side of the bed, and it was twitching.'"

"Maybe you were really shaking," I said.

"That's not the point!" he yelled. "There is no 'her side of the bed.'" He stood and walked back and forth like he was still in the dream. "We're married. It's all one bed. And besides, I bought everything here. If we want to split hairs, both sides of the bed are mine."

"Is Nicky with her now?"

"I guess you've heard a lot in your house. The truth is he's not my son. Let this be a lesson. I was away for a few months, a year actually, and when I came home, Jeanie says to me, 'Here's our son.'" His eyes opened wide, his mouth dropped with surprise, and he smiled, bewildered all over again, an infectious puzzlement that I immediately felt. Then he looked at me and at my plate, which was empty except for the tough end of a giant dill pickle. Instantly cheered, he said, "You liked the sandwich! And don't leave the schtickl. When I was a kid Borsleman kept a jar full of them, the ends. They're good. Borsleman, he's still there, used to say, 'A nickel for a schtickl.'" He jumped from his chair and grabbed the two cylinders of cookies. "Something to take home." He dropped them in a bag. I put the schtickl in my mouth. I had never seen anyone change so quickly, from grieved to astonished to ecstatic, ecstatic over a schtickl.

At the subway entrance, Fred put his arms around me and kissed me. "Back to Queens," he said. "I really don't see how you can stand staying home at your age. The place reeks of mothballs and garlic, and your mother's roping you into those hobbies."

"I'm not really there, Fred," I said, surprising myself with that crazy statement. I started down the stairs, along the smudged white wall.

"Next week we'll pick up the suit. You can come next week, huh?"

"I'm sure I can," I said, as I hung on the staircase railing and watched him light a cigarette. The burnt match flared out as it fell to the cement and I inhaled the sulfurous smell.

"Hey," he chuckled. "How'd you like the way I won the martini contest?"

"That was great," I said, delighting again in the way the beam from his flashlight streamed through the green bottle, igniting his glass of gin.

Times Square

"What are you doing here?" my mother asked as I met her in the hall, where she and my Aunt Linda each carried a basket of bed pads.

"I thought you were going to Yankee Stadium," Linda said.

"Fred had to do something," I said.

"You must be disappointed," my mother said.

"Not really. The game's on TV." I decided I would mask any emotion, as Fred instructed me to do with the burning coffee. I handed the bag of cookies to Linda. "These are from Fred." She took one look at the fancy wrapping and sneered. Linda, my mother's younger sister, thirty-eight, never married, and lived downstairs from us, alone in the apartment since my grandmother's death the year before.

"Just glad to be home, I bet," my mother said, putting the wicker basket down and leaning against the wall.

"Fred dumped him," Linda said.

"No, he didn't. He's got things to do."

"Without the mob he'd be a big zero," she said.

"Well, you're home now," my mother said, walking toward me and trying to straighten the crooked part in my hair with her fingers. Linda opened the hall closet and said, "Look!" as she brought out a jacket on a wooden hanger. She unwrapped the plastic from a new sport coat. It

17

was pale blue with pink pinstripes. Every pocket had a flap and every flap a button. "I got it on Fourteenth Street."

"Jazzy!" my mother said, and I thanked Linda.

As I put it on, Linda said, "It fits! Isn't next Saturday the end-of-year dance? Wait till they see you in that."

"I probably won't be going," I said. "Fred invited me back."

"Again?" Linda asked, as she smoothed her palms across my shoulders.

"Yeah, he bought me a suit at Brooks Brothers and I have to pick it up." Linda took the jacket off me roughly.

My mother and aunt looked at each other. "That's an expensive store," Linda said. "Very generous of him."

"Well, it's not from him exactly," I said. "Some guy gave me a watch, and Fred took the watch and traded me for the suit."

"What guy?" my mother asked.

"A guy Fred knows, an old man."

"I told you!" my aunt yelled at my mother. "I told you!" She held the flamboyant sport coat low, so that its vent scraped the ground. It was a single vent.

"He's a nice man," I said. "Fred knows him for years."

"I knew something like this would happen," Linda said.

"Oh, it's probably nothing," my mother said, her face darkening nevertheless. She grabbed the basket and headed downstairs.

"You think it's nothing," Linda called after her, "but the next thing you know he's arrested for unloading stolen TVs from some warehouse in New Jersey."

We went out for dinner. My aunt wore a yellow summer dress, backless, white powder dusting her spine and collarbone. In spite of the warm weather, my mother hugged a blue wool cardigan as we walked. My new blazer stood out on the street where a sport coat was rarely seen, but this jacket would have turned heads anywhere. The route to Phil's Luncheonette took us through the church courtyard, an empty quadrangle strung with the convent's clotheslines swaying with black habits and snowy underthings so strange no one knew their names. As boys, we played tag through those strands and flags of linen, fragrant with ivory soap, wrapping our faces, scarflike, in their immaculate folds, inhaling the pure and bewildering scent.

At Phil's, we all had the special: pot roast, mashed potatoes, and green beans, and when the jello arrived, we recited our litany of fullness, my mother pushing it away, saying, "I'm too full."

"I'm full too," my aunt said, looking down at the trembling red square.

"I hate to see it go to waste, but I'm full," my mother said.

Linda put some bills next to the pale green check and glanced at me. "You're not eating your jello either?" she said.

As I was about to answer, my mother said, "He's full," and we left.

That night at ten Fred called. My mother answered in the kitchen, where she and my aunt had been talking while I read Ginsberg in my room instead of watching the ball game. A phone ringing that late usually meant bad news and, in my aunt's eyes, Fred's call was just that. I put on my bathrobe and walked to the sink, getting a glass of water. After a few polite phrases, my mother gave me the receiver. I pulled the knotted cord around the corner and leaned against the dining-room wall.

"What do you have to say that's so secret?" Linda yelled.

"Great day," Fred said. "Everyone who met you really liked you, especially Gail. She said you have *presence*, whatever she meant by that. Next week we'll get the suit, right?"

"Sure," I said.

"Are you free this Wednesday?" Fred asked. "No need to wait. It's summer, school's over. You should get out of there." I knew that a date with Fred so soon wouldn't be welcomed, and I told him I had a few things to do with my mother.

"Like what?"

"She wants me to trade in her plaid stamps, pick up some feathers, stuff like that."

"Don't be stupid," he said, and I could hear him sucking in a Chesterfield, and then the clink of ice. He whispered, "Can't someone else run those errands?"

"There really isn't anybody, Fred."

"God bless you," he said, and hung up.

When I came into the kitchen, Linda said, "We'll see about him phoning you at all hours and making plans. I have some plans of my own."

On Monday morning I was looking through the *Village Voice* for poetry readings when Linda called from her office at Paramount Pictures, where she was secretary to the purchasing agent. "I got you a job," she said. "You start in the mailroom tomorrow. A position like this can change your life."

This meant riding the subway back and forth with my aunt every day. It meant the end of Fred except for weekends, her strategy. The more I thought about it, the more encouraged I became about working in the city. I'd spent the previous summer playing checkers in the park with the other boys from St. Bartholomew's or taking the bus to Rockaway Beach, hoping for a sip of beer or a chat with a girl. I visited the pale and acne-ridden boys of Elmhurst Lanes, guys with pencils behind their ears who were getting interested in horses and learning the numbers. I hung around La Ronga's Beverage Warehouse because Tommy La Ronga's father owned a distributorship and his office, a desk next to the loading platform, was always open. The warehouse itself, with its tall ceiling and dark walls, seemed half-cathedral, half-dungeon. Tommy's job was to fill orders for quarts of orange, lime, cherry, and grape that glowed fluorescently even in the poor light of the bulbs hanging from the rafters, and we helped him clunk the radiant bottles into their wooden cases.

I hardly saw my best friend, Mark Cooney, the son of the police commissioner, a patrolman who rose to that office through a series of scandals and deaths. Mr. Cooney feared his son's association with our local gangs, the Gladiators and the Majestics, and he put Mark to work at our local precinct, the 110th. Mark could be seen though its dim windows in his gray rookie uniform, kneeling at a filing cabinet or mopping the floor. When we did meet, we walked from his stoop to mine and back through the humid air, watching children play stickball in the streets as we had done, their game halted every few minutes by passing cars. We were too old to play and too young to drive.

"Who knows where this job can take you?" Linda continued while I stood next to my mother, who had known about Linda's plan. She pumped her cupped palms toward the chandelier in gestures of great enthusiasm, showing me how excited I should act toward the offer. Linda went on, "I wouldn't be surprised if you got hired permanently. You could end up a movie executive. Forget what Fred told your mother about needing a man's company. This job will make you

20

a man. You'll be in the company of real men. You should see who comes in here—Tony Perkins, Steve McQueen, Richard Burton ... " I couldn't hear the rest of the list because my mother suddenly forgot I was on the phone and started the vacuum. Then she seemed to forget I was there at all and pushed the loud nozzle around my feet, so I had to prance across the rug to say good-bye.

The next morning I pulled on my chino pants and knotted my Hawaiian tie in the mirror above my dresser. My mother's favorite disc jockey, Ted Brown, sang his theme song:

> *Am I blue?*
> *No, I'm Brown.*
> *Got a smile on my face*
> *Not a frown.*
> *Each day at 6 o'clock,*
> *I come on after Martin Block.*

No matter how humid the day, my mother insisted I eat a hot breakfast, and a square of polenta, freshly fried and topped with a melted slice of American cheese, steamed into my face. Even the driest English muffin in our house burned with a twinge of garlic, a smell never wholly removed from the counter or cutting boards. Evenings, the fragrance of onions and peppers frying in olive oil streamed down the stairs. My grandmother used to say, "A woman will never lose a man as long as he smells onions and peppers when he comes home at night." My mother took those words to heart, but she still lost her man, to a paper and envelope company and interminable business trips.

Before I left, my mother straightened my tie, patterned with the profiles of pagan idols. I walked down the stairs toward my aunt, who waited at the newel post, and my mother called after me, "Next time, try to get a god directly on the knot." Linda had an hourglass figure, wore fitted suits, and carried herself with a strictness she practiced, walking room to room balancing *The Complete Lives of the Saints* on her head. Making her even more forbidding was her sharp widow's peak, so that her profile, body, and carriage formed a presence of unapproachable angles and rigid softnesses. She never dated, having had her heart broken by a soldier named Mac to whom she had been engaged. Older teens on the block asked me teasingly if she had any boyfriends, and their fathers inquired about her in front of their wives to arouse their jealousy.

Seeing her in her tight tan suit at the bottom of the stairs, I realized she was an attractive woman, a stranger though I had lived upstairs from her and my grandmother all my life. She took my arm as we walked to the subway for the half-hour ride from Queens. Hooked to her in this way, I felt captive, yet she pressed my arm so firmly against the side of her breast that I didn't move. At Forty-Fourth and Broadway we entered the Paramount Building, where Linda had worked since she was my age, sixteen, and where she would work for fifty years.

Entering the mailroom for the first time, I tried to place the smell. A very strong cigar. Moldy parmesan. Burning rubber. Cat box. Four green tables abutted each other, forming one gigantic square. Posters from Paramount's films covered the walls, except for the back, which held a rack of pigeonholes. A dumbwaiter lifted packages to the floors above. At the entrance, pneumatic tubes fired capsules of "Rush" envelopes up to the receptionists, and every so often one of these quart-sized brass-and-leather containers shot down, landing heavily in a cradle of rags. A long shelf contained postage-metering machines, steel tape dispensers, and packing materials. At four o'clock each afternoon, this shelf would be whirring.

The head of the mailroom, Bob Gates, stood before his desk and greeted me. Red-haired, with a red mustache and a black patch over one eye, he twinkled and menaced. A curved pipe never left his mouth as he shook my hand. A giant mousetrap hung on the wall above his head. Over it, a sign read: Complaint Department. Gates contributed a column of nostalgia to the house organ, *Paramount World*, called "When the Times Were Square." I would soon learn that his missing eye was no handicap in detecting the messengers' shenanigans around the table. If voices rose too loudly, Gates cocked his head to the side like a bird, and soon the worst offender's name would be called for an errand. He showed me the cafeteria, the men's room, the time clock and left me with Mr. Scott in Personnel to sign my working papers. Scott took the finished forms and handed them to another man, saying, "This is Linda Bertolotti's nephew. You know, the one with the legs."

When I returned, the table was circled by messengers drinking coffee and reading the *Daily News*. Gates introduced me to the boys, all in their late teens. "Did you ever see a white asshole?" Harold asked as we shook hands. Since he was black, I thought it over for a second. "Me neither," he said. "I'm looking for a white asshole. Let me know if you see one." Ruben, a tiny man with a Spanish accent, said, "I won't be around long. I'm taking night classes at the New York School of Printing. But for the minute," and here he stretched his short arms across the cramped room, "welcome to my world!" Sitting down, listening to them discuss the Mets, I looked over my clothes and winced. They wore T-shirts or bright tops they called "Italian knits." My outfit didn't match theirs, but my madras jacket, narrow Hawaiian tie, and pale poplin pants would be worn all summer.

In the afternoon one of the messengers, Brian Beardsley, returned from a cross-town pickup, hoisted himself onto the table, and said, "You know Evelyn? The redhead? She said, 'I'm glad to see you, and you haven't lost your good looks.'" That spring, Beardsley had crashed through a windshield that left a deep and still raw scar furrowed diagonally across his face. His right eye fluttered and strained in its wake. He carried photographs in his breast pocket taken just after the bandages had been removed, and he often shuffled them like a deck of cards.

"Bullshit," Ruben said. "She wouldn't give you a second look." Ruben leaned his metal chair back from the table, dangling his tiny legs. His little red Converse high-tops gave him the appearance of a child, although his pencil-thin mustache showed his age—nineteen. He was exactly five feet tall and kept hoping to outgrow his clothes.

"Bullshit yourself. I know women, man, and she's got it for me."

"From the way you talk, you know nothing about shicks and that's the truth," Ruben said.

"Shicks! You can't even speak English, you dinky spick."

"Knows nothing about them," Ruben said again, calmly shaking his head.

This angered Beardsley, who said, "You probably don't even fuck your girl."

"None of your business, man."

"I knew it, he doesn't fuck her! Ruben doesn't fuck his girlfriend, everybody!" Beardsley cupped his hand to the side of his mouth, broadcasting, although Gates and I were the only ones there.

"Hey, man, I respect my girl. I French-fuck her."

"French-fuck? What's that shit?"

"I just put the head in. I don't go ape on my girl." Ruben spoke with such conviction that Beardsley stared at the table, chastened and brooding. Ruben continued to read *Billboard*. A few seconds later, pointing at a chart, Ruben said joyfully that Jay and the Americans had another number one, and he drummed the table with his fingertips.

"Ruben, pick up 812," Gates called.

As Ruben walked out, Beardsley yelled after him, "If you like that crap, why don't you go to the opera?" And he made a donkey sound.

In the quiet of the mail room, I considered both the French-fuck and whether Jay and the Americans were operatic. There was nothing to do but read and comment on the reading. We leafed through the well-worn morning papers, stepped-on, splashed pages that the boys picked up in waiting rooms and on trains and buses. When Gates went to lunch, Ruben's radio blared and Beardsley unlocked his briefcase of pornographic magazines, which he made a big deal about keeping secret as he tossed the key into the air and caught it. I scanned those glossy pages and feigned indifference before the coupling bodies, enema bags, and women wearing Nazi regalia. The secret cache of magazines and the calm that held at odd times allowed me to reorganize myself. I was used to hiding things, the small treats a schoolboy smuggles into his desk, and accustomed to silence, which I had practiced since I was six and entered school taught by nuns. In the mailroom I was silent in the quiet and silent in the roar, listening, flipping pages, shrugging and smiling when the din was turned on me. Beardsley's stealth gave the mailroom a schoolhouse air in which I felt secure. I imagined the French-fuck, and I wondered if it were the gentlemanly, the sophisticated thing to do. I tried to imagine Ruben's penis, the big head of a small penis of a small man. Or was the head small too? That was easier to think about than the place it entered. My friend Cooney, who had sisters, explained sex this way: a man has a penis, but a woman has nothing. I imagined my penis, just the head, entering nothing, where it disappeared.

Gates sent Beardsley out and then yelled, "Don't pay attention to anything you hear this summer." He walked over to the table. "These guys are crazy," he said. "Their everyday lives are screwed and God help their private lives." He whispered, "Some of them are into unnatural acts. You don't want to know." He went to his desk, whistling. I opened *Billboard* to the charts and found them filled with doodles of breasts, penises, and buttocks drawn by many hands. I wanted to know about unnatural acts—they might be more easily described than the natural acts, which had so far eluded me. I was holding the magazine sideways to get a better view of an anus like an asterisk when Mario, who ran the dumbwaiter, leaned his face over my shoulder, and I jumped. He hung his thumbs in his belt and asked very thoughtfully when I was born. I told him and he said, beaming, "You were born on a Sunday." Mario hardly talked unless to figure the day of someone's birth. He had been a passenger on the *Andrea Doria* but would never describe the sinking ship. He was twenty, with the face of a child's drawing: round with round eyes. Most of the time he wore no expression, but on the rare occasion that he smiled at some joke or pratfall, everyone noticed and the dim room brightened. When I lifted the magazine, he interrupted me again. "Do you think shit can heat a room?" he said. "A room this size, for instance?" I said enough of it probably could.

At the end of that first day, I told Linda I had saved some carfare by walking instead of riding the subway. She pointed to a graph of the skyline on the front page of the *Journal-American* illustrating air quality. That evening, and for most of the summer, the artist blackened the entire atmosphere, meaning, *Poor*. Linda mocked my suggestion to remove my coat and tie, saying, "You'll have to make a good impression if you want to work here someday. And it'll keep you from the service elevators. You'll see the hotels and penthouses as if you lived in them." I wiped my forehead with a white handkerchief that turned gray with soot.

Each night when we got off the train in Elmhurst, Linda stopped at Horn & Hardart for a tray of baked macaroni or a roasted chicken. Every inch of the bag I carried for her was printed with the slogan: *Less Work for Mother*. As I placed it on her kitchen counter, I couldn't help look into the dining room at my grandmother's chair and end table, where she had spent long hours until last year. The table served as a small altar at which she prayed throughout the day, even in her senility. Her wax statues included St. Francis, who held a sparrow on his finger; St. Peter standing on a rock; Jesus exposing a red knot of a heart by parting his robe; and St. Sebastian. Sebastian, martyred by an executioner's arrows, had been knocked too close to the radiator during vacuuming. Now he stood at half his original height, arrows still protruding but his legs melted into a puddle, his face and torso dripping. Once, on scanning the altar, my grandmother shook her head, obviously moved, and said, "What they did to that poor man!" The kitchen, silent and odorless, resurrected Linda's grief. When she sighed as I left, I wondered if it was from missing her mother or about the empty evening ahead of her.

Upstairs, my mother stirred a huge pot of minestrone even though the temperature had hit eighty-five. We sat in the hot kitchen and she filled my plate. "Who else?" she asked.

"There's John Wayne and Rory Calhoun. And Carroll Baker, the new star of *Harlow*."

"Suddenly your life has taken an exciting turn. By the way, what are you doing with Fred this weekend?" I invented the ridiculous excuse that he wanted to take me someplace special for meatballs.

"Meatballs? Everything better be on the up and up," she said, and took out a dozen potholders she'd knitted that day, arranging them on the table like a game of solitaire.

"They're beautiful," I said.

"Go down and tell Linda how nice your first day was, that you're glad to have the job."

"I already thanked her."

"Tell her again. Just thinking about your trips with Fred makes me appreciate what she's done for you."

Linda sat at the dining-room table, her slip loose at the shoulders; she had pulled down the straps to relieve the heat. The *Journal-American* and *World-Telegram* covered the dining-room table next to a glass of iced coffee. When I knocked on the frame of the open door, she looked down at herself, but waved me in. I sat across, staring at the top of her breasts, exposed further as she pushed the sports pages toward me. I tried to amuse her, reading aloud Jimmy Cannon's column, "Nobody Asked Me, But . . . "

26

In my neighborhood, an old man wouldn't shake hands with an undertaker.

Why do most soft-drink stands feature unappetizing bowls of black-speckled oranges?

The plainest of women look exciting in a polka-dot dress.

"Mr. Joyce wouldn't shake hands with the undertaker. You didn't know him. His widow still has your mother's plate," she said, and went to the kitchen for more coffee. I couldn't help staring at her legs. I finished the sports, but when I slid the front page my way, she tugged it back. "There's some business in England, nothing you need to know." She took a sip and the thin cubes clicked.

"About what?"

"A scandal. Sick." She inserted the sections into each other, creased them, and wiped the back of her hand over the top page, very official. I knew that later I could get the papers from the orange crate under the basement stairs. Linda looked at me and smoothed her widow's peak with both hands, hoisting her breasts high. "There's so much you don't know," she said. "You'd be surprised at how many sick people there are, especially where you're working." She sighed. "I should have thought twice about your going, but I was in a rush to keep you from getting too mixed up with Fred. Those jobs aren't easy to come by, you know."

"It doesn't seem that bad," I said.

"You just started," she said.

"Don't worry about me, Linda," I said, thinking about my new world of Fred and Gail, straining to read the upside-down print. My tone irritated her.

"You think you know everything?"

"No, not everything," I said.

She stacked the papers in a pile. "You'll have questions. I'm sure you know more than we did at your age. Everything's sex now. But remember, you can always talk to me."

"Okay," I said, unable to imagine asking her anything. She kept her eyes on me, and I tried to keep my eyes from the front of her slip.

"I just hope Fred doesn't fill your head with garbage."

"He won't, Linda. I've already met some nice people."

"Really? Who?"

"Mr. Ret, who gave me the watch, and a woman named Gail."

"Probably a floozy, like Jeanie."

"Not really, Linda," I said. "She's a businesswoman—she owns her own place."

She smirked. "You have a lot to learn."

"Well, I can tell she's professional."

"Professional? That's a good one. You don't even realize what you're saying."

"I think I do," I said. Defending Gail made me believe I had something to defend.

"You're a babe in the woods." We were both silent, and then she said, "I was eighteen before I discovered that women have two places between their legs. Did you know that?"

"No," I said. A moth flew in circles around her head, and she looked almost angry.

"The place where your penis enters to make babies, and the other place, for peeing," she said, her head high.

Growing up, I'd known little of Linda, and the little I knew had always been teacherly, righteous, so I mostly ignored her. But her tone on this night was convincing, highhanded yet vulnerable, and her half-naked body kept my attention.

"And that's just the beginning," she said, "of what you don't know." She shifted in her chair and I shifted in mine. Her saying "your penis" made me feel both capable and concerned. Earlier in the day, my penis was entering nothing, and now it was entering a place between my aunt's legs. I said I had to go, and Linda pushed out her chair, saying, "We'll talk more."

That night I found the paper in the basement and carried it to the empty coal bin, which had the brightest bulb. The front pages of the *Journal-American* had been neatly clipped, a rectangle and a square missing, like a cutout of the skyline. I was dying for the "sick" news, and I quickly tied the scandal to unnatural acts. In the hallway, Linda's *Vogue* magazine rested on the radiator with some junk mail, and I took it to my room, searching for any trace of flesh, even the airbrushed models bound in starched foundation garments. I found all the women irresistible, and I snipped the thin, the matronly, and the adolescent. I looked into their eyes as I swayed before them. When I finished, I stuck the clipped ads into a manila folder in my bookcase.

I looked at *Vogue*'s front cover: July. I had destroyed the current issue. Instead of replacing it with the mail, I tiptoed to the cellar, where I buried it in the crate.

When I got to the mailroom the next morning, I fished through the papers. The *Journal-American*'s front page featured a long story on John Profumo, England's minister of war, and two call girls, Christine Keeler and Mandy Rice-Davies. He had resigned two years earlier, and while the piece focused on his current retirement, it was simply an excuse to reprise the depths of the scandal. I savored the details of how these girls, dressed only in high heels and black stockings, whipped men with a variety of implements. One minister, dressed as a woman, complete with eye makeup, lay across a bed, his dress lifted over his buttocks, caned in alternate strokes by Mandy and Christine. Mandy used a horsewhip on her customers, who paid her a pound per stroke. I looked up the words *tawse* and *flail*. I was shocked that Linda knew about these things, and I wanted to prove to her that I wasn't naïve. I would wait for the right moment to impress her, to work *tawse* into one of our conversations.

Is Another World Watching?

I met Fred on the front steps of St. Pat's on Saturday. "A good friend of mine has passed away," he said. "And we have to go to the wake." Fred walked with his head down, none of his usual looking around.

My mouth was dry, as it had been all week running errands for Paramount. On my first day I bought LifeSavers, then gum, until I realized I was spending the money I saved by walking, which had made me all the more thirsty. Looking for an alternative, I rummaged through my mother's spice rack, filling my madras jacket with cloves, which I chewed and spat out, a cheap refreshment. I snuck a clove into my mouth. "First, let's get that suit," Fred said, suddenly exuberant.

I loved walking into Brooks Brothers, doing my own errand instead of someone else's. We passed the counters filled with wallets, suspenders, and shavers and headed upstairs. Fred paced around the three-way mirror, yanking my cuffs, putting his fingers into my waistline, and patting the edges of my shoulders. "I'm surprised at you, William," he said to the salesman. "These are over half an inch too long." He pointed at the sleeves, truly angry.

"I think they'll be all right, Mr. Bertel. With wear, they should rise."

"Don't give me that. I'm not stupid. You think I was born yesterday?" He looked at me and pointed at William with his thumb. "He thinks I was born yesterday!" He kept tugging on my sleeves to show

how long they were, while William pulled the shoulders up to prove the fit was right. "Get him a cotton oxford. Blue. What is he, 14/32?" William nodded. "Then make it a 33, William, so the cuffs will show under this behemoth." Fred grabbed the shirt and removed the pins. He held them in his teeth, and I understood that I was to take my shirt off right there and not in the fitting room. The cloth felt thick and robust, unlike any shirt I'd worn. "See this," Fred said, as he held the collar with his thumb and forefinger and turned my head to the mirror. "That's the Brooks Brothers' roll." I stuffed my chinos and shirt into a shopping bag and walked out in the suit, which felt weighty, as if it held someone else's shape. The silky lining glowed, and I flung the jacket open again and again, glancing at it. We had our shoes shined in the lobby of the Almanac Hotel and our hair cut next door, in a long, narrow shop with a sign in the window that read, "All Haircuts, 75 cents." It was a barber school, and we waited for Pasquale, who Fred said would surely have his own place someday.

Gail sat at the front table of Close Quarters, writing the menu on a blackboard. "Forget the shepherd's pie," she said in a stage whisper as we walked in. Fred ordered mulligatawny stew for me and burned toast for himself. "There's no calories that way," he explained. He reached across the table and grabbed my wrist. "I'm glad you're here," he said. "You're a good kid. Today you'll probably see Jeanie, she was a friend of Dick's. Maybe Nicky will be there. Don't let them get to you, they might say things." The waiter brought our plates, and Fred leaned back and looked at me. "In that suit, you're a different person." I smiled, because that was exactly what I wanted to be. "It's good for you to get out of Queens. How you stay there is beyond me. Puzzles with your mother, Jesus—that's a puzzle itself. What do you do for fun, hang around under a streetlight?"

"Yeah," I said, "that's about it." I was afraid to say that when I did go out, I went to Alexander's department store and read the liner notes on record albums, trying to get beyond rock and roll and into semiclassical. And that besides helping my mother with her hobbies, I lay in bed, reading and tuning my radio, listening for the pipes to rush, signaling Linda's bath. Then I planned my visit, hoping to catch her undressed. Sometimes I'd arrive prematurely, hearing her still bath-

32

ing, and I'd return to my room, only to fly down when the bathroom lock clicked, a sound I gauged by tilting my head over the banister.

Gail joined us, bringing a cup of coffee. "Is that toast black enough for you?" she said to Fred.

"That's how I stay slim," he said, patting his waist.

"Bullshit," she said, and called over to the bar for chicken salad. "I made this myself, Fred, you've got to taste it." She turned to me. "You look great. So this is the new suit." Her lips seemed wet. I had developed a way of staring so I didn't flinch when caught. I pretended to be lost in thought and gradually moved my eyes away. Fred told Gail about the funeral.

"Not for me," she said. "I know he was your friend, but I couldn't stand him. Even his name was fake, was really Carridi, a wop like you two."

"Love your friends with their faults," Fred said as he put a fork into the plate Gail ordered. "This is terrific. What are these, walnuts?"

"Yeah, but the meat's the thing. From Jersey."

"Jonathan, try this," he said, holding a chunk on a soup spoon. "You'd have to be a rooster to get a better piece of chicken."

"Nice," Gail said.

"It's great," I said, nodding at Gail.

"I like you more and more," she said to me before noticing the man leaning over our table, holding himself up by two metal braces. "Well, if it isn't that old asshole Van Forkenberry!" Gail said, "The thieving gimp of Third Avenue."

"It's nice to see you again, too, Miss Close," he said.

"This is my old friend," Fred said to me, and then he greeted Van. "John's a bookworm like yourself. Pull up a chair."

"I have bad news, Fred," Van said. "They took Miller to the hospital last night, maybe a heart attack . . . "

"Christ!" Fred said. "First Richards, now Miller. Gail, is that florist still there?" He was already on his way out the door.

"No," she said, "but there's a Fanny Farmer three blocks down. Why not send candy? It wins over the nurses." A salesman came in and Gail took him to the bar, leaving me with Van, who called for two cups of coffee. He wore horn-rimmed glasses and a straw hat. He had no beard; his hairless pink cheeks shone. Van's coffee came with a shot of whiskey, which he dumped into the cup. "I like the brown milk," he said, and asked if I remembered a recent traffic jam on the TriBorough Bridge. "Well, I caused it. It was my fault," he said, and hung his head. "I parked there and I was going to jump, I planned to jump. You don't know how hard it is being a cripple. It's lonely, no one wants to talk to you—your uncle excepted, of course. He's always nice to me. I just wanted to end it."

"I'm sorry," I said. I felt sympathy but also a weird pride in getting to know a survivor.

"Thank you," he said. "I'm better now, I realize I have things to live for. This day, for example, the cool air, the trees, this coffee, and meeting someone new, like you. I'm glad for all these things," he said, fluttering his eyes.

"That's good," I said. I was drinking coffee and getting thirsty at the same time. I searched for a clove but realized I was wearing the new suit.

"Yes, it is. And you should be grateful too, for the things you have. Just look at you." He glided his hand in front of me, like a showgirl displaying merchandise. "Good-looking, a nice blue suit, a young buck. I can tell you care by the way your shoes are shined. You're a fine young man."

"Oh," I said, "Fred and I just stopped at a stand."

"Learn to accept a compliment," he said sternly.

I tried to change the conversation. "Do you work with books?"

He puffed himself up. "Reading is an interest of mine," he said. "I deal in rare stuff, curiosa, arcana. Your uncle has a fascination with the occult I try to nourish. That's what I like about him, he's open-minded, been practicing ESP, did you know that? I got him some books on it. He loved *The Predictions of Nostradamus*."

"He did?"

"Telepathy was the first form of communication. We can still read each others' minds if we try. I also work in prisons, reading to the inmates, teaching them to write."

"I bet they have some good stories."

"They do," he said, "but also a lot of filth, filthy words. I spend most of my time crossing them out." He pulled the tablecloth, smoothing the wrinkles.

34

I recoiled at his idea of editing, which I thought would have censored my beat heroes, who let their minds go free. "The beatnik writers used those words," I said. "Suppose you're suppressing a masterpiece?"

"Masterbusiness!" he said. "They write a lot about that too, yes, they have nothing else to do. How old are you?"

"Sixteen."

"You live where?"

"Queens."

"With your parents?"

"Right now, with my mother. And my aunt."

"Pets?"

"I have a dog."

"Good. A boy needs a dog. Male or female? What's the name?"

"Major. A male."

"Major, an old-fashioned name. Do you let him out, so he can get together with other dogs?"

"No, it's a busy neighborhood. We have to keep him on the leash."

"That's a shame. He's a boy like you. He's got to roam the streets!" Van pointed toward the avenue, as if Major was happily trotting there, from bar to bar. "Even if you let him get on male dogs, it would be good for him. Of course, he wouldn't procreate, but it would give him exercise."

I memorized *procreate* to look up later. The fast questions unbalanced my composure, and I could tell Van's last sentences were unseemly, but I didn't know exactly why. At the same time I was intrigued by Fred and the occult.

"So you're alone with two women? Your aunt's not married?"

"No."

"Uh oh," he said, laughing.

"What do you mean?"

"Well, you should watch it. You're not a child, your aunt might find you attractive and want to sleep with you."

"Not really," I said, crunching ice.

"It happens. Haven't you ever slept with a woman?"

"No."

"Oh God!" he called out. Then he leaned halfway across the table, his face crawling along the taut linen, and he asked in a forceful whisper, "Don't tell me you're a virgin, you never had your dick sucked?" I stood up and pushed my chair aside. "Now I've done it!" he said, straightening with great dignity. "Now I've offended you!" I was a few steps away when he yelled, "Everyone shuns the cripple!" I turned back, feeling I had abandoned him, when Gail came over, stuck her finger into Van's face, and said, "If you propositioned Fred's nephew, he'll tear off your good leg and hit you with the bloody end of it." She pinched the sleeve of my suit and pulled. "Come over here, I want to show you something." I sat at the bar with Gail and her ledgers. "Van can be a royal creep," she said, and she ordered two Camparis that lit up like votive candles when the sun hit them. I recognized the man in tweed, Mr. McGuire, sitting a few seats away. "Do you think I should try serving quail?" she asked, mostly to herself, as she eyed the smudgy lists.

"Thanks for getting me away from Van," I said. "I thought he was supposed to be a writer or do something with books."

"He does do things with books," she said. "He steals them. He was caught last year in a rare-book room removing a page. Imagine that, a page. I hear they really watch over you in those places. They're totally silent. Know how he took it? He had a string in his mouth, got it nice and wet, then laid it down so it dissolved the paper. He pulled it away from the binding without a sound. But still, they caught him." I was sipping the bitter drink, imagining Linda's designs on me and what Nostradamus predicted, when Mr. McGuire said, "Get with it, Gail, and don't start introducing one so young to sins of the flesh." He crossed himself dramatically.

"There's a devil in every bottle, McGuire," Gail said, and twirled her finger around her temple in the cuckoo sign. McGuire, still wearing the heavy wool jacket, jumped off his stool, ran around to the other side of the bar, and made a yanking motion with both hands, as if tugging a long rope. He returned to his seat and ordered another martini.

"What's he doing?" I asked.

Gail's index finger continued down the supplier's pages. She said, "Every so often he feels the need to pull the spear from Christ's side." A few minutes later Fred stood next to us, grinning and holding a big heart-shaped box of chocolates from which two pink inflated legs rose, complete with taffeta garters and fishnet stockings.

"I couldn't resist," he said.

"That must be the sweetest pussy this side of the East River," Gail said, looking over her reading glasses.

"Tell Lenny to deliver this," Fred said to Gail, throwing a handful of dollars onto the bar. "We have to get to the wake."

"That'll be great for your nephew," Gail said. "Every small-time hood in the city will be there."

Fred looked at her seriously. "Plenty of the bosses will be paying their respects too, Gail, not just the little guys."

On the way out, Van half-turned in his chair and said feebly, "Fred, I have to talk to you," but Fred rushed right by.

We took a cab to Chelsea, where a crowd surrounded Gilmartin's Funeral Home. Limousines double-parked on Twenty-Third Street and chauffeurs chatted with police. Boys bounced a pinkie off a stoop, playing Single-Double-Triple, and every so often the ball careened skyward, landing at the feet of a mourner, who flung it back. We edged through the men on the porch but, just before entering, Fred took me aside and pointed to the street, saying, "Look at the old men—see how they walk together, their hands behind their backs? That's one way to tell they're Italian." I watched the men, in pairs, wearing dark suits, bent and downcast, from another country. "Listen," Fred said. "When you meet the family, shake their hands firmly and say, 'Sorry for your trouble.' Be calm and remember they lost someone. Also, remember the names of the people you meet and address them by their names, using 'mister.'" He gave me these instructions with a scary severity, as if I were already trying his patience.

"I hope I remember them," I said.

A couple whisked past, and Fred leaned his whole body against mine, pushing me into the railing, his face red. "What do you mean you 'hope you remember them?' You're supposed to be smart, right? Use memory tricks. Like that guy we passed, named Balzone. Look for something on him that will remind you of his name, like he's bald, Bald Balzone. I do it all the time, didn't they teach you?" Fred looked me up and down and saw the Brooks Brothers bag that held my pants and shirt, which I had been hiding behind my leg. He ripped it away and stepped off the porch, flinging the sack over the hedges. "You don't need those anymore," he said.

We walked into Gilmartin's foyer, and I worried about what pants I'd be wearing to work. The ornate rooms smelled of smoke, and black furniture glistened against fuzzy red wallpaper. Fred kept his hand on my shoulder as we passed life-sized statues of Saint Joseph and the Blessed Virgin. In the hall a man held a small radio to a priest's squinting eye, saying, "And here's a compartment for keeping valuables." When he saw me staring, he said, "Do you know what I'm doing?"

"I'd say you're selling," Fred said, and kept walking.

"I got a deal for you, Freddie," the guy with the radio called.

"N. O., baby," Fred answered.

A female voice boomed from the room where Richards was waked. Two women stood before the coffin, arguing. The loud one insisted Richards should be wearing his glasses, since that's how everyone knew him. The other wailed with a grief that sounded like crazy laughter, but the first pulled a pair of black horn-rims from her purse. Her companion slapped her hands, saying that glasses were for seeing, and now that his eyes were closed, what was the use? The first woman opened the glasses above Richards' collapsed face, while the second tugged at her forearms, looking around for help. An elderly woman arrived, put her arms around their shoulders, and they all returned, crying, to their seats.

We knelt by the coffin, and Fred crossed himself fervently, eyes closed, lips moving in prayer. The strong fragrance of the hothouse flowers and the scent of the heavily powdered corpse made me light-headed. We shook hands with the widow, the woman who had tried to replace the glasses.

"Sorry for your trouble," I said.

"Thank you," she said. "Fred, so good of you to come. You know, next week would've been our twenty-fifth anniversary." She began to cry, and Fred patted her hair as she leaned against him. Suddenly, she pulled away and reached under a chair, bringing out what I thought was a painting. But inside the frame, twenty-five silver dollars made the shape of the number 25 on red velvet. "I found this in a drawer," she said. "All wrapped up. It's what I wanted for this occasion, and he had gotten it for me."

"That was Dick," Fred said. "Always thoughtful."

"I'm burying it with him," she said, and turned to greet another mourner.

Looking over the crowd seated in folding chairs, I recognized Jeanie, Fred's ex-wife, the woman I had eyed as a child. I had always tried to sit near her, enthralled by the sunglasses she wore, even indoors. My mother later told me they hid a perpetual black eye given to her by Fred. I had once overheard Linda and my mother discussing Jeanie. My aunt said, "Her eyes are so hard you could scratch them with a pin." My mother said she had "a bad skin," referring, I guessed, to the few pockmarks on her cheeks. I didn't like the phrase, "a bad skin." The *a* was the startling bit of diction. It separated her from her skin, which I thought looked just fine. Fred noticed me pause in the aisle and said, "Go back and say hello." Jeanie still looked young, wore a black suit, black stockings, and crossed her legs so that I could see the little bows on her insteps, part of her tiny shoes. An older man draped his arm across the back of Jeanie's chair. She shook my hand and pulled me down to her, kissing my ear. I lurched and almost fell. Then I stood clumsily at her knees until she broke the silence, saying that her son Nicky was in the lounge outside the men's room. Jeanie looked closer to my age than my aunt's.

I had not seen Nicky since we were kids, and I wondered how he'd be at sixteen. From the way Fred talked about him, mentioning that he'd lived all over the city, taken numerous odd jobs, I knew I'd fall short in comparison. Nicky sat in a high-backed armchair cleaning out his wallet. He balanced different colored cards on the knees of his glen-plaid suit, its pattern similar to my old one, but it "draped" over his body, as Fred told me good cloth should. I realized that my wallet contained only an Elmhurst library card and subway pass, and I vowed to beef it up.

"I've got something to show you," were Nicky's first words. The suit looked even better as he led me toward the door. "Let's go where we can be alone." We walked past Red Hickey's Garage, whose neon sign read, "Cracked Heads and Blocks Repaired." In a concrete, graffiti-filled underpass once used for trolleys, Nicky pulled a book from his inside jacket pocket, flipped to a page with a folded corner, and handed it to me. I wanted to see the cover, but when I tried to turn the book over, Nicky grabbed it and insisted on the text. Was it a book on the Mafia? On the city's secret places? I read, staring every so often at the large script over his head, "Monk and Joanne L.A.M.F." Like a Mother Fucker. Nicky shifted from one foot to the other, very close to my face. Each time I finished a passage, he darted to a new one, thumbing expertly through, saying, "Pretty good, huh?" and I nodded. Some of the sentences were so enticing and encoded that I memorized them for the time they would come clear.

"Upstairs Jack plunged his hand down the front of his partner's dress. Outside, a sailor bargained for the charms of a shopworn streetwalker," and "She began to whimper, then gasp, until she screamed with an intensity he never thought possible."

I was deep into imagining what went on in these words when I felt a presence behind me. I expected Nicky to jump when he saw Fred, but he stood still. Fred turned the book over, indifferent to its cover, a line drawing of a half-naked woman tied to a bed, and its title, *Bound for Lust*. I guessed this was "sophistication," the only good characteristic of Fred's my mother could concede. I took it to mean that you didn't show your feelings, and I made up my mind to make this change: not to be bothered by anything, even what tortured me.

Fred took my arm, saying, "I want you to meet someone," and walked me back to the funeral home. No word to Nicky, no word from Nicky, who seemed content to stay behind, reading slogans sprayed over the years in blood-red enamel. As we walked, Fred said, "You know who's here? Long John Nebel. Ever hear him? On all-night radio? He's a talk-show host."

I hadn't.

"Well, you should. He's smarter than most, and what he has is common sense, experience, more important than anything you get in school." He flicked his cigarette into the roses that clung to the chain-link fence separating Gilmartin's from Hickey's. "In fact," Fred confided, "he's a genius."

Long John sat in a folding chair in the last row, his knees sticking out from his six-foot, four-inch frame. The pocket of his white short-sleeve shirt held a plastic shield containing a pen and pencil. He kept rubbing the heel of his palm against the tight lawn of his crew cut to keep it upright. He didn't look like a star but like a guy selling vacuums door to door. Fred introduced us and left. Nebel's voice was deep, and he spoke slowly, as if an involved and weighty thought process churned before each phrase. He said, "I hear you're intelligent and study hard. That's important, but your uncle thinks you should see more of the world." I guessed Fred had compared me unfavorably with Nicky, and I squinted. Nebel told me that Fred thought college was a waste of time but he didn't agree, that he prized the company of graduates of Ivy League schools, had been a close friend of Henry Luce from Yale and sometimes attended functions there, arriving by private car or plane. He made references to names and places I didn't know, and I tried to memorize them but most went by me. I was glad I got Luce. He mentioned that he didn't attend college, saying, "I never did matriculate at university." He concluded that I should go to Wesleyan. "Connecticut. A big step for you. My friends can arrange for scholarships and the like." He stressed the importance of connections and asked me to tell him when I made my application. He said he would try to accompany me to my interview.

"Now," he said, "I'm going to give you my private phone number, a number everyone in the city would like to have, a number the phone company secured for me personally. Not more than a dozen people in New York know these digits, although I have over a thousand friends." He took a pen from his shirt pocket, shifted in his chair for his wallet, removed a ten dollar bill, and printed his phone number on it. "Write it down and take your uncle to lunch." I shook his hand and headed over to Fred, who leaned against a wall with a few men, watching. As I made my way down the aisle, Long John called to me, smiling. "And remember," he said, "it's not *who* you know. It's *whom* you know."

Fred introduced me to Joey Archer, a middleweight contender. To my surprise, he was shorter than me. "Big boy," Joey said. "All you need's a couple more pounds." I had seen him on TV, on the Friday night fights, and now, up close, I couldn't take my eyes off his twisted nose, his very pink face made brighter by the thick white scar tissue above his eyes. Fred said, "Sometime, you, me, and Joey'll have a night on the town." Joey nodded in agreement, although he looked in another direction. Fred pulled me aside, saying he had to "take a meeting," and he pressed his key into my palm. He'd be back for dinner. "I can't believe we might go out with Joey Archer," I said, hoping we'd make the date firm.

"We will," Fred said, distracted.

"His nose was really flattened," I couldn't help saying.

Suddenly alert, Fred said, "It's been broken a lot. He finally had the bone removed." He tapped his nose. "He doesn't have a bone in that nose at all. I'll meet you later."

On my way to the men's room, Mr. Gilmartin, the funeral director, stopped me. "John? Fred asked me to speak with you." I followed Mr. Gilmartin into his office, where he introduced his son Francis, a heavy, disheveled boy who rose from his chair. "He's just graduating from Stonehill College," Mr. Gilmartin said, "and then he'll join me in the business." From its name, I thought Stonehill must have been a school for undertakers.

"I've had a lot of fun there, near Boston," Francis said. "You might like it." He bent over the desk and wrote down the name and address. The tail of his white shirt stuck out like a poncho.

"Is it Catholic?" I asked, tired of the Dominican nuns, Franciscan brothers, and now Christian brothers in high school.

"Yes, but it's not strict—we don't have to go to mass or anything."

Mr. Gilmartin shook his head. "Believe me," he said, "go to some state school and the Jews will have all the seats and you'll be sitting off on a windowsill somewhere."

I turned to Francis. "Do you work here now?"

"I plant a few," he said, and sat back before his catalogs of caskets. Mr. Gilmartin and his son gave me the creeps. I had known another undertaker, Mr. Spinelli, who owned a funeral home in Elmhurst. I played baseball with his son, and he drove us home from a game once, setting the air conditioning so high I could see my breath.

I walked into the men's room, feeling for the key. It was three o'clock. I was thrilled to be going to Fred's alone. I had at least two hours to be Fred. I imagined walking into a nightclub with Fred and Joey, all heads turning at Fred's stylish suit and Joey's strut as we took a table. Then I thought about Long John's description of the Ivy League, where I'd attend banquets and meet girls different from the quiet virgins who brought bouquets of hydrangeas to the nuns or the Majestics' molls, who leaned against the park fence, stretching their legs across the sidewalk, glistening their ankle bracelets in the sun, daring pedestrians to ask them to move. I stared into the mirror for several minutes and drank three times from the water cooler, using a different cup each time. I checked again for the key, Long John's number, and the index card from Francis, souvenirs of who I was in Manhattan in spite of who I was everywhere else. I printed *Wesleyan* on the bill so I wouldn't forget. I started uptown, but half a block away I remembered my old clothes and doubled back. I sidled between the faded brick and the thick privet and retrieved the bag holding my orange shirt-jac and chinos with the let-out hem.

When I approached Fred's building, Fitz just nodded. I waited for the elevator and saw Miss Mahon enter the lobby. I stood still, not wanting to talk, but she came my way, down the narrow hall leading to Fred's elevator. Hoping she'd pass, I flattened myself against the wall, wincing when my bag crinkled. Miss Mahon gripped her dog's harness, talking to Tippy. Tippy's hazy eyes shone up at me, unalarmed. They kept coming, and just when Miss Mahon drew even with me, she whipped her bony hand high, grabbing me full in the face. I yelled, "Hello, Miss Mahon!" as if I had just been strolling down the hall, but she dug her fingers around my eyes, screeching for Fitz. "It's me, Miss Mahon. John. Fred Bertel's nephew."

"You scared me, you," she said. "Is your uncle here?"

"No, Miss Mahon, he's at a friend's wake."

"I hope he croaks too," she said and walked on.

Being alone in the apartment made me giddy. I opened a small leather case on the counter, a manicuring set. From the terrace I watched boys push sailboats around the pond. I sank into the big white leather couch in the living room, getting up to switch the channels between the Yankees and the Mets. In the bathroom I clicked on Fred's shaver and splashed my cheeks with a cologne called "Sportsman." I had the urge to call my mother. Then I felt stronger for resisting. I enjoyed just breathing Fred's air and wrote my name in the nap of the thick rug and brushed it away. I tuned the radio to the Living Strings playing "The Sunny Side of the Street" as I sorted through the stack of newspapers. A familiar face appeared on the front of the *Long Island Star-Journal*, a Queens paper. It was my classmate Sal Colletti's graduation photo from St. Bartholomew's Elementary, and the headline read, "Elmhurst Teen Murdered in Greenwich Village."

Sal was found dead in a vacant apartment, where he had been bound by electrical cord, soaked, and plugged into a live current. I couldn't understand why his death took place in the Village, the home of espresso and free verse. Sal, a bully who founded the Majestics, had often stationed himself at the schoolyard gate, making everyone call him "Your Majesty." He kept a pack of Kools under the sleeve of his T-shirt, which was rolled almost to his shoulder, and exhaled smoke straight up, stirring the carefully curled lock over his forehead. He held court in the boys' room, hanging out in one stall, the front of which he taped with photos of naked women. He used to clear his throat in the other stalls, letting fly upward enormous "hawkers" or "lungies" that stuck to the ceiling, which hung with stalactites of phlegm. Gobs of mucus dropped, little by little, onto those who followed. He invented "The Punk Test" and tortured every boy in the school. He held my fist, rubbing a nickel very gently across the back of my hand, over the same inch for ninety seconds. Another Majestic stood next to us with a watch. At first there was no pain, but then the skin wore away, layer by layer, watering, then peeling, and finally leaving a stinging raw and wet oval. If you pulled away, you were a punk.

I looked again into the forced smile on Sal's face. The obituary described his hobbies as chess, cars, and gun collecting and his occupation as "stock analyst," though he worked at the A&P as a stock boy. The part about chess was true. Mr. Wittikund, a retired fireman turned teacher, interested Sal in chess as a battle strategy, and soon Sal hunched over the board in the park at noon instead of spitting or scraping flesh. But when he didn't make the finals of the parish tournament, he quit, staying away from school for a few days. When he returned, there was no chess set under his arm, but in his bathroom stall the centerfolds were taken down, replaced by a photo of Sal at age five. Naked, standing next to an inflatable pool on the sidewalk, Sal had curls even then. But by a photographic trick, his penis had been elongated and stretched in a slow blur all the way to his ankle. Now Sal and his long dick were dead.

The funeral took place in Queens, ending in Calvary, where most of our family was buried. I had never seen a cemetery in Manhattan, just a few green courtyards outside churches marking the lives of patriots. I was considering what happened to corpses in the city when Miss Mahon called.

"I'm sorry for what I said about your uncle," she said.

"That's all right, Miss Mahon."

"There's something between you and me, you know."

"There is?"

"Oh, yes, I can tell. I felt it was you in the lobby, I know those things. When I walk into a room, the dead start rocking in their rocking chairs! Come down here, I want to show you something. A beautiful painting."

"I can't, Miss Mahon, I'm waiting for my uncle."

"5D," she screeched. "You must!" And she hung up.

She waited at the door, facing me in dark glasses, dressed in her usual black. "This way," she said, and walked with one hand a few inches from the wall. Tippy slept in the living room, where Miss Mahon handed me a glass of ginger ale with a long gray hair circling the rim. The phone rang in the kitchen. "I'll be back in a minute," she said. "It's the grocer."

Oval paintings of saints filled the walls, with name plates under each portrait and the cause for which they were invoked: St. Gertrude wards off fever; St. Ambrose, protector of bees; St. Hillary defends against snakes. Miss Mahon placed her order, yelling, "No, not the bite-size!" She repeated a list of brand names as I walked among the holy figures, pausing at a robust array of roses. Two fallen petals lay next to the vase. When I lifted them, I realized they were fake, as was the bouquet. Miss Mahon had pulled them out, as if they had dropped there, once alive.

"Hurry now," she said, rushing toward me. "The delivery boy's coming. In here." I followed her through a curtain of beads. It was dark and smoky with incense. Miss Mahon directed me to an individual pew I could barely see, and I knelt on the padded cushion. "Ready?" she called from the doorway, and then she flicked a bank of floodlights that illuminated an enormous painting. I shielded my face, trying to ward off the flare. When I adjusted, I saw a woman in a long white robe leaning against a canopy bed, her cheeks pasted with round wafers of rouge, staring at a bald man who knelt in the center of the picture. The temptress had lowered the folds of fabric at her breast, exposing the nipple, but the man hid himself from the sight by pulling the sleeve of his brown cloak across his forehead. Miss Mahon announced, "St. Jude resisting temptation." I complimented it and got up, my eyes still stinging from the flash, and she pulled me from the room, saying, "Will you make that choice?"

"What choice?"

"To turn away, to resist!"

"Yes, Miss Mahon."

As we walked to her door, I stopped at a crucifix on the wall, a large black Christ hanging from a gold cross. Above his head, in the crossbeam, a clock ticked. She felt me pause. "You're looking at the Lord," she said. "He's quite at home here." She put her face close to mine and whispered sweetly, "You'll resist temptation, won't you?"

"Yes."

"No, you won't!" she screamed. "I can see you won't. Now, shoo!"

I was still seeing spots when I sank into Fred's couch. I started to think Miss Mahon wanted to blind me, even for a few minutes, and that St. Jude was forever blind in her apartment. I thought about her last words to me, "I can *see* you won't"—that she could see when I couldn't. I continued to blink, then I noticed a stack of magazines behind the mesh screen of the stereo cabinet. I chose one called *Smoothies*, in which the models, both men and women, were entirely shaved, head to toe, and oiled with lotion. Then I thought of Miss Mahon, with the eerie feeling that she watched as I fulfilled her prediction.

Fred woke me at ten. "I'm sorry I'm late," he said, "but it gave you a chance to get the lay of the land." I got up from the couch and followed him into the kitchen, where he put a carton of milk in front of me. "I've been thinking that maybe I've been rushing you, with the Jack Black and all. You're still a kid, Madeline reminded me of that tonight." He poured the milk and said, "That's ordinary milk, right? Now watch." He lifted a box of straws from the counter. They were Flav'r Straws, each one lined with a thin strip of chocolate. He dunked the straw again and again into the glass, and a brown ribbon leaked out, discoloring the milk. I took a sip of the sweet drink, and he said, "That's more like it, huh?" He put a few packs of oysterette crackers on the table, saying, "We'll have a big breakfast tomorrow." I told him about Miss Mahon, and he balled me out about going to her apartment but changed the subject quickly to Long John Nebel, saying his guest that night was a man who believed a race of demons lived under the earth's crust. "They're called Deros," he said. "This guy found a lot of garden hoses on Long Island were yanked underground. Who knows what they're doing down there?"

The decor in the guest room was entirely feminine, pillows everywhere and heaving, ruffled drapes. A frail antique desk where it was impossible to sit. I climbed into the canopied, four-poster bed next to a dresser holding a chamber pot of straw flowers. Books piled on the nightstand included *The Autobiography of a Yogi, You Can Take It with You, Eyeless Sight, How to Live Forever*, and volumes by John Cheever, Sigmund Freud, and Mickey Spillane. The first sentence of Spillane read, "I shook the rain off my hat and walked into the room." When Fred came to say goodnight, I was skimming the *Village Voice*.

"This is your first overnight in the Big Apple," he said. He wore only pajama bottoms, and when he held the poster, I noticed his shaved underarms. He saw me staring and said, "It's not skin that causes odor, it's hair. Why should women be the only ones to shave their arms?" He sat on the bed. "It doesn't mean I'm queer." When I said I didn't think that, he said, "Hush your mouth! I met a hockey player the other night at Junior's. A big guy, all his teeth knocked out. He removed his plate at the bar." Fred made a buck-toothed face and grabbed his front teeth with this thumb and forefinger. "Guess what! He's queer! Who cares? You could tell he was a 'man's man.' That's a man men love." He pointed at me. "Richards was like that. Gail didn't care for him, but he was a man's man and I miss him." He reached over for a book by Upton Sinclair called *Mental Radio*. "Here, try this. The introduction's by Einstein. I've practiced some of these experiments for the fun of it. Amazing what the human mind can do. Good night." I held Sinclair's book, the same Sinclair who wrote about the meat-packing plant. The cover said, "If you want to learn the art of conscious mind-reading, this will tell you how." I sifted through the pages. "It explains the step-by-step methods on how to be conscious and unconscious at the same time."

I put it back and read a Cheever story about a businessman taking the train out of Manhattan to the suburbs of Westchester. I tried to guess why he wanted to live outside the city and switched off the lamp, still thinking of Fred's underarms, wondering if he was a secret smoothie.

In the morning the floral room filled with light. In Queens our bedrooms were in the center of the flat, always dark, and the weather remained hidden until you walked to either end. Fred and I went to a cafe called Flamingo's for breakfast. At the small bar in front Fred spoke Italian with two old men. I recognized their Camparis by the way the sun illuminated their glasses into two ruby lanterns. When they left, they strolled past the picture window, their hands behind their backs. Fred smiled at everyone, mostly couples, who nodded. He wore a gray sharkskin jacket and a black knit shirt, the first time I had seen him without a tie. His bald head shone, and he smelled strongly of "Sportsman." I felt very formal in my blue suit, and I placed the books Fred urged on me, *Is Another World Watching?* and the Sinclair book, next to the bud vase. The white tablecloths, the classical music, and the quiet unfolding of the *Times* represented to me more of the "sophistication" my mother touted as Fred's one virtue. I had narrowed the definition to two possibilities: the first was having good things or at least knowing what they were; the second, not being shocked by anything. After chicken livers, eggs, and bagels, Fred signed for the bill. When he noticed that the waitress had left her pen, a cheap black ballpoint with a cracked barrel, he handed it to me immediately, saying, "John, a pen!" I understood that I was to put it in my jacket, which confounded my definition.

We walked the empty streets to the subway. The little saplings in front of the shops stretched toward the sun. At the window of an antique store, Fred spotted a bright brass eagle with a yard-long wingspan. "I'll take the bird if you ship it," he said to the clerk. He flipped open a leather address book and wrote down the destination. I walked around the shop, eyeing the diver's suit, the Tiffany lamps, the carousel horse, while he joked with the clerk and signed the gift card. When we left, Fred looked at the name of the shop, Simple Pleasures, and then again at the window. He pointed to the small gold lettering that I hadn't noticed: *To the Trade.* "That means they don't sell to the public," he said flatly, with no sense of paradox. "Just to other dealers." The day before I had watched him write a check at a liquor store as he stood below a sign that said, "Absolutely No Personal Checks." I guessed rules didn't apply if you ignored them, and I longed to send an eagle to someone. I pictured Cooney's mother answering the door, puzzled at the pine crate held by two delivery men who set it down carefully on her living-room rug. She calls Mark, who sees his name on the label, the return address announcing *Simple Pleasures, Second Avenue.* They crack it open with screwdrivers and a crowbar, and he and Mrs. Cooney lift handfuls of excelsior into the air, uncovering the greeting card signed with my name. Then Mark digs in with both hands and, as Mrs. Cooney stands back, he smiles and holds the brassy eagle aloft.

"How were the meatballs?" my mother asked when I walked in. She sat at the terrazzo table, sorting the mail.

"Not as good as yours," I said, but I had paused for a second, forgetting what I told her was the purpose of my date with Fred, and she knew it.

"This came from your father." She handed me a postcard from California, where he was visiting a paper mill. The picture showed a drive-in restaurant, The Beacon, which the caption explained served three tons of onion rings a week. My father wrote, "This is some place—they go through sixty thousand gallons of ice tea a year. Miss you both."

"I don't like onions that way," my mother said, getting up to stir a pot of tripe. I walked over to the stove and showed her the books, hoping to further muddle my trail, and she immediately grabbed *Is Another World Watching?*

"Can I borrow this one?" she asked.

"Okay," I said. "I think it's kind of weird."

"Interesting," she said, leafing through.

I told her about the wake and meeting Joey Archer. She was not impressed. I described Joey's nose as being soft and twisted, hoping to add a little vulnerability to his portrait, but it had the opposite effect.

"That sounds real nice," she said, lifting a spongy strip from her ladle and chewing it.

"Fred said I might go with him and Joey to the fights sometime."

I heard Linda slowly making her way up the stairs, greeting Major at the top, where he slept. She had been waiting for me. "So that's the suit," she said, walking into the kitchen.

"It does look good on him," my mother said, without turning around.

"He'll pay for it forever," Linda said.

"It was a gift," I insisted.

"With Fred, every gift has a long ribbon," she said.

"Fred invited him to Madison Square Garden, to the prizefights," my mother said.

"Another promise. It won't happen," Linda said.

"Fred was serious, Linda. He introduced me to a guy who could hold the title."

"Your mother doesn't want you with those characters," Linda said.

"One doesn't have a nose," my mother said.

"I know we'll get ringside seats," I said. "And he has a nose, it's just that the bone's been removed."

"No fights with Fred, and that's it." She put down the ladle. "Conclusion." When my mother said, "Conclusion," she drew a box in the air with her forefingers. Her two fingers started out together, traveled apart, down, and then back along the base of an imaginary rectangle until they met again. In that box all rebuttals shriveled and vanished.

Vanishing Cream

On paydays, Linda took me to lunch, to places she thought a man should know. On these occasions, I wore my suit. She taught me to pull out her chair when she left for the ladies' room and to stand when she returned. We ate in German restaurants clotted with heavily carved furniture; sporting spots with paintings of hunting dogs on the walls and suits of armor in the corners; delicatessens where the sandwiches were named after the city's athletes; steak houses where mats of beef hung over the edge of the plates and a potato cost five dollars; sections called "Men's Grills," where women were not permitted unless escorted by a man and, on entering one of these, it hit me: Linda was showing me the world but showing it to herself as well. She would never and, in some cases, could never have gone to these places alone. To teach me how to pay a check, she slipped folded bills under the tables of Luchow's, Tofenetti's, The Blue Ribbon, Gallagher's, and Jack Dempsey's. At these lunches she often remarked that someone was looking at us and trying to figure out our relationship. Every time a restaurant's doors closed behind us and we were back on the bright street, she snuggled close, taking my arm. All summer I pretended to pay and she pretended to be treated by her escort.

As secretary to Mr. McBain, the purchasing agent, Linda ordered drapes for the executive dining room, inspected linen invitations to

first nights, and catered screenings and openings. McBain, an alcoholic, usually returned from lunch in a drunken enthusiasm for an in-
novative piece of stereo paraphernalia, soft shirt, or brochures for
cruises. He often rushed into the office, saying to Linda, "Hold my
calls. I've got to rest." Linda's efficiency covered for McBain's flushes
of exhilaration and incompetence, and I felt sorry for her getting none
of the credit. Each night at five I took the elevator to her office and
we walked down Broadway to the E train, past Hector's cafeteria and
storefronts of electronics whose sheet-sized posters announced, "Closing Out Odds and Ends." Tad's Restaurant advertised steaks at $1.19,
and I longed to have dinner there, to see what Times Square was like
after business hours. On the subway Linda whipped through the *Journal-American* while I read William Burroughs' *Junkie*, which I used as
a guide to the neighborhood.

The crowded train made conversation impossible, but on the walk
home Linda gave her opinion of the top executives: Reardon from
Harvard, very tough; Boasberg, shrewd; Adamo, a gentleman. She
wanted me to emulate them, to be captivated by her descriptions, to
be serious and suave. She said, "Adamo comes in from upstate, where
he has a mansion and two mastiffs. Know what they are? Big dogs that
guard the grounds in England. He told me." When she spoke like this,
she smiled a smile that pictured her nephew heading toward such an
estate, up from the mailroom all the way to the top, into the company
of these men, protected by mastiffs.

But I hardly saw them. I dealt with those outside their doors, the
porters, secretaries, and elevator operators. The most ambitious person there was Ruben, his desire to leave the mailroom emblazoned on
the T-shirt he wore from the New York School of Printing. When I told
Linda a funny story about Ed, the air-conditioning man, she repeated
his name in disgust, as if I had soiled her vision. At home she only nodded to our neighbors or spoke a word or two, but when we were alone,
her opinions poured out. I mentioned this to Fred, who said, "Give
a lonely woman company and she'll talk more than anyone." She
snapped the back of her fingers at my lapels, saying, "Clothes make the
man." She sneered at policemen swinging their billy clubs on corners.
"Thugs in uniforms," she said. Stopping at Borsleman's on the way
home, she terrorized the butcher. "Know how he makes these chops

look good? With the lights!" She pointed her finger toward the ceiling, accusing, "The lights!" Her tone in these moments was heated but matter of fact, more verdict than opinion, a touch of Fred.

On Times Square we passed window after window of frilly lingerie, half-naked mannequins, sex books, and magazines, storefronts I savored on errands. If I turned my head in their direction, she snapped, "Don't look at that garbage!" Once, though, when we approached a bar called Billy the Kid and a very pretty woman stood in the doorway, wearing only a slender bikini top and tiny shorts, we both gawked. The woman knew it and smiled. She was in her late thirties, my aunt's age. A few steps past, Linda said, "Sometimes I do wonder what goes on in those places." Her opinions were all warnings, and her stories, parables. The gist of them was to avoid things. As we walked through the city streets together, she elbowed me and said, "Stare straight ahead, don't look anyone in the eye." Half a block later, she softened, "Okay, look if you want, but don't let anyone know you're looking."

In July Linda asked me to meet her at restaurants instead of our usual going together. At first she said she'd be shopping in a certain area, and it was inconvenient for her to get to Paramount. Then she said she wanted me to learn how to meet my party. Reservations were under my name, which I gave to the maître d' who escorted me to her table. Linda was always there, already on her second glass of chardonnay. I had to kiss her and take my seat. Once she whispered, "Everyone thought I was alone," and I saw that I was part of a dramatic fantasy. The first time I kissed her, I leaned forward, and she quickly tossed her high cheekbone toward me, embarrassed. But over the summer she relaxed, and sometimes her lips lingered on mine, the tiniest half-bite that left me tasting the astringent wine.

One Saturday I agreed to accompany her to Calvary to tend her parents' grave. I stood in her kitchen, waiting, while she rubbed her heels with a pumice stone. "I'm making coffee," she said, getting up and pouring milk into a pan boiling on the stove. She stirred in some sugar cubes, creating a sweet smell that reminded me of the close scent of the hothouse flowers at Richards' funeral. She placed a biscuit next to each cup. I recognized Fred's gift by the Queen of England's stamp on the package, the fancy cookies he favored.

"Why he buys these things when he doesn't have a dime is beyond me," she said as she poured.

"He seems to do okay," I said.

"At times," she said, "then he loses everything gambling or playing the big shot. He ends up borrowing twenty here, twenty there, no way to live. What exactly do you do with him in the city?"

"Go to restaurants, see his friends. Does he pay you back?"

"He's always selling junk," she said, not listening. "Have you seen where he gets that stuff? What do you talk about?"

"The city. Some sports. He told me about Jeanie and Nicky."

"When he was married he was never home," Linda said, "and Nicky's not even his son."

"I know that," I said. Fred had taught me to drink coffee black, and the creamy, bitingly sweet mixture in front of me had a foreign taste.

"He thinks he's so clever, but he goes and marries a girl when she's no more than seventeen . . ." She made a long tisking noise as if she were calling a cat.

"He's smart about some things," I said.

"He was always intelligent, no doubt about that. But he didn't use his brains. At your age he was already arrested."

"For what?"

Linda's bathrobe opened slightly. She leaned over and poured more coffee. "His group tried to rob the safe in a jewelry store in the Heights. Kwastel's on Seventy-Fourth, and they all got caught. Mom gave me twelve dollars to get a lawyer. I went to see Mr. Fremont. He was a nice man, and Fred got off."

"Weren't you just a kid too?" I asked.

"My mother put me in charge, even though I wasn't the oldest. In some ways I never had a childhood. Anyway, he ran right out of the courtroom with his friends, didn't even thank Mr. Fremont. I could have killed him."

"But Fred's given us some good stuff over the years," I said.

"Really?" Linda said, walking over to a clock whose minimal numerals were impossible to read. The late July sun was already hot, and she glanced at the inscrutable face. "Like this piece of junk, for example."

54

"But remember the telephones?" One Christmas Fred brought phones and showed them off as we sat around the table. "There's a light on the dial which glows when you answer," he said, holding the phone to his ear. "The dial is inside the receiver! And look at the shape, compact and slim, for a nightstand." Soon we saw them on television: princess phones, a new item, and one of Fred's friends came over and installed them, all at no cost, without the phone company.

"Yes," Linda said, "but remember the cherry trees that turned out to be sick, and your mother had to pay someone to dig them up? And the gimmick that gave us color television? A piece of swirling plastic stuck to the screen?" She laughed. "I hate to say this about a member of the family, especially my brother, but he's a bum. It's that simple. He has no job. He gambles and hangs out with floozies who have God knows what kind of diseases, and he's a fake. He says he loves family, but we never see him. He never came to see Mother when she was dying."

"Why not?"

"Who knows? Except that he takes the easy way. He didn't want to work roofs like our father, or lay bricks or deliver milk like his brothers. He wouldn't type letters for a living like me. Remember, do a good job this summer and you never know, you could make it in the movie industry." Linda's eyes widened as she transformed herself into an interviewer, then a guide, someone I didn't want to disappoint. "But the first thing is to get through the summer. Between Fred and where he takes you, and the cheap sex all around Times Square, you could hit a roadblock." She crossed her legs and smoothed her palm over her heel. "Before we go," she said, "help me change the bathroom light." She opened the hall closet and handed me a halo-shaped fluorescent bulb packed in corrugation. Then she carried a tall, three-legged stool to the bathroom. When she flicked the switch, she laughed. "I keep forgetting it's out," she said. She pulled the chain on the light over the bathroom mirror and stepped onto the stool.

"Hold me," she said.

"Let me do it," I said. "I'm taller."

"No," she said, "it's tricky. I'm good at it. Just hold me." I paused. "Go ahead," she said. "Don't let me fall." I held her waist while she tried wrenching the glass ring from its metal casing. It wouldn't budge, so she tugged harder, swaying back and forth on the stool, which rocked slightly. I had to tighten my grip and, as she twisted, my hands slid down her hips and I could feel each lurch of her shoulders rippling through her buttocks. Finally the bulb popped free and she handed it to me, getting down. Flustered and warm from the effort, she took off her bathrobe and hung it on the door. Her sleeveless nightgown reached only to her thighs, the material worn and flimsy, a transparent curtain that wavered as she unwrapped the new bulb.

"I'll put it in," I said, but she cut me off.

"I've done it all my life," she said. "This time, hold the stool. The linoleum's sagging here." I had to squat to press the stool firmly to the floor, leaning my palms on the seat. When Linda stretched her arms toward the ceiling, her nightgown lifted, and I looked directly at her white backside and the patch of brown hair starting between her legs. For a moment she leaned on one foot, raising the other slightly. "There!" she said, as it snapped into place. She took my hand and stepped down. I left the bathroom quickly, hiding my erection. Linda hit the switch, but the room stayed dim. She said, "I guess you better try it after all."

"Now?" I said from the hall.

"Yes," she said. "Then we can go."

"Let's do it when we get back," I said. "It's getting late."

"It'll take a second," she said.

I climbed the stool, and Linda held my waist as I fiddled with the bulb. It flickered, then filled the room with a brash ping of light. My hands were trembling as I started to step down, but Linda turned me by my belt loops so that I faced her. "Stay there," she said, and she turned to the sink, an edgeless porcelain oval marred by black nicks. She slid open the medicine cabinet and brought out a squat tub of Pond's vanishing cream. I had seen this jar before, when she smoothed it into her forehead and cheeks after a bath, sitting at the kitchen table, her hair wrapped in a towel. She unscrewed the lid, smearing her fingertips with the white paste, and faced me, my bulging pants even with her breasts. I felt like a museum piece, a statue in the alcove of our church, a patient about to have his temperature taken. I thought of a conversation with my mother earlier in the week, when she asked if I had met any nice girls at Paramount, and what kind of girl was I looking for. I said, "Probably someone like Aunt Linda," and I saw I hurt her feelings—did she want me to say someone like her? Now I was sure my answer was right, that under Linda's formal carriage was a woman who understood men and sex, and things would change between us. But I couldn't gauge the expression on her face—stern, then blasé.

"Do you feel like you might lose your balance there? I think the floor is really tilting. I almost lost mine."

"I'm okay," I said, and I spread my feet farther apart to keep steady.

"Do you like this smell?" she asked, holding her hand, fragrant with the floral cream, up to my chin. Before I could answer, she said, "You can have it," and she looked into my eyes, the tiniest smile on her face, so faint I could hardly tell if it was a smile at all. I put out my right hand, as if to shake, and she tenderly transferred all of the white grease. I stepped off the stool. "You can take this too," she said, giving me the jar. "We should leave soon. Come back in a few minutes."

I ran up the stairs, bringing my palm to my nose and inhaling. In the bathroom I used the cold cream that only minutes before was in her palm. I thought how close I was to having her do it, and I gasped, surprising myself, immediately afraid she might have heard me through the air shaft that ran through the house, bathroom to bathroom, from roof to cellar, the vertical tunnel that vented our private moments.

Outside Calvary, Queens' largest cemetery, buses fired long streams of greasy exhaust into the air as the children inside screamed and hung out the windows on their way to Rockaway Beach. Crowds entered Stevens' Appliance Center, a discount warehouse, whose big lighted sign flashed the TV in its name. As we made our way on the narrow path, Linda pointed out the untended graves. Next to my grandparents' plot, a red banner left over from the holidays read, *Christmas in Heaven*. Linda turned her shopping bag upside down, dumping a trowel, garden gloves, and plastic tulips. I stabbed the tough crabgrass with the trowel, making a small bed so she could stick the wire flowers onto each grave. Spindly and bright, the tulips looked like something from a cafeteria table. There was no one else in the massive cemetery, and Linda gazed at the wide green expanse serrated by markers, saying, "I suppose there are more dead than living now." The sun grew stronger and began to heat the paths. Linda dropped a glove and we bent for it at the same time, knocking our foreheads together hard. She tipped slightly backward, eyes closed, and I caught her, thinking she might pass out, though I was dizzy myself. She pushed me away, trying to shake off the shock, but she fell into me again, and we hugged until our heads stopped spinning.

That night I couldn't sleep, the beginning of a persistent insomnia. My mother heard me getting a glass of water and called from her bed, "I finished *Is Another World Watching*? What else do you have?" She got up and sorted through the others, choosing *The Thinking Body*. Fred had lent me a book called *Sleep*, a lucky coincidence. I read, "It is comparatively unimportant whether the head or feet are at the north end of the bed, but it is very important for the body to lie south-north or north-south."

I turned to the radio, dialing WABC, where Cousin Brucie played hit after hit, each followed by a loud bell—ding! I had never heard Long John because I had always been asleep, but after midnight I tuned him in. I paid attention to his words like I listened in school, weighing every syllable and, as I did, I pictured his tall frame at the microphone, knowing I met him and had his private number. His voice faded in and out, my cheap transistor pulling weakly, and I perched it between my headboard and the wall.

Long John's first guest, who called himself an analyst and appraiser of unseen human vibrations, introduced the Mantong Alphabet, a language used throughout the cosmos. Nebel ridiculed the man, who was also assaulted by Nebel's panel of friends. The second guest, Florence Psychic, spoke about her experiences aiding the New York Police Department. Once, she pointed the way to a kidnapped girl in the basement of a madman's house simply by holding the girl's scarf. She was smart and articulate, and I believed her. She said she did not accept payment, but once a grateful police commissioner insisted on granting her a wish. Her lifelong dream was to be listed in the Manhattan phone book, even though she lived in Jersey. "So if you look me up today," she said, "you'll find Florence Psychic, right there, the only person with a Jersey address and number."

Nebel's show wakened me even more, and the heat made it harder to sleep. I took off my undershirt and fluttered the sheet. Then I tiptoed into the kitchen, where I lifted our phone books from the bottom drawer of the cabinet and brought Manhattan to my room. When

I found *Psychic, Florence*, I entered a secret world. I tried to get her to feel my finger as I ran it across the letters of her name and address, 46 Golf Road, Tenafly. It was 4 A.M. when I finally fell asleep, just as Orfeo Angelucci, the third guest, spoke about zooming from one solar system to another in the company of a blonde who was five inches tall.

Hard Luck Suit

"I have a tip on a horse," Fred said on the phone. "Want to get in on it?"
I said I did.

"How much can you get?"

"Money?"

"Of course 'money!'" I could hear him chuckling.

"I have about a hundred and thirty nine," I said. I left off "dollars."
I was always halting my sentences with Fred to make them jazzier.

"Bring it, and more if you can." I thought I could scrounge through
my junk drawer, where a few stray bills lay crushed among old keys,
gum wrappers, whistles, and stubby pencils. I told him I had been listening to Nebel. "Which night? With the guy talking about BHT? To
keep stuff on the shelves longer? You know, there is more knowledge
on the airwaves alone than in all the colleges in the world. I've gotta
run, love to your mother. Oh, one more thing—how about I line up
a girl to meet us later, for dinner?" When I paused, he said, "Okay,
don't worry. I heard about your talk with Van. It's nothing to be
ashamed of. I'll ask Madeline to bring a girl. And this will be another
first too, your first job with me. We're a team now, right? See you
then." Since we were a team, I thought Fred might give me the key to
his place. I wanted to take it out during the week and run its teeth over
the tip of my finger. I wanted to throw a party and greet Long John and

61

Florence Psychic at the door. I wanted to show Linda the fancy bed. When an errand brought me anywhere near the Upper East Side, I looked toward Fred's and felt a pang close to homesickness. I mentioned this, and he said, "That's not homesickness. You don't live there. You've got away-sickness—you just want to get away."

My sleeplessness continued, and I listened to Long John interview the man Fred mentioned who claimed an evil race lived deep in the earth. The Deros, short for Detrimental Robots, rigged certain elevators in New York, so that if passengers pressed basement twice, they would travel straight down, three miles, into the boiling hearth where these monsters made their home. During one of Long John's endless commercials for a disinfectant so strong that one drop could deodorize an airplane hangar, I worried about the money I risked, Christmas money saved to buy a Zenith TransOceanic radio. For a long time I'd wanted to hear overseas broadcasts, which wasn't possible on my cheap transistor. I started to replay Linda's words about Fred, and I worried. I worried about the promised girl. Not only about what would be expected of me, but because of my obsession with Linda. Of all the women in the city and all the mailroom's thumbed-through magazines showing overinflated blondes pushing their mouths into succulent shapes while lifting gauzy underwear, nothing excited me more than my prim, officious aunt. I worried whether any other woman would be able to arouse me. I looked down at my penis, which had shrunk to the size of a hazelnut, and I worried.

I met Fred at Rumplemayer's on Saturday morning. It was mid-July, and the lips of the carriage horses around Central Park foamed with a frothlike meringue. I looked forward to going to the track, thinking of the train that sped through the stations without stopping, leaving commuters in its breeze, the train that blew straight to Aqueduct, the train marked S for *Special*. I arrived early and spun twice through the St. Moritz's revolving doors just for the luxury of entering and leaving. Rumplemayer's marble soda fountain stood in the center of an enormous pink room whose walls were hung with stuffed animals. Fred waved from a booth. He wore a dark pinstriped suit. As I slid in, I straightened my lapels. He asked where I got my tie.

"Tie City." All ties were ninety-nine cents. "I just bought it, for today."

"Don't go there anymore," he said. "That's a junk shop." I looked down at my chest, at the wildest tie I could find, a tie for the racetrack, a tie of good luck. Horse heads and horseshoes covered the kelly green background, pinned to my shirt by a new tie tack, a horse's backside and long tail.

"I have to go to Whitehouse and Hardy later to pick up a suit. I'll get you one that goes better."

"I thought this would bring good luck," I said.

"And I'm sure it will," he said, "but I want you to look more formal. You know, if you go off to college, you'll never learn how to dress. You'll be a bumpkin forever." Fred glanced at the menu and said, "Did you see Gail's putting game on her blackboard? Weird stuff, mutton, venison—she even has tongue! I'll never eat anything from an animal's mouth." He paused. "Let's have eggs." He ordered eggs Benedict for both of us. He had a habit of snorting when he was excited, and he breathed loudly through his nose. His grin never let up, and he called for more ice water whenever I took a few sips, annoying our waiter, an older man.

"We should talk about Van Forkenberry," he said. "Gail told me about what he said to you."

"It's okay, Uncle Fred," I said. "It wasn't your fault."

"I didn't say it was my fault!" he yelled. "I didn't apologize!" I took another sip. Then he whispered, "Never apologize, remember that. Things are too complicated for any one person to take the blame. Van's fallen a long way since his gigolo years at the Commodore Hotel." He yelled again, "Waiter, more water!" And to me, "I feel sorry for him." He looked down at his plate. "How did you feel?"

"I got mad," I said.

"I know you did, but look at it this way. I mean, if a woman flirted with you, you wouldn't feel mad, would you?"

I said I wouldn't.

"Then why feel mad at a man? It's the same thing, isn't it? And like I told you before, drop the 'Uncle.' Just call me Fred, okay?" My glass was three-quarters full, and this time the waiter stopped, looked at Fred, and said, "He still has a full glass."

"Do what I say!" Fred ordered, and the waiter went off, returning a moment later with the pitcher. When he had finished, Fred said,

"Now, waiter, he'd like more coffee." My cup was empty, but I had had more than enough. I started to object, but Fred shut me up and the waiter smiled a fake sweetness. Fred was onto another subject, hotels, describing the upstairs rooms in the St. Moritz, when the waiter arrived, carrying the tall silver pot. He filled my cup, lifting the spout, which was shaped like a swan's neck, higher and higher as he poured. Soon the coffee began to stipple onto the table, and the cup was still only a third full. He continued to raise it until the droplets thickened into drops, scattering onto my saucer. Fred talked without noticing, stretching his arms to show the size of a honeymoon suite, telling how he sat in the middle of the enormous bed, leaning against the headboard, and had to crawl a long way just to set his drink on the night table. Drops were hitting the cuff of my sleeve, and I moved my arm to my lap. I nodded to the waiter, who kept smiling, his eyes fixed on the cup, which he had filled to the brim. He turned on his heel as Fred continued. I pressed my sleeve with a napkin. The old waiter stood at attention across the room and, when I caught his eye, he looked left and right, lifted his hand from under the towel draped over his forearm, and gave me the finger.

After breakfast Fred said, "We're partners, right? You'll get a kick out of this errand. Get a few things around town and drop them off later. Simple."

"Before we go to the track?"

"The track? Oh, no," he said. "We don't go to the track. We make the bet in town." I was disappointed, but my disappointment changed quickly into wonder about the job. I remembered Gail's description of Eddie, the runner Fred had fired while grinning. We got in a cab, and Fred asked the driver his name. "Paul, we have some errands to run. It involves a bit of waiting here and there, but I'll make it worth your while." He handed a bill over the seat.

"Fine with me," Paul said, tucking it into his shirt pocket.

Our first stop was a shoeshine stand on Lexington Avenue. Fred said, "Remember Mike? Go tell him you're picking up for Fred. I'll wait here." Mike was buffing the shoes of a huge blond man. When he finished, I said, "Good morning. Fred sent me to pick up something for him." It was just like my job as a messenger. Mike stared; after a few long seconds, he answered, "Good morning." A car horn blew hard, but I couldn't tell if it was Paul. Mike shuffled over and gave me an envelope, holding it by the corner so he wouldn't taint it with shoe polish. When I opened the cab door, Fred yelled, "What the hell took you?"

"He was shining a man's shoes."

Fred smiled, but he was irritated. "Kid, don't *you* wait. I'm waiting out here, Paul's waiting, the meter's running, and we don't have time to wait for you to wait."

"I know, but Mike was shining the shoes of a really big guy, Fred." I thought size would impress him.

"Big, schmig," Fred said.

The next stop was Marino's fish store, where the owner spoke with a heavy Italian accent and tried to get me to invite Fred for lunch. "Tell him I've got fresh calamari. I'll fry it in the back. Little lemon." He made a circular, squeezing motion with his fingers, as if over a plate.

"We're in a hurry," I said, taking his envelope.

The counterman at Nat Sherman's didn't trust me and walked outside to look in the cab. I thought of buying a cigar for Fred. As I looked at the case, the man said, "Brazilian cheroots, mild and sweet." I paused at the door, over a small barrel that held great, fat cigars I pictured in Fred's mouth. The sign read, "Five Cents." From behind the counter the man called, "Those are strictly five-cent cigars." And he held his nose. I made my way through a coin shop, several newsstands in hotel lobbies, Mr. Ret's, and a liquor store. I looked at my reflection each time I had the chance and smoothed down my hair. Mr. Ret gave me another Toblerone candy bar wrapped in tissue, and his shaking hands held mine as I turned to leave. He pressed more tissue into my palm, saying, "This is for Freddie. Tell Fred that this is for him because I don't know who will be getting my things." His mouth quivered as if he were about to cry.

Fred separated the crumpled paper and shook out a gold ring. "This is nice," he said, using his jeweler's loupe to stare at the stone. "Mr. Ret must be dissolving his estate, not feeling well lately. You hold it. You got it from him. Good work." I shifted in my seat to put the ring into my pocket, a deep pocket, unlike my other pants that tossed change onto cushions around the city. Fred had settled into the cab as if it were his office. He pulled money from each envelope and marked the amounts in a little book. Paul peered through his rearview mirror. The bills expanded like sponge when Fred opened the envelopes;

the stacks were thick and filthy. He put a note under the rubber band that circled each pile. He saw me staring and said, "Like this?" holding up the black leather book. "It's a *New Yorker* date book, from the magazine. Ever read *The New Yorker*?" I had spent the summer reading everything on the stands, even the odd papers that news dealers hung from the frame of their shacks like fringe, papers of different sizes, tints, and typefaces. I read Breslin in the *Tribune*, loving Fat Thomas and Marvin the Torch. I read the *Wall Street Journal* and the *Sporting News*. I thumbed through the *Hollywood Reporter* as well as *Variety*. I scanned *Cue*, but I had skipped *The New Yorker*. I didn't like its looks—its cover seemed drawn by adults trying to draw like children. "Madeline gave it to me. She loves it. You'll meet her tonight. She's a model, went to college, some kooky place upstate. In a funny way she reminds me of you." He continued to fiddle with the envelopes while I watched, disappointed that I reminded him of a woman when I wanted to be a man's man. "Paul," he said, "take us to the west corner of Fifth-Sixth and Eighth."

Paul pulled in front a fire hydrant, saying, "How about I idle at this 'drant?"

"Fine, Paul," Fred said, "but I want to talk to my nephew in private." He handed over another bill. "Won't be long." Paul got out and leaned against the car in front of us, looking down the block. It was hot, and sweat showed through Paul's yellow T-shirt that said, "WMCA Good Guys" on the back. Fred asked, "Did you bring your money?"

"Yes, but I could only get the one-thirty-nine."

"All right," he said. "The money in these envelopes is going on different horses. If you want to put your money on my horse, I'll add it. You have to remember you could lose. But today, I feel sure we'll win."

"I guess I'll bet," I said, "if you think we'll win." I took the money from my wallet and he added it to his stack. He looked at his watch again. "This is what you have to do now. Very simple. But you have to do it right." He slid the stacks of bills between a folded paper and then into my inside jacket pocket. "Ours is the first stack," he said.

I had to use a bathroom. I had drunk several coffees at Rumplemayer's and countless glasses of water. I tried to concentrate on Fred's words while I shifted in the sticky vinyl seat.

"Bernie's waiting at the end of the block, on Ninth Avenue. You just walk down the block and give him the money."

"What does he look like?"

"A little guy. A twerp. But don't worry, he's waiting for you. I told him you look like Prince Charles. I told him, 'Prince Charles is coming in a blue suit!'" Fred was grinning hard and wide. "There's one thing," he said, "and this is what it all comes down to." He stopped smiling, lifted my hand off my leg and pressed it between his palms as he looked at me in a deadly way. "Take these," he said, showing ten strips of bond held together by a paper clip, each with a number written in big letters. "Put these in your pants pocket, and keep your hand on them as you walk."

"Then what?"

"Listen!" When he said this, he raised his hand to the side of my face as if he were about to hit me. "Somewhere down the street you'll pass a guy. He'll be standing next to a building. There should be a number written in chalk right next to him. If it isn't, wait a minute, tie your shoe, something like that. Then look again."

"Suppose it's not there?"

"It'll be there. This guy is gonna write it. Could be there now."

"What do I do with the number?" I was following Fred's words as I had never followed instructions from anyone in school, at Paramount, at home. I was studying every phrase when Paul's profile jutted through the open window, and I jumped, hitting my head on the high roof. Paul was red, and sweat beaded on his face and neck. Fred exploded at him, instantly as flushed as Paul, screaming, "What the fuck do you think you're doing? I'm paying for this time, you miserable little hack!" Paul opened the front door and reached in.

"Just getting my hat, for Christ's sake. It's broiling out here." He grabbed a Yankees cap and left.

Fred turned to me, totally calm again. "You get the number from the wall. Then you count these papers, which will be in your pocket, right? Till you come to the number he wrote. Take it out, keep it in your fist, and then slip it into your breast pocket, under the rubber band of the stack nearest you."

"Our money?"

"Right! But remember, Bernie will see you coming, so don't make a big deal with moving the number."

"Suppose I get the wrong piece of paper?"

"Can't. Feel the first one." He held it out.

"It's rough."

"Yeah, it's sandpaper. You feel for that and then count. One, two, three. Okay?"

"I think so," I said.

"Don't count the sandpaper, start counting after that, then stick the number into our stack." He grabbed me by the elbow. "You know what to do, right? You'll do fine, I know." I checked the stack and put the papers in my pocket, holding my hand there, not wanting to mess up the order. "Remember not to count the sandpaper," he said. "And remember, there's a nice girl waiting for you at the end of this day. Now, go!"

I opened the door, keeping my hand in my pants pocket at the same time. My full bladder ached. Paul jumped into the cab as I left, and as I passed the window, Fred leaned out and whispered, "Good luck, nephew!" It was a weird, harsh whisper.

The white sidewalk steamed in the sun, and I knew why Paul wanted his hat. I was sweating after a few feet. I thought I saw Bernie at the end of the long block, but then he disappeared. I walked too fast and couldn't get myself to slow down. Fred hadn't told me the pace. No one was on the street, and the windows of the brownstones had a sooty look along their sills. I sneezed and restrained myself from yanking my hand to my face, so that instead I twisted around, my hand in my pocket, my elbow out, like a bird with a hurt wing. I saw Bernie on the corner, walking back and forth along the avenue, facing me once in awhile.

I decided that if no one gave me the number, I'd return to the cab, but then a man walked up from the basement stairs, looked at me, and wrote "6" just below the yellow and black arrow that pointed the way to a fallout shelter. I touched the cardboard and began counting. I pulled the sixth strip free and, pretending to sneeze again, brought it to my mouth. I opened the folded paper in my jacket with my fingertips and eased the number under the rubber band. I walked with longer strides. Bernie was now staring at me and then at some pigeons around a lamppost. As I got closer I saw him clearly: gray fedora, tiny features. His nose, eyes, and mouth so close together they formed a circle on his face. It struck me how sophisticated the man in the doorway had looked, a pencil-thin mustache. I thought I should grow one like it. Bernie lit a cigarette just as I reached him, making me wait. Then he shouted, "Let's have it!" as if I held him up. I slapped the envelope into his palm and he stuffed it into his front pants pocket and stalked off. I wanted to dash to the cab, but I walked slower than I had ever walked in my life despite the heat. When I reached the fallout shelter I felt a great ease and confidence and love of the world. I went down the three stairs and relieved myself in a corner. Fifty-sixth Street teemed with objects I suddenly found fascinating, a plastic tricycle, a cracked slate stoop, a litter basket crowned with heaps of dried-out carrots and heads of lettuce. Paul had the radio on, but not to WMCA. Instead, we listened to Ed and Pegeen Fitzgerald discuss pillows made of hops, which they slept on in Austria. Fred didn't even look at me when I got in, but ordered Paul to Whitehouse and Hardy on Fifth Avenue.

"Everything went fine," I whispered to Fred, who nodded indifferently.

As soon as we got out of the cab, he changed. All smiles again. "You got the number?"

"It was six."

"And Bernie?"

"Yes, he didn't say much."

"What's to say?" he said, cupping his palm on the small of my back and escorting me into the clothing store. Fred held the sleeve of his new light-gray suit so that I could inspect it, and I touched the fine colored threads that ran through the fabric. He asked endless questions about the alterations and took almost as much time choosing a tie for me, wrapping each one around his fingers and holding the improvised knot under my chin. He settled on light blue with yellow stripes. On the way out, he paused at rows of slippers that seemed more like shoes, shiny and hard. "A pair of these would last me ten years," he said with a faraway look. "Know why? Because I'm never home." He fit one onto his hand and held it in front of me so that I could see my face.

At dusk the traffic changed, delivery trucks giving way to limousines and sports cars. Fred swung the suit over his shoulder, humming. We ate hot dogs from a vendor and walked to his apartment. We passed a tiny men's shop, Pink's, and Fred looked in the window. "Someday I'm going to have my shirts made," he said, shaking his head in appreciation of the collars and cuffs. "Know what their slogan is? 'Any color, as long as it's Pink!'" A block later, he said, "You'll meet

69

Madeline tonight. You'll really like her. And of course, she's got that girl for you."

"I didn't need a date, Fred."

"Of course you do. You'll have fun. Don't be nervous."

"I'm not nervous," I snapped, sounding like Fred.

"Don't worry," he said, "Madeline has some nice friends."

"Have long have you been going out with her?"

Fred seemed thrown by the question, as if he hadn't asked it of himself. "Since February or so. Sometime in the winter." As soon as we entered the apartment, Fred put on the radio and hummed along. Every so often a voice gave the call letters and said, "The Mellow Sound." He took a can of Dr. Brown's Cel-Ray tonic from the refrigerator and held it high. "This is for you. Can only get it in delicatessens. Delicious." He poured it into a wineglass. The radio gushed a sentimental song dominated by intensely vibrating strings. Fred ran over and spun the dial. "I hate the mandolin," he said. Long John Nebel came on, doing an ad for the world's best shoeshine. He said, "The leather is softened by rubbing it with the tibia of an elk, polished to a high gloss by a lamb's wool buffing bonnet on a power drill." The method was invented by a bootblack in the St. Louis airport, where you had to mail your shoes. Nebel continued, "After an application of Van-Van oil, the shine is baked under Cooper-Hewitt lights."

"I'd like that shine," Fred said, "but I'm not sending my Church's." He sat at one end of the kitchen table making phone calls while I sat at the other, drinking the tonic and paging through papers and magazines Fred had picked up. He pointed dramatically to a stack of old *New Yorkers*, and I picked one to read in preparation for meeting Madeline. When I thought I'd neared the end of a long piece on amphibious cars, it continued for five more pages. I walked out to the terrace, suddenly very tired, and lay down on a lounge chair next to Fred's new acquisition, three identical sculptures of the Venus di Milo. The evening air felt cool, and I reviewed the places I had been. I particularly relished peeling off the number six. Realizing again that I'd done it right, I laughed with relief. I couldn't wait for the results of the race and imagined celebrating if we won. I also wanted to see Fred with a woman. Would he be gracious or gruff? Would he be both a "man's man" and a "ladies man"? I didn't want to see myself with a woman. I wanted to learn how to act first, as I had learned other things, like how a drink or two could change a dull evening. For the first time, I wanted a drink just to see how much better things could get. Fred took a shower and changed into his suit. I knotted my new tie, and he inspected it. "Beautiful," he said, but then he brushed my shoulder and examined my hair. I thought he would criticize the crooked part I could never get straight, but he said, "You know, you have a piece of dandruff on your head as big as a dime."

I hadn't had anything like that before. "Is it okay if I take a shower too?" I said.

"Sure," he said. I'm going out for a few groceries. Back soon."

I rushed to the bathroom mirror and combed my hair with my fingers, exposing a ruddy scalp. Raw patches on my arms began to itch, and skin flaked on my chest as well. The shower made the hives brighter. My face was spared, but for how long? Skin continued to loosen on my scalp and, in a panic, I searched the apartment for a remedy. I found a vacuum cleaner in the hall closet and removed the attachment. I knelt in my underwear and vacuumed my head with the aluminum pipe, praying that Fred would not walk in. In the bathroom I saw the treatment had pulled my hair into triangular points, as if a dozen tents were pitched around my head. I took a can of Ajax from under the sink and washed my hair again, scrubbing it ruthlessly. I poured Ajax onto a hot washcloth and rubbed my chest and arms. When I wiped the mirror clear, I saw I had found a kind of solution. I had made my entire chest and arms bright red, but a pink aura outlined my forehead and sideburns, like I had worn a helmet for a long time. In the medicine cabinet I found something I had never seen before: flesh-colored talc, and I dusted my hairline. I was grateful Fred did not inspect me when he returned. As he put the groceries into the closet, I sat in a chair away from the light.

"I've been thinking," he said. "You did a good job today."

"Thanks," I said. "It was fun."

"Fun! Yes, it was!" he said, as if he had never thought of it that way. He laughed and said, "Let me have Mr. Ret's ring." I opened the tissue and Fred plucked it out, shaking it in his fist. "I'll give it to Madeline tonight." We got on the elevator and Fred jingled the coins in his pocket, humming again. It was a tune I recognized but couldn't place, a song I knew, one we had heard together. Then it came to me. The jingle from WNEW, the station where Fred heard "The Make Believe

Ballroom." As we walked down the street, he said, "I have a wonderful evening planned. We'll meet Madeline and her girlfriend, and then we'll have drinks, dinner, maybe music. She's bringing Shelley, I think it's Shelley. Christ!" he said suddenly, "You'll need to get her something too."

"Like what?"

"Just something. Like I have this ring, you need something, like flowers, but not flowers. Let me think." He walked faster.

"How about a silk scarf?" I said. "They're selling them around the corner."

"A great idea," he said. When we got to the vendor's stand, I lifted up a red square brightened by a silver pattern. Looking closely, I saw they were punctuation marks: rows of exclamation points, asterisks, ampersands. Fred showed no interest and just nodded his head. After he paid, he began going through his pockets, searching his pants and jacket. "Do you have that ring?" he asked.

"No, Fred. I gave it to you." I could hear a whine in my voice.

"Where? In the hall?"

"Kitchen."

We started back to the apartment. Fred did not return Fitz's greeting. After inspecting the counters, sink, and drainer, Fred moved the table and chairs and explored the floor and molding. He emptied the vegetable bins. I combed the thick white wall-to-wall rug of his bathroom on my hands and knees, crawling before his closet doors that formed a wall of mirrors. "No luck?" he asked, poking his head in.

"No luck," I answered. He stood in the doorway in his tight white undershirt, jockey shorts and black socks. A few minutes later he bent over the dining-room table, rubbing the heel of his palm over every inch of the suit. "Maybe it fell into the lining," he said.

But it hadn't. Fred put on another suit. Before we left, he opened the refrigerator and took a long swig of Cel-Ray. I stared at his back. When he turned, he looked at me holding the paper bag with the scarf, as if he suddenly remembered I was there. "Leave the scarf," he said. Fred carried the new gray suit over his arm. Instead of getting on the elevator, he walked to the incinerator and stuffed the suit down the shaft. "That's a hard luck suit," he said. "It lost that ring. I don't want a suit that loses things."

I thought he could have given it away. I'd seen how much Fred had paid and, as we left the building, I couldn't help saying, "Maybe we should have dropped it off at the Salvation Army—you know, for the poor."

Fred kept up his brisk walk and looked over at me, puzzled. "Why? Give away bad luck? To the poor? So they can lose what little they already have?"

He was adamant about hard luck, and I became even more quiet, remembering the words, "You're through, Eddie." I also felt fortunate I hadn't lost the ring myself. I had gotten attached to my blue suit.

We were meeting Madeline at a club called "A Little Table in Every Corner." Fred touted the long beads that hung from ceiling to floor around three sides of each table, so every party had privacy, its own corner. Fred snorted as we walked in and saw the women at the far end of the bar, laughing. "It *is* Shelley," he said. "A gorgeous redhead." Their teeth flashed in the dim light as they talked. Madeline was in her twenties, tall, pretty, and very pale. Her long black hair was pulled straight back, then it rose and fell in a lofty ponytail onto her backless dress. She wore no makeup except for dark lipstick that accentuated her wide mouth, reminding me of an angelfish. Even her sweptback hair looked like a dorsal fin as she moved toward us. And the bar itself, with its ferns and lanterns, the little bridge to the dining room, seemed like the bottom of my aquarium. Shelley was not more than twenty. Her reddish hair, cut in a pageboy, and the smattering of freckles across her nose gave her an even more girlish look, although lines crowded her eyes. Her plaid skirt and pleated blouse were like those in *Esquire*'s college issue, which I had seen in barbershops and waiting rooms. I liked the bump in the center of her nose, one of those features that hints at what the person will look like when they're older. As an old woman, she would look good.

Fred dragged them away from the bar and into the main room, where we sat around the truncated piano, two feet from the pianist, a young man with a long neck so skinny you could see his vocal chords vibrate as he crooned. Fred handed him card after card, with dollars folded into the names of Madeline's favorites. We heard "Bewitched, Bothered, and Bewildered" twice. Madeline's choice for Fred was "Mr. Lucky." The women ordered champagne cocktails, and Fred called for Jack Daniel's. When our drinks came, Fred looked down at his glass, turned, and yelled at the waitress, "Let me speak to the manager." Madeline sipped her drink, and Shelley said she didn't want a scene. The manager was a tall and hefty man in a double-breasted powder blue suit. I recognized his strong cologne, English Leather, popular in high school. Fred held the glass up to his face, just under his goatee. "Look at this glass," he said.

"What's wrong with it?"

Fred pinched its thick side, saying, "It's a sham glass, a sham glass!" and he dashed the whiskey into a clean ashtray, where it pooled, barely covering the bottom. "This is something you'd serve a child." Fred was loud, and the pianist hit the keys louder, hammering out "My Favorite Things." The manager began to explain standard measurement, but Fred cut him off, pushing his chair from the table and standing. The power of this sudden gesture was diminished by the manager's size, and Fred had to gaze up into the big man's face. Still, he yelled, "Bring us some real drinks!" The manager walked away, and Fred shrugged and smiled, calm again. "Did you get a load of that suit?" he said.

The waitress brought water glasses of whiskey, half-full. Fred said nothing when she placed the drinks before us, but then he lifted his glass toward me, repeating his old refrain, "Sipping whiskey, John, sipping whiskey." Madeline and Shelley begged to leave the piano, and we finally took a table surrounded by the promised beads. I was glad to be out of the spotlight, because I wondered how my talc was holding up. Shelley looked right at me and said, "I hear you're smart." Her left eye was out of focus. She had what my mother called a turn in her eye.

I hesitated to answer, but then Fred said, "He's always been smart in school, right from the start. Like me, really."

"Where were you all day?" Madeline asked. "I kept calling and got no answer."

"We were running errands. John made his first bet on a horse."

"That's exciting," Shelley said, raising her eyebrows.

"But we didn't go to the track," I said. The bourbon gave me the courage to ask what had been on my mind. "When do we find out if we won?"

Fred did a double take.

"Win?" he said. "Win? Of course we won."

"That's great," I said, relieved.

Madeline and Fred talked about her new apartment. She was unhappy with the men delivering carpet.

I wanted a little ice in my whiskey and was about to sneak some from the ice water when Shelley said to me, "Did you know I used to work at Saks? I did, but I quit. I'm thinking of going back to school."

Fred caught part of our conversation and said, "I gave Shelley a book last Christmas. Know what she said? 'I already have a book.'"

"Bullshit, Fred. I read more than you."

Fred was already back to Madeline and the carpet. Madeline said, "It was supposed to be a thicker shag."

"Your uncle can be tough to take sometimes," Shelley said, lighting a cigarette. She was easy to talk to, and I didn't have to rely on the drink to lift my shyness.

"Let's go," Fred said. "I don't know about you gals, but we're starved." When we stood up, I measured myself against Shelley, glad to be taller, and I thought I felt her nestle by me as she walked out, like Linda at our lunches. I held the door and, when the women were on the street, the manager stepped out of nowhere, spun Fred around by the shoulder, and punched him hard in the stomach. Fred's gasp and the fist hitting his belly sounded like someone swinging a bat into a shower curtain. Fred doubled up against the window as the manager walked quickly away. Turning to us, the whites of his eyes large against his tan skin, the manager said, "Have a good evening, Slick." I put my arm around Fred and looked for the women, who kept walking, unaware. Fred glanced over at me, clearly in pain, and said, "That didn't hurt." He straightened, smoothed his shirt, and trotted toward Madeline and Shelley. Madeline held dollar bills above the heads of gypsy kids, who jumped and snatched at them.

Fred described the restaurant, La Machinetta, saying, "The gnocchi's the best in the city, and if you want veal, there's no place better. The chef's name is Quattropane, which means 'four breads,'" and he held out his hands as if grasping the loaves. I recalled seeing a review of it in the *Times* on a slow day in the mailroom. "I read about this place, Fred," I said.

"Then it's packed for sure," Madeline said.

"Will you stop worrying?" Fred said. He and Madeline walked fast, arm in arm, and Shelley and I bounded next to each other to keep pace. At one corner Fred led us down the subway stairs and into an arcade. "We'll miss the lights this way," he yelled over his shoulder as we cut past hot-dog vendors, pinball parlors, and newsstands. On our way out, up a long flight, we passed a nun holding the railing and putting her black suitcase down after each step. Fred stopped, bent to the nun, and said, "Let me give you a hand." He lifted the bag, which surprised him by its weight. "What do you have in here, Sister," he asked as he climbed the stairs, "pennies from heaven?"

There was a long line outside La Machinetta, and Madeline said "Cripes." Fred grabbed my arm and took me to a phone booth, leaving the women in front of a florist. He dialed information for the restaurant's number and handed the phone to me. "Ask the name of the maître d'."

"It's Marcus Venturi," I said, hanging up.

"Now we'll just wait a minute," he said. He put his hands in his pockets and gazed over at Madeline and Shelley. "Aren't they pretty there," he said, "among the flowers?"

"Madeline's nice," I said.

"She wants to talk with you, when it's quiet." He got on the phone and asked for Marcus Venturi. He had to wait, but then I heard him say as he closed the door to the phone booth, "Mr. Venturi, I have a fifty dollar bill in my pocket. My name is Lotti, party of four." I was surprised by his new version of Bertolotti: sometimes Bertel, sometimes Lotti. I guessed he used the Italian name in Italian restaurants. The four of us lingered by the front door, to the side of the line. In a few minutes a voice yelled, "Lotti!"

Fred shook hands with Mr. Venturi, who led us to the dining room. The walls were stark turquoise, with bright white molding. The ceiling held one large skylight, and a willow tree reached through it. "This guy owned The Orangerie," Fred said. "They have those drinks you like here, Shelley."

78

"That's what I'll have then," she said, looking over at me. "Champagne and orange juice." She cranked the handle of one of the antique coffee grinders, the *machinettas* placed on every table.

Madeline said, "John, I got you a subscription to *The New Yorker*. It's 43-26 Judge Street, isn't it?"

"Yes," I said. "Thank you."

"What I'll get you next year, when you're in college, is *Daedalus*—do you know it?"

"No, I don't." I was memorizing the name to look up.

"It's not as au courant as *The New Yorker*, but it's more in depth."

Shelley finished her veal marsala and ordered rack of lamb. It was easy to place the order, as waiters never left the table but stood behind us, bending to refill our drinks or to light a cigarette even as Fred or Madeline reached for their packs.

"I hate the way people say, *the* lamb or *the* bass," Fred said. "It's pretentious."

"Another dinner?" Madeline asked Shelley.

Fred looked at Shelley and said, "What you eat, eats you in the next world."

"I don't care for your theories, Fred. I'm ravished," Shelley said.

"That's *famished*! What a dummy!" Fred said, but Shelley pretended not to hear. She was buttering a huge heel of bread.

After dinner we heard Roy Eldridge at Jimmy Ryan's. We sat up front, and Fred listened so completely it was as if he had left the table. He said, "When this guy blows like he can, nobody blows better." Then he whispered to me, "That's a musical expression." Shelley said to Madeline, "You really don't get anything good to eat in a place like this."

"Hush your mouth," Fred said. "Listen how he builds his solos, like a book—an introduction, then chapters, then a climax. He learned that from Satchmo."

"Sounds like something else," Shelley said, giggling. Fred ignored her and got into a conversation with a guy at the next table. I could hear him saying, "Nobody blows like him." Eldridge was doing "St. James Infirmary," which I'd heard on my easy-listening station. He went so far away from the tune, I thought he'd never come back. But then he did. The day's errands, the bourbon, the wine at dinner, and my nervousness about being with Shelley had me babbling. I was in the middle of telling stories about the mailroom and describing Beardsley's awful scar, but Fred cut me off just as I was saying, "It runs right through the eyelid so it waters, like his eye is drooling . . ."

To make up for it, I waited for Eldridge to finish his set and then told Fred how much I liked the band that took his place, but he looked at me with scorn. "That's the house band," he said. "They're paid to kill time." Still, I requested "To Each His Own," which I recalled as one of Madeline's favorites. I admired the way the piano player said, at the end of his set, "This is Frankie Dash at the piano, playing 'You've Changed,'" and I pranced my fingertips at the edge of the table.

We had more drinks at The Brasserie, where a costume party had ended up. A beautiful woman tied a helium balloon to each of her pigtails, lifting them six inches above her ears. Two men in gorilla suits sat at the bar, their masks at their feet. Fred said, "The men usually go for the gorilla suit and women for the Cleopatra." Shelley said, "I think it's pretentious to say *the* gorilla suit or *the* Cleopatra," and she began to laugh hysterically. Fred looked at her glass to see how much she was drinking. Her laughter started to attract attention, so she leaned into me, pressing her mouth against my shirt. Instead of calming her, I began to laugh uncontrollably myself, just from having a woman in my arms. Fred looked amused, then embarrassed, and finally angered. He said to Madeline, "Take her to the ladies' room."

When we were alone, Fred handed me a roll of bills, saying, "Here's your share."

"Your tip was right on the money," I said, squeezing the wad into my pocket.

"Jonathan John," he said. "There wasn't any tip. The guy on the street knew who won. The race was over at that minute. Your timing was good, and Bernie suspected nothing because he saw you the whole time."

"Holy shit," I said, laughing again.

"Don't start," Fred said, but he was laughing too. "A few weeks ago I was playing golf with another bookie." He put his hand on my forearm. "This is a good one. On the fifth hole a kid comes along and asks if we want to buy some golf balls. Don't tell Shelley this stuff. This is business, between us."

I brought my drink to my lips and inhaled its fumes. That was all I wanted to do with it. It was a stinger, white crème de menthe and brandy, that Fred ordered for me, saying it tasted like Christmas.

"The kid has two balls in his hand. We don't want them and he leaves. A few seconds later I pretend to remember I wanted to play a horse in the fifth race. The race is over by now, but the bookie doesn't care. He's been with me on the links, we're in the middle of nowhere. He takes my bet on the second horse, a long shot that pays pretty well."

"How?"

"The kid, John. Sent out at the right time, the fifth hole, two balls for the second horse. Remember, don't tell Shelley. Oh, and I hope you like her. We'll bring her back with us. She's a nice kid, a little dumb, but nice."

"I don't think she's that dumb," I said.

"Oh ho!" he said.

I took out the money. "How much is this?"

"$350. Listen," he said, "there must be something you've wanted for a long time. Now's your chance. What is it?" He leaned over with a smile that took credit for my good luck and showed real pleasure in what it would bring. I felt invited enough by his expression to tell him the reason I'd saved the $139. "Well, there's a radio called a Zenith TransOceanic. You can get stations from every country . . ."

Fred interrupted. "There aren't enough stations in New York? The best in the world isn't enough? You got Long John, Big Wilson." He counted on his fingers. "John Gambling, William B. The top guys are right here."

"This goes all over the world."

"Don't be like the nitwits who study how dolphins talk when people can't even speak to each other. Just promise me that," he said, getting up. "I've got to make a call." I sat alone at the table looking over the half-finished drinks and the crumpled, lipstick-smeared napkins. I asked myself why I wanted a worldwide radio when I hardly knew New York. I felt worse because I'd just bought a book by John Lilly on dolphins. Perhaps Fred knew it through the ESP he had been investigating. I lifted my stinger and began to drink. An older man wearing a straw fedora and a seersucker suit stared at me from a nearby table. When he caught my eye, he walked over and sat in Shelley's chair. "I like that girl you're with," he said. "She's pretty."

"Thank you," I said.

"My days for that are over," he said, "but then again, one always hopes."

I nodded.

"You know, I live alone, and every night I go to the store, get a little something for dinner. Last night I got liver." He flagged a waitress and waved his glass, holding the stem between his thumb and forefinger. Fred had taught me the different shapes and I recognized a Manhattan glass. Moving his face close, he told me about carrying the liver home in a little white box, and how two dogs fought just as he passed them, aroused by the scent. He had just finished describing how their hunger got to him, and that he divided the meat between them, when Fred returned.

"Who's your friend?" Fred said.

When the man began to introduce himself, Fred simply said, "Go!" The man was slow to rise, and when he did, he lingered, saying, "So, I had a can of tuna for dinner."

"Would you get out of here!" Fred said, and gave him a shove.

"They really wanted my liver . . ." the man continued, shaking his head as he wobbled back to his table.

"Someone wanted *your* liver? I wouldn't wish your liver on a dog!" Fred called. "What were you doing with the rum-bum?" Fred asked, and I started to explain that it wasn't his own liver but that there were dogs involved, which maybe Fred intuited by his use of ESP. I was drunk, confused, and Fred made a weird face at me, when we were interrupted by Madeline and Shelley's return. Shelley sat down, wiping tears from her cheeks, and Madeline stood behind her chair for a moment, looking at Fred and rolling her big eyes.

In the cab I sat on a little folding stool in front of everyone's knees. We got out at Fifth Avenue, and Fred bought the early Sunday editions as well as an *Architectural Digest* for Madeline, who carried a thin bottle of wine that she had admired somewhere during the evening. Once Shelley had to pull me back to the curb when I toppled off.

Madeline whirled around the apartment as if it were hers, while Fred took a shower. She hung up my suit jacket, flung open the terrace doors, and lifted windows. Shelley began frying bacon, and Fred walked in wearing a silk bathrobe. He whispered to me, "I hope you like your sheets. I got them just for tonight." I recognized the scent of lavender soap, Yardley's, that I'd seen stacked in the medicine cabinet. He had unwrapped each bar, which he told me made them last longer. "Good night, everyone," he said.

Madeline said, "Shelley, make sure the door to the terrace is shut."

"Okay," Shelley said, as she laid out strips of bacon across my new *Village Voice*.

I had expected some advice from Fred about Shelley, who filled two water glasses from the thin bottle. "I like tumblers," she said. "You don't have to worry about knocking them over." She ate the bacon with a piece of toast. "Your uncle's a lucky man," she said. "Madeline's a gem."

"Are you good friends?"

"I've known Madeline Turner since grammar school. We were kids together. Awhile ago she used to go out with my father, but don't tell Fred." The more she drank, the more her eye wandered.

"Really?"

"Yeah, but I didn't mind. My mother was really sick at the time, really sick, and Madeline was good for him. He gave her a pet name, used to call her, 'Turner Over,'" and she laughed. Shelley knew where my room was, and she threw her purse onto the bed, but the leather bag hit the gold sheet, skimmed right across the slick surface and off the other side, spilling everything onto the shag rug. "Oh, God," she said. "Satin sheets! I hate them!" I ran my hand over the tempting sheen, pleased with the watery, lingerie-like feel. Shelley came from the bathroom in a towel. I stood by the dresser, dialing the radio and looking at myself in the warped mirror. I got Long John, who said, "In case you tuned in late, with me tonight is a man whose name you know, and whose face you would recognize, but what he has to say is so shocking that he prefers to remain anonymous. For that reason, we have altered his voice . . ." Shelley turned it off and kissed me. She lay down and said, "Come on, get undressed." I fell into the wall as I took my pants off. I hadn't realized how much I had drunk, and the white wine and my nervousness dried my mouth. When I was naked, she looked at me and said, "What happened?"

I had forgotten my splotches. Glancing down, I saw they had gotten worse. They were clearly scratched and torn from the Ajax.

"I was in a fire," I said.

"A fire?" she said. "When?"

"A few days ago," I said. "Just a little one. I put it out."

"I hope you're not into weird stuff," she said. Then, "Hold your dick, stroke it. It turns me on." She patted the place next to her and unrolled the towel. In bed she swayed over me, kissing my neck, nipples and, as she hovered over my stomach, she said, "Want me to go down?"

Most things I could look up later, but this seemed spoken in a code I couldn't crack. The elevator passed through my mind. I said, "I don't know."

"Oh yes you do," she said, and took me in her mouth. After a few seconds she turned out the light. She tried to put me inside, but my knees slipped on the sheets, and I lurched on top of her. When my penis rubbed on the satin, I didn't know where I was or what I was doing. I tried to balance myself on my elbows, but they splayed and I banged my chin against her eye. The dark made it more confusing, although I knew I was sliding around on top of something new, sometimes a woman, sometimes a satin sheet. With one long and sloppy kiss, it was over. When I lay next to her, she said, "That was great."

"Really?"

"Yeah. Anyone who can do anything on these sheets has got to be good. Let's have more wine."

She slipped into my shirt in the kitchen and turned the radio on. Long John's callers harassed him in a way I had never heard before, one after another. He answered the phone the same way: "You're live on WOR," and each time a voice greeted him with, "How did the fuehrer miss you?"; "You're all washed up"; "We have the ovens ready"; and "I'm coming down to the station and I'm gonna clobber you." Long John insisted these calls did not bother him, but he kept losing his temper, ranting and cursing. Shelley changed the dial to the all-news station just after he yelled, "Crawl back into your jar of formaldehyde, you yellow bastard!" The top story reported a woman hit in the head by a window pole that fell from an office building. The point had entered her skull, and firemen had to chop the pole on the sidewalk to fit her into the ambulance.

"That's what I mean," Shelley said, drinking more wine. "Just walking along and *bing*!" I couldn't understand her saying "that's what I mean." It was as if she had reached a great philosophical conclusion after long thinking and discussion, but she hadn't said anything. Then again, I admired the easiness with which she claimed that ground with no prior evidence. Somehow I felt our encounter in bed was related to her theory. I stood by the sink wearing only my pants as she sniffed a few strips of pastrami in front of the open refrigerator. "Yech," she said, putting it away. "I better go."

I wanted her to stay. "I bet we have a wonderful breakfast at Flamingo's," I said.

"I'm sure you think all I do is eat," she said, and laughed. "I'd like to, but I really have to leave."

"I have something for you," I said, and gave her the scarf we bought earlier.

"What? For me?" She slid it from the bag and said, "Thank you, it's lovely."

"I'm glad you like it," I said.

Looking at the scarf again, she said, "Oh, these are little question marks. You are funny."

I thought how beautiful she was and wanted to take her face in my hands. I noticed some redness high on her cheek. "Is your eye okay?" I asked.

"It'll be fine," she said. "I put on extra makeup. Listen, tell Fred you had a good time. You did, didn't you?"

"Oh yes," I said. "I'll tell him."

"He worries about you, wants to make sure you have fun when you're with him. Just tell him how much fun it was." At the door she dropped her purse with a bang and put both arms around my neck, kissing me. "Maybe I'll see you again," she said. "And remember to tell Fred." Watching her walk onto the elevator, I leaned against the doorframe and almost pressed the buzzer with my shoulder. Closing the steel door softly, I tiptoed into the apartment. I had to remake the bed, but the top sheet kept diving to the sides. As I picked it up, I wished I could recall what had happened.

I woke with Fred standing over me, saying, "Where's Shelley?" It was late, around eleven o'clock, and too bright. I felt sick to my stomach. Fred seemed angry. "When did she leave?" he asked.

"She left after four. I had a really great time."

"Good, good," he said. "You did? Good. How'd you like the sheets? They're the best, aren't they? Come on, get ready. We'll have breakfast at Flamingo's."

I took a shower and got dressed, but Fred and Madeline were still in their bedroom. I drank a glass of water and walked onto the terrace. Looking down, I imagined that a ton of lead was compressed into a tiny round ball and the ball balanced on the edge of the railing, right above the traffic. Would it take much strength to knock it off? And when it hit, what kind of hole would it make in the city?

In my fantasies I walked into Flamingo's with a beautiful, sophisticated girl. That Sunday I felt I had lost her twice. Once, by having no memory of our night, and the second time by her leaving. I became a nephew again when I entered with Madeline and Fred. As each couple came through the door, the others looked up from their papers. There was never much talk, you could hear the pages turning, and the sound of a dropped spoon on the marble floor startled everyone. Our booth was at the window, where a red-and-white checked curtain blocked some of the harsh sunlight.

Madeline asked if I knew the poem, "Purple Grackles," and I said no.

"I always think of that poem this time of year," she said.

Fred ordered sausages and pancakes for himself and Madeline, then added, "Tea and dry toast for him."

I felt surly and I couldn't tell why.

"Edna Millay's sonnets are out in a complete edition, and I'll get you a copy."

"Thank you, Madeline."

"I'd recommend my alma mater to you, Sarah Lawrence, but Fred thinks you're too much of a beatnik already."

I was surprised by Fred's opinion. "I like beat poetry, but that's about it."

"Beat comes from 'beatitude,' did you know that?" she asked.

"I thought it came from 'dead-beat,'" Fred said. "Besides, why should he go to college? The city's an encyclopedia, and it's free."

I was not the bright nephew Fred wanted me to be. I couldn't raise myself to meet Madeline's inquiring mind. My hand shook when I lifted the teacup to my mouth, and the sight of the fat sausages made me queasy.

"Look," Fred said, "Roy Eldridge just walked in."

"Where? Oh, that *is* him," Madeline said.

"Maybe he moved around here," Fred said, excited.

"I didn't think he'd be up this early—doesn't he play all night?"

"John," Fred said, "Go tell him how much you like his music." He reached across the table and pushed my forearm while he kept his eyes on Eldridge, who took a table in the back, in a dark corner I envied. Fred almost knocked over my cup and saucer. "Go on," he said. I turned to Madeline for support, but she looked as if this was another opportunity for me, and she said, "He's one of the greats."

"I wouldn't know what to say."

"You liked what you heard last night, didn't you?" Fred said. "Just tell him you were there last night, at Jimmy Ryan's, and you heard him. For Christ's sake, you don't get a chance like this very often."

"You mean I should just go up to his table?"

"Yeah, go up to the table and tell him. Say, 'I really liked the way you were blowing last night,' something like that, so he knows you're a real fan."

Madeline reached over, took my hand, and said, "It'll make your uncle happy if you meet him. And this will be something to tell your kids."

There was no way out. "How should I start? Should I say, 'Excuse me, sir . . . '?"

Fred pointed his finger at me. "Don't ever say 'sir!' What are you, a servant? Don't call anyone 'sir.' You're not a peon, a slave . . . Just say what I told you."

"Enough, Fred," Madeline said. "Go on now, before you take the fun out of it."

I headed for Roy Eldridge's table. He was reading the paper. I repeated to myself, "Mr. Eldridge, I was at Jimmy Ryan's last night, and I really liked the way you were blowing. My uncle is a big fan." Was "mister" all right? Then I thought I shouldn't mention my uncle. I went through variations in the heavy seconds that passed. But as I got nearer, Eldridge slid out of his booth, glanced at me, and headed toward the back. I stopped to look at Fred. He and Madeline waved for me to continue. They didn't see him go. I tried mouthing the words, "He left," but their arms were both in the air, pushing me on like fans at a baseball game urging a deep drive to stay fair.

I could hear the kitchen, and I peeked at the hanging pots and long black stove. He wasn't there. I found the rest rooms. The first one said, "MA." I thought the "N" must have fallen off and I walked in. There were only stalls and I rushed out. The other was labeled "PA." Thankful no one saw me, I entered the men's room, staring at Roy Eldridge, who stood at a urinal.

I thought about lying to Fred and telling him we had talked, but then I knew I could never invent what Eldridge might say.

I loitered behind him, blushing, and said, too quickly and in a soft, embarrassed voice, "You were really great last night."

He didn't answer.

"Really great."

Without turning around, he said, "Sorry, Jack, I don't go that way," and he began to zip up.

I left the men's room fast, before he faced me. I rushed into our booth, with Fred and Madeline asking how it went.

"He just said, 'Thank you.'"

"That's class," Fred said, slapping the table. "That's class, to talk to a kid who's just learning his way." He looked approvingly at Madeline.

"It wasn't so bad after all," Madeline said, smiling directly into my eyes. "You shouldn't be afraid to meet people, to take on the world."

"I'm not afraid, Madeline," I said.

"It gets easier with time," she said. "And experience." Then she turned to Fred. "I wouldn't call it 'class,'" she said. "I would call it 'dignity.'"

"Yes," Fred said. "That is a better word," and he craned over again to look at Eldridge, who was being served.

We walked to the subway, and both of them kissed me. Fred always kissed on the lips, hello and good-bye, no matter where he was. On my way down the stairs I heard Madeline ask Fred, in a very low voice, very concerned, "Are you sure that was Roy Eldridge?"

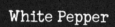

"You look awful," my mother said. "Are you all right?"

"Fine," I said. "I had a great time. I'm really seeing the city."

"Taking you along is quite an expense. Be sure to write Fred a note."

"I will," I said.

"Tom Peck from next door and Linda are coming over for dinner. He caught some fish on the island."

Tom Peck was fifty years old, fat and simpleminded. Earlier in the summer, my mother sent me to help him buy an air-conditioner. As we walked the store's wide aisles, we passed the beach umbrellas, grills, and coolers. Tom paused, reaching out to touch the small containers sold to keep drinks cold called Blue Freeze, whose labels promised, "Colder than Ice." After placing his fingertips on the plastic for a few seconds, he pressed them to the side of my arm, saying, "Feel. They're not colder than ice. How can they get away with that?" He worked for Con Edison, in the sewer, and came home each night smelling foul.

My mother served cheese and crackers before dinner. Tom fell back into our one good armchair from a standing position. When his bulky frame hit the cushion, the springs winced. I brought glasses of wine to Linda and Tom, and I sneaked a swig of whiskey that I hoped might perk me up but instead created a deep drowsiness. When the fish arrived, Tom asked us to play a game. We had to name our five favorite seafoods in reverse order. "Start with your least favorite and work up to number one," Tom added. My mother and aunt were upset with my lack of conversation, and when I inattentively gave the number two spot to escargot, they both yelled.

"That's not even in the seafood family," Tom said, so I changed it quickly to squid.

"Squid second best?" my aunt asked. "Ridiculous!"

"Don't be stupid," my mother said. "Over shrimp?"

At dessert Tom asked for another game. "If you had to be a spice, which would you be?"

"I think you'd be nutmeg, Olga," he said to my mother. "You're a little nutty."

Without enthusiasm, my aunt said, "Rosemary."

"I'd be clove," Tom said. "A girl in the singles' group at church smokes clove cigarettes. A tiny girl, short and small. I kind of like her."

Before I had a chance to name my spice, my mother pointed at me and said, "He'd be white pepper, because he's a sneak and hiding something," and she walked out of the room. I immediately remembered the bills in my pocket and berated myself for not taking everyone to dinner. I missed Shelley terribly and wanted to rise from the table with her on my arm and get in a cab.

"No, Olga," Tom called after her. "He's just salt," and he lifted the cylinder and dangled it by his fingertips in front of my face, spilling a few grains and then tossing a big shake over his left shoulder for good luck.

My aunt looked at me sadly, a knowing and sympathetic expression on her face. "You're a thousand miles away," she said.

The next day my mother woke up unable to speak. Even whispering strained her throat, and she forced out only a few words. Still mute by midweek, she saw her doctor, who referred her to a specialist. Linda and I stopped at Walter's Stationery and bought a blackboard. Polyps on the vocal cords were suspected, but tests showed nothing, and the word *Psychosomatic?* appeared in chalky lettering. Fred told me that's where the word *psycho* came from. My mother added churchgoing to her hobbies, receiving communion at the six o'clock mass each morning and confessing her sins every Saturday afternoon to Father

Magno. Magno suggested she make a novena, which meant attending a Monday-night service for nine Mondays in a row, so her wish would be granted. Father Magno put it this way: "Her intentions would be heard." I wondered if her sudden silence was related to her father's yelling "Parola!" when she was a little girl, words that reached her only now.

Linda's conduct changed. She became cold, and I felt somehow she knew about Shelley—there was an air of jealousy about her. She spoke little and, when we got off the train at Times Square, she walked more quickly than ever. One Friday we rode up to Paramount's offices alone, in an empty elevator. At my floor she said, "Don't think you're better than everyone who works here. You'd be very lucky to have a job like mine one day."

"I know I would, Linda," I said, as the doors began to close.

"Then stop trying to imitate Fred!" The elevator rose and she yelled down, "You'll end up like him, a bum in a fancy suit."

When I reached the mailroom, I found Gates had started his vacation and put Beardsley in charge. Beardsley swaggered under this authority, wearing a clip-on tie and a polyester short-sleeve shirt instead of tropical pastels. The crimson scar across his face and his habit of banging a mop handle on his desk to get our attention gave him the look of a mutineer, not a boss. In late morning the phone rang, and he called me over. It was my aunt. "We're leaving early today, I've arranged it. There's something you'll enjoy taking place in Central Park."

"What is it?"

"A Bob Hope Special. They're filming. You've never seen how they do TV, have you?" I said I hadn't. "Come to my office at three. This is an NBC Special, something my precious brother Fred would never take you to." She was ebullient with the idea, but then she lowered her voice, saying, "I'm sorry if I was a little harsh this week."

When I hung up, Beardsley leaned into Gates' creaking chair and said, "So your aunt is Linda Bertolotti?" I thought he would mock me, but instead he was impressed. "How about joining us for some Chinese food before you meet her? Ruben and Mario are coming, along with the whole print department."

At the China Bowl the maître d' gave us an out-of-the-way table in a sunken cove off the main room, where we caused a ruckus, ordering the family dinner for twelve, turning away silverware but later asking for its return, and calling for numerous cocktails protruding with swords and parasols that arrived in snifters, tankards, and fishbowls that were tasted and passed along the table fire-brigade style. The coconut and pineapple flavors made me appreciate the simple smolder of bourbon all the more.

After we paid the bill I walked behind my group, the last to leave. I saw my cousin Nicky by the bar at a little table for two, and he jumped up to greet me.

"Are you alone?" he asked, looking around, as if I were a puppet broken loose from its strings.

"I'm with guys from Paramount," I said, envying his dark pants and the fake front of a tuxedo, a rippled white dickey with a black bow tie.

"I'm right around the corner, at Hubert's," he said, pointing to the gold name embroidered on his shirt. It took me a few seconds to read the whole thing: *Hubert's Freak Museum and Congress of Strange People*. I had passed the arcade on Forty-Second that housed Hubert's. The hand-drawn posters along the walls, rain beaten and faded, still enticed tourists and residents with a creepy, bygone allure. I had heard Paramount's elevator operators snickering about Princess Wago, who danced nude with her pet pythons, and debating whether Albert/Alberta was really half-man and half-woman. The posters promised Waltzing Dogs; Professor Heckler's Flea Circus; and The World's Smallest Man, imprisoned in a birdcage. In the corner of each painting, the word *Alive!* flared in an official-looking medallion. So startlingly fake, they lured me all the more. "Come over next week for lunch," he said. He reached into his back pocket for a little appointment book and thumbed through it. "Wednesday. At noon. We'll eat at the Automat, and I'll have you shake hands with Sealo, Half-Boy and Half-Seal. He's got flippers."

"What's going on here?" a voice behind me asked. Beardsley stared suspiciously at Nicky.

"I ran into my cousin," I said, and introduced them.

"You work at Hubert's?" Beardsley said. "I been there."

"How'd you like it?" Nicky asked.

"It stinked," Beardsley said. "Let's go."

"See you Wednesday," I said as we walked out.

"You have relatives all around here?" Beardsley asked. "Still, I have to watch out for you, seeing who your aunt is and all."

In the mailroom new stills had arrived, from *Beach Ball* and *Girls on the Beach*. Beardsley sized up Leslie Gore in a bikini. It was a fallow time for Paramount, except for John Wayne's *The Sons of Katie Elder* and *The Family Jewels*, with Jerry Lewis playing seven roles. Among the new glossies Mario found pictures from *The Ten Commandments*, and he held up a shot of Charlton Heston as Moses, poised at the edge of the Red Sea, jaw set and eyes righteous. "Beardsley," Mario asked, "Is that Charlton Heston, or is it really Moses?"

At three o'clock Linda and I walked out of Paramount's brass doors just as pages from Westinghouse pressed free tickets to Merv Griffin's television show on all pedestrians, trying to swell the audience. We rode the bus to Central Park, facing our reflections in the window: a prim woman in her thirties, wearing a gray business suit, her hair dressed in a style from years ago, a single curl oiled and fixed to the side of her forehead. Her job at the moment: to show the boy next to her the world but to shield him at the same time. And the boy: trying to stand straight, sixteen, gangly, wearing a wrinkled jacket of brown and orange checks, crumpled further from soaking in summer showers and drying out on a metal hanger. His hair parted in a zigzag, like the route of his ambition to get behind the shield.

In the busy meadow sweaty crews shifted on a stage surrounded by cameras, booms, trucks, and trailers. A few secretaries and business people joined the audience, drawn mostly from those already in the park, old folks on benches, dog walkers, vagrants, kids playing ball. From the expanse of grass, I gazed at the office buildings and hotels around the park, trying to guess where we were in relation to Fred's. Once in a while a figure appeared on a rooftop garden and peered over. I imagined having a flowerbed that high, a place for guests in lounge chairs, close to the sky, surrounded by blossoms and shrubs, different from the hot roofs of Queens, which we called tar beach. I mentioned this to Linda, who poked her finger toward the clouds and said, "They still get the soot."

She edged our way through the crowd to the stage, while voices counted into microphones. After half an hour, three vendors in back yelled, "Free pretzels, courtesy of Mr. Hope!" and everyone rushed the tiny carts. The sellers, fearing the stampede, began winging pretzels, but when the crowd kept coming, they fled, wagons at their heels. A noise boomed from the sky, mechanical, threatening, and everyone ducked down and looked up at the same time. On stage a local disk jockey, Jack Spector, one of the "WMCA Good Guys," introduced himself with, "This is your main man Jake, your leader, the boss with the hot sauce!" Then he pointed and yelled, "Let's welcome Mr. Hope," as the helicopter swooped and settled. Hope ran right up the steps and launched into a series of jokes that he read from gigantic cue cards for five minutes. Then he introduced The Hullabaloos, a rock group whose equipment problems stalled the show for another half-hour. NBC bought out soda vendors to keep the crowd from dispersing, and the song was finally played.

The newly crowned Miss America, a tall blonde, walked out in a bathing suit, holding a wand with a star on the end. Her small scene with Mr. Hope was repeated again and again. The lines were supposed to go:

"Where are you from, Julie?"
"I was born in Toledo, Bob, and I still live there today."
"Well, it's certainly great to have you with us."
"Thank you, but who are all these people, Bob?"
"Oh, just a bunch of bird watchers."
But Julie answered:
"I was born, Bob, and I live in Toledo today."
Then:
"I was born today, Bob, and I live in Toledo."

A crowd of kids, who had quit their baseball game to watch, started heckling. Miss America laughed each time she got it wrong, with genuine astonishment at the difficulty of her task. Hope remained good-humored despite the heat, pointing and saying, "Just read the cards, Julie."

When the director shortened Julie's response to "Toledo, Ohio," one of the kids slapped his head with his mitt and cried, "Oh, man!" Julie could not recite her next line either, asking who we were. She complained that she couldn't say the line and wave her outstretched arm at the same time. Linda asked me if I wanted to leave. We had been there for two hours, and I said I understood how television was made. As we walked toward the subway, we could hear the kids coaching Miss America, chanting, "*But who are all these people, Bob?*"

We got caught in rush hour, and there were no seats. In spite of the pressing crowd, Linda managed to read *The Journal-American*, folding the paper into quarters. I opened the thin paperback Fred had lent me, *The Flying Saucer As I Saw It*. As we held onto the straps, I scanned the eye-level ads along the top of the car and faced a Miss Subways poster unlike any other. Every month the Transit Authority chose a female commuter whose photo and résumé appeared in each car. It gave date of birth, job, and interests—modeling was always prominent. The photograph, like that from a high-school yearbook, showed airbrushed skin, hair in a stiff wave, smile a second too late. But the Miss Subways before me wore no clothes and lay on a bed, legs spread. Someone had pasted her picture over the head shot, its border the perfect size. I couldn't take my eyes from the triangle of pubic hair, but— so as not to appear to be staring—I looked at my book, then away, as if considering a particularly mystifying passage. Licking her fingertips as she squared each page, pressing the heel of her hand over her paper, Linda raised her eyes to the photo, and I felt her face me. When her head bent, I squinted upward once more. If Linda looked over, I went back to my book. Getting off the train at Roosevelt Avenue, I tried to see if it was an *E* or an *F*, and exactly what car we rode, and what time we got on, but I never saw that Miss Subways again.

On Judge Street police cars and an ambulance sounded their sirens among the small crowd in front of the home of Mrs. Roche, our elderly next door neighbor. Linda asked a cop what happened, and he said, "DOA, second floor." My mother and Tom Peck, Mrs. Roche's downstairs tenant, stood on her steps with the police. Mrs. Roche was found dead in front of her television, and a young cop grilled Tom suspiciously, asking if he had found the body. "Did she keep much money in the house?" he asked again and again. His loud and vehement questioning of dim Tom drew loud whoops and Bronx cheers from some of the kids gathered around the hedges, and my aunt glared at them, almost disguising her sneer at the cop.

Tom shielded a lit candle with a cupped hand as he answered. As ritual demanded, he was waiting to escort the priest to the body for last rites. My mother walked to our place and returned with her blackboard, writing, "Father Greene is on his way." Tom nodded, still guarding the candle flame although the evening air draped heavy and still.

Reading my mother's message, the cop turned to her and said, "Is that what he's doing with the candle?"

My mother gave a puzzled stare, but my aunt looked right into his freckled face. "Did you think it was your birthday?" she asked, and left the stoop.

"Just watch it, lady," the cop called. "Just watch it!"

A few minutes later we all sat at our kitchen table while my mother cooked. Tom said that he had accompanied Mrs. Roche to the doctor a few months back. "We went to St. John's," he said. "And when we passed the chapel, there was her doctor, kneeling in a pew, praying. She said it was a bad sign." Since my mother had been at Mrs. Roche's, I asked for details, which she provided on the blackboard: the old lady sprawled on the rug next to a half-gallon of melted ice cream, the television on static. When I speculated how long she'd been there, my aunt said, "Now you sound like the cop. That thick Irishman." My mother put her board down, mouthed the word, "Conclusion," and drew a rectangle in the air. To change the subject I mentioned meeting Nicky at the China Bowl, and both women turned toward me. "I was with the mail boys," I said, "and he was eating there. He works at Hubert's Freak Show."

"Good place for him," Linda said, and my mother wrote, "Not related to us!" for Tom's benefit, and she made the exclamation point very big.

"That's nothing to be ashamed of," Tom said. "My family had a lot of freaks. My cousin Chickie could stand on eggs. And when my father died, I found photos of bearded ladies in a trunk in the cellar, naked bearded ladies. I don't know what he got out of them ... they were very blurry."

"I'm going to meet Nicky next week," I said, "and he's going to show me Hubert's. It's really famous."

"Don't be ridiculous," Linda said. "With all the museums, that's where you're going? You really need to get away to a good college." She looked at my mother and asked, "Is Nicky still living with Jeanie? I wonder what's become of that cheap bit of fluff." My mother just shrugged. Linda said her neck was stiff from standing in the park and asked me to massage it while she read aloud from Bennet Cerf's column, "Try and Stop Me." It made fun of the police crackdown on jaywalking, for which we had both received warning citations. I stood be-

96

hind Linda's chair, kneading her neck and shoulders, glad there was no follow-up on Nicky.

"Not too hard," she said, which made me do it harder. "Don't!" She jerked. "You'll leave a bruise." I massaged her all the more deeply, my thumbs pressing the flesh around her spine and sliding under the back of her dress, which she endured for longer than I expected, eyes closed, before calling out.

In bed that night I nursed my memory of the fake Miss Subways, superimposed her onto Shelley, and involved my aunt. Then I opened another of Fred's paperbacks, *Strange Dimensions*, and read a chapter on hermaphrodites. It contended that Freud believed in their existence and documented his belief with some facts about the testicles of an eel. Another said all hermaphrodites were women with enlarged clitorises that were mistaken for penises. I looked up *clitoris*, another missed feature on my blurry night with Shelley, which was getting blurrier. I whirled the radio dial from one end to the other for something even weirder than Nebel, whom I now tuned in every midnight.

I searched for what I really liked, because I didn't have the chance during the day when I was being agreeable. I was trained in agreeability by nuns who forced us to sit still at our desks, no smiles or tears, a practiced rigidity that unwittingly gave us champion poker faces. My mother instructed me at dinner to take the piece of chicken closest to me on the serving plate. Teaching drinking manners, Fred told me to say, "I'll have what you're having" when asked by my host. By not choosing I was spared imposing my tastes on anyone, and so I left them undiscovered, even to myself. But now, making my way through the city as a messenger on weekdays and as Fred's shadow on weekends, by listening to the airwaves late at night and thumbing through Fred's books, I surprised myself by what attracted me. I badly wanted to see the freaks at Hubert's, long before running into Ricky. But I had a distraction. My penis began to itch, and I called Fred.

"Shelley's clean," he said. "Don't worry about that. Just a minute." He muffled the speaker with his hand and then said, "Yeah, Madeline says she's clean. It must be something else, but you should check." He gave me Dr. Roberts' address in Manhattan. "Just show up. I'll call ahead." After some small talk he laughed and said, "Well, if she did give you something, at least you gave her a black eye." I flushed, recalling the debacle in the satin sheets and how I'd banged her with my chin, now a joke among the three of them. I wrote the phone number on a torn corner of the *Daily News*, something serious for my wallet.

My mother began the Monday novenas. Strained by continually writing on the blackboard, she slammed it down more than once, cracking the slate so her scribbling wobbled even more crazily over the fractured tablet, and one Saturday night she left it propped in the bathroom sink. Covered with tiny script, the message asked me to receive communion for her. The next morning I sat before the side altar of the same church I had attended for the eight years of grammar school, at the same nine o'clock mass, the service required of all St. Barth's students. Although it was summer, the pews filled with children, perhaps sent by their parents out of habit.

I squirmed through the sitting, standing, kneeling, as I hadn't summoned the courage to visit Dr. Roberts, and the itch had worsened. Although I hadn't prayed in years, I prayed for my mother. I made the prayer I'd always made as a child: I thought about the response to the catechism's question, "What do we mean when we say God is eternal?" The answer dizzied me, "He always was and always will be." No future and no past. I thought about it again and had a vision of the Milky Way streaming back in time, over lush continents stalked by dinosaurs, and further, above a dark planet that disappeared into a sticky, decaying fume—where He always was. And then the rush of stars roared into the future, over the same ground, and into centuries beyond ours, over space stations and huge antennae spiraling into the skies—where He always will be. The familiar mental blur took hold. When I opened my eyes I looked around at the martyrs in alcoves, the old women fanning themselves with church bulletins, my neighbors shuffling to the altar for communion.

A girl of ten walked by, dressed as if from the earlier part of the century in a thick, boxy dress and round brown shoes. Her hair a Buster Brown cut, old-fashioned and out of place. I recognized her. From where? I tried to place her as she approached the altar. Then I got it: she looked exactly like my mother as a little girl, in the photo of her on a pony in front of our house. The same haircut, similar dress. The picture taken for a few cents given to the old Italian man who walked the weary animal from door to door. The girl had a kind of infinity about her—as if my mother always was . . . I felt sorry for her, for her awkward haircut and odd, sturdy clothing. I said a prayer, kneeling into the bench as she took her place at the rail. I strained into my knuckles, saying, "God, do whatever you can for this girl." I raised my head from my closed fists, with the bizarre sense I had aided my mother through this anachronistic replica.

I stared again, and the girl, still kneeling, waiting for the priest to make his way to her with the sunny chalice, suddenly stiffened and fell backward, hitting her head hard on the marble floor, arms and legs in four directions. She twitched for a moment and then lay still, eyes closed. One of her brown shoes had come off and turned on its side. Two ushers rushed toward her, and the pale girl, even paler now, was escorted from the church. Dizzier than all my thoughts about eternity had made me, I knew I had harmed the girl with the power of my prayer, which I had somehow worked in reverse, probably since I had-n't taken communion in years. I slipped out the side and sat on the steps under the shade of a buttress until mass ended.

My mother was washing laundry and cooking, so the apartment smelled of oregano and soap. She looked at me in alarm and wrote, "There were an odd number of doves under the bird feeder." I said, "So what?" She wrote, "One must have died. Always in pairs." Her se-ries of superstitions began with that perception. Later that night, she began walking through the rooms, stretching out her neck and bring-ing her chin to her breastbone. Then she sat at the dining-room table, reading pamphlets she had ordered from an address in one of Fred's books. She began mouthing syllables exaggeratedly, hoarse sounds. I looked at the sheet, following what she tried to sing:

COO AH FA FA

COO AH FA FA

COO AH FA FA COOOOO

She gargled with Castile soap and started eating raw vegetables. When I questioned her, she wrote, "No animal eats cooked food," and went back to her carrots. I worried for her health and asked her if her belief in God wasn't enough, but she simply wrote, "Faith AND Science."

I needed science myself. I wiped my penis, a regimen now, as it of-ten dripped. I couldn't put off the doctor any longer.

Fever

Dr. Roberts' office was near the Museum of Natural History, on West Seventy-Ninth, a block of apartments studded with brass plates inscribed with the names of surgeons and specialists. Roberts' plaque simply stated: Dr. Anton Roberts. There was no MD after his name, something Linda once warned me about on the subway as she read consumer tips in the *Daily News*. Everyone in the reception area propped their legs on footstools, creating an otherworldly atmosphere, like Lourdes, where pilgrims dropped their crutches and rested. On the registration form, where it asked the name of a referral, I wrote Fred Bertolotti, Fred Bertel, Fred Lotti. I was paging through the Sarah Lawrence catalog I'd borrowed from the Donnell Library when a nurse, emerging from the back to call the next patient, made straight for me, yelling, "Feet up!" She spun toward another patient who'd crossed his legs. "You too! If you won't obey the rules, see another doctor!" I followed orders and read a laminated page on the benefits of keeping your ankles higher than your hips. Another leaflet touted orificial therapy, the practice of relaxing the openings of the body. When my name was called, a nurse wrote down my complaint and then took me to Dr. Roberts, who chain-smoked behind an enormous desk, not a page on it. His huge stomach deluged out of his gray vest. He looked at my folder and said, "Were you drinking a lot when this started?"

I denied it. It was like being in confession, and I lied, even though that night of bourbon and wine washed through me.

"And you were with a woman, right? Is this your girlfriend?"

"She's a friend of the family."

He let out deep laughs, sinking his double chins to his chest and wiping tears from his eyes. "Oh yes. Your uncle told me, but he didn't quite phrase it that way."

"It's nothing from her, doctor. At least I don't think so."

"Well, I think it might be, but your uncle says he knows the girl. Let's take a slide anyway." He moved so slowly around his desk, I couldn't understand how he moved at all.

I smeared a slide.

"Here's some sulfur pills. Three a day till they're gone. It's probably just urethritis."

I had brought my roll of bills, and I swayed in front of the receptionist's desk, but she just said, "See you next time" in a significant way, so I left.

The pills did the trick.

The next Monday evening, when my mother was at her novena, I lay on my bed listening to a new Nebel show called "Long John Versus." The format was simple: Nebel opposed the opinion of every guest. Linda knocked on my half-opened door as Long John grilled an expert in "spirit photography." The photographer developed a picture of a woman and, to his surprise, an image of a little boy appeared at her side. When he showed the customer, she became hysterical, demanding to know how he could play such a cruel joke: the boy was her dead son, killed the year before in a car accident. Nebel politely inquired about the quality of the photographer's equipment. He was preparing to launch his assault as Linda arrived. "I thought you and Olga might come down for some coffee. I got Yuban." Linda loved Yuban coffee, which our A&P rarely kept in stock. Fred ridiculed her indulgence, for the indulgence itself and for the poor quality of the product. Before I could answer, she said, "Oh, that's right, she's making the novena," and she cinched the belt of her robe tighter as I followed her downstairs.

I drank the coffee at her dining-room table, complimenting it and scanning the evening papers. She placed a fat glossy on top of the *Journal-American*. It was the *Vogue* I had ravaged, and I blushed. "I found this in the basement, when I was helping your mother with her papier-mâché. You're lucky she didn't see it." I didn't say anything. "I don't care about the magazine, but I'm worried about you, going to all this trouble." She fluttered the pages, shaking her head and pursing her lips, saying, "Ads for bras, panties... You're so tall that I forget how young you are, how much you don't know." She was in that official mode, when she would lecture and brush everything aside but the points she made. "And I know where this comes from," she said. "From all those displays on Times Square, that stupid lingerie. That's for tourists. They sell sex that way. Come with me." I walked out of the dining room, my eyes fixed to her spine. We passed through the doorway of my grandmother's empty room to hers, a double bed covered by a shimmering tan comforter. The dresser held a large mirror, and its glass top displayed a few postcards, a bottle of potpourri, a lamp, and a mahogany hairbrush. Linda put her cup and saucer down and closed the door. The other end opened into the living area, a wide entrance, so it seemed we stood on a set. She pulled a rope, releasing purple drapes that swung down, and suddenly we were backstage, in the dark. She turned a little key on the lamp, which gave off a yellow light. I leaned against the dresser.

"I know what you're feeling," she said. "Remember, I was engaged. Someday I'll tell you about Mac. And like I said, I haven't mentioned a word about the magazine to your mother. We'll keep that to ourselves." The secret raised my feelings to a new power. I felt in some ways she understood me, that we had traveled together to this private place, and the dim room shrank.

"You can sit there." She pointed to the vinyl hassock at the foot of the bed. "I'm going to give you a fashion show," she said, smiling. "What women wear. It's no mystery." I counted squares in the comforter. She opened a dresser drawer and held a bra so close to my face I couldn't see it. "It hooks like this," she said, and twisted its stiff lace, which she placed on the bed, its two cones pointing to the ceiling. She pulled another drawer and dangled a garter belt. "Know how I learned how to put this on? From Bob Hope!" She laughed. "I couldn't figure it out when I was young, then I saw him on TV, pretending to be a woman getting dressed, and he bent like this." She hiked her robe and leaned over, making fastening gestures with her fingers around her thighs. I couldn't follow the method, but I smiled, my hands on my knees, as she laughed. "Simple," she said, and laid the belt in the middle of the bed.

She lifted a long black slip by its straps and snapped the bottom. She laid it down over the bra and garter belt, saying, "Slip. You've seen me in this." Opening another drawer, she said, "Half-slip," and she held the sheer white material by its frayed waistband. She placed it over the bottom of the whole slip. The half-slip was my favorite, with its lubricated finish. "Nylons are seamed or seamless," she said, stretching a stocking from top to bottom. "This is an old pair I'm showing you because they run easily and they're expensive. When you want to give a girl something nice, you give her good stockings." She nodded after this statement, agreeing with herself. When the nylons were added, I looked at the flat thing on the bed, a scarecrow without straw. I wanted Linda to go on, and I wanted her to stop. What I really wanted was to be in my room upstairs, watching. I told myself a story: his aunt put a slip on the bed in front of him. I thought of myself this way, from above, and I started to relax.

"There are all kinds of panties," she said, and foraged around, shaking out different colored underpants and putting them back. Then she walked behind the hassock and untied her robe. She put her hand on my shoulder for support, stepping out of her underpants. "These are what I was looking for," she said, and held the warm fabric next to my shoulder so I could see the brocade around the edges. "Feel," she said, "they're not like those ridiculous things on Forty-Second Street, but they have a nice texture." I touched them with my thumb and forefinger, like shooting a marble. "Really feel them, with both hands," she said, and I rubbed them until they felt slick, almost liquid, then seemed to dissolve. She draped the silky triangle right over the half-slip. "That's all there is to it," she said. "Slip, panties, garter belt, bra, stockings. That's what I put on every morning while you're upstairs. Let's see if you can hook the bra," she said. She picked it off the bed, and I fastened the hooks into the loops. "It's harder getting off," she said. She turned her back to me and rolled the robe off her shoulders. I stood and pulled the straps together and undid one hook. "Take your time," she said. I stretched and pulled the elastic left and right until it came undone. "That's it," she said, letting the straps down and holding the bra in front of her. I stared at her smooth back. Then I saw our reflection in the mirror, my head over my aunt's shoulder, her eyes closed, her breasts cupped just above the nipples in her loosened brassiere. I struggled to keep from pressing my face to the side of her neck. She placed the straps onto her shoulders. "What are you waiting for?" she asked.

I considered what she meant.

"Fasten it!" she said. I clipped the hooks and she tugged the robe around her snugly, as if against the cold, and I sat down.

"Well," she said, lifting her coffee cup and looking at me sitting stupidly on the stuffed round plastic. "I still haven't addressed what you did to the magazine. I should spank you. You're not too old, you know." She sipped the cold coffee, and when she placed the cup back in the saucer, her hand shook and the china rang. "Do you think you should be punished?" she asked.

"I don't know," I said.

"Maybe it's time you took some responsibility. It's not the magazine, but someone else's property." She crossed her arms. "Would you like me to spank you?" she whispered. When I hesitated, she said, "You deserve it."

I knew I should say no, but the boy upstairs watching said, "Yes," and she almost jumped to the head of the bed, saying, "Take your pants off." I unbuckled my belt and let my khakis drop to the floor.

"My underpants too?"

In a bored, almost annoyed voice, she said, "I believe I'll leave that up to you," and she calmly straightened the comforter at its corners. Even the boy upstairs lacked the courage to reveal his erection, and I kept my shorts on as Linda glanced over, fluffing the pillows. She smoothed her hair and circled behind me. "Lie down, like this." She gently pushed me onto the map of lingerie. Her hand moved over my buttocks, pressing firmly against them, and she slapped my left cheek and then my right, lightly, with her open palm. Then she picked up the hairbrush and it really stung. I heard her breathing with the exertion and once I let out a small cough, which encouraged her.

"That was thirty," she said. "I bet your backside's nice and pink." She pulled down my boxers and smoothed her fingers over the hot skin. "Some saints did that to themselves, did you know that?"

"No," I said, talking into the white cones that had made their way to my face.

She continued the massage, using her palms, each time with more force and for longer seconds, so that I got caught up in the rhythm and began to rub against the lingerie. At night, when I tired of my homework, I'd rest my head on a pile of books stacked on the dining-room table, daydreaming about diving into an empty pool from the highest board. I'd focus on a fissure in the blue floor and concentrate on it until I was plunging, headfirst, into the ragged split. I liked the feeling of simultaneous courage and fear, the courage to have leaped headfirst into the unknown and the fear of hitting bottom. I had dissolved into this stupor-dream often, wincing awake each time. Now I felt that same shudder under Linda's hands.

She rolled me over with a nurse's efficiency and wiped my stomach with her panties. I tucked myself together. "Come down next Monday," she said offhandedly, and tossed the panties into her cabinet of soiled laundry. As I left, I heard her slamming the dresser drawers.

I couldn't concentrate on the program that followed the Versus show, about women drivers, and I tuned the dial to WLIB, a black station, where Billy Taylor played jazz. During a long drum solo, I threw myself into the walls, crashing into the big toy chest where I kept my underwear and banging the door shut with my bony shoulders. I roiled around until the song ended. I thought of Linda and the spanking. I wanted the burning sting. I decided to give up masturbating so I would be ready for the next Monday.

My mother returned from church and grilled a snack of homemade pizza: English muffins topped with mozzarella, oregano, and tomato paste. I ate three crisp disks and went to bed, for once falling asleep right away. I dreamt that Fred walked down Judge Street and invited the Majestics to board a long bus parked in front of our door. Sal leaned in the driver's seat, smiling and joking. Shelley walked down the aisle, looking for a place. Fred gave me the once-over as I sat on the nub of a fire hydrant. Then he climbed the bus and ordered Sal to sweep the doors shut. I cupped my hand to my mouth and yelled, "Don't go! Sal's dead!" The bus roared off and I woke up, parched, and went into the kitchen for a glass of water. Then I dreamt again, about something the nuns told us in grammar school. That God would let us know our vocations. In my dream God poked a long tongue down from the clouds. There was a mouth on its tip and it spoke, transforming me into a fireman. I threw buckets of water up to a burning window, but they kept falling back, soaking me. In the morning I had a high fever, and my mother sat next to the bed, opening *The Family Book of Best Loved Poems* to "Gunga Din," which I read.

> *'e lifted up my 'ead,*
> *An' 'e plugged me where I bled,*
> *An' 'e guv me 'arf-a-pint o' water-green:*
> *It was crawlin' and it stunk,*
> *But of all the drinks I've drunk,*
> *I'm gratefulest to one from Gunga Din.*

The poem made my thirst grow all the more, and when Linda came upstairs, she said, "How much water can be in him, to sweat so much?" Linda stayed home, something she never did, even when she was sick. My mother went to a later mass, and Linda put a cold washcloth on my forehead and sat quietly by the bed. Her silence reminded me of her nurselike conduct in her bedroom and her bathroom, and my mind continued to steam. I fell into another delirium, a dream in which I tried to impress Linda and Fred by making reservations at an eastside restaurant called "Moi-meme," but Pearl Bailey answered their phone and told me it had been closed for years. I woke to find Linda still sitting in the chair. I realized the restaurant's name meant "myself," and the trick my subconscious had played made me burn hotter.

"Have you been dreaming?" she asked.

I said I had, still dazed.

"You have some imagination," she said. "You're too sensitive. Like a turtle without a shell. I'm going to make a novena for you, just like your mother's. I'll go with her on Mondays. Maybe that will help." Then she left.

It took me a minute to realize this meant I wouldn't be seeing Linda on Monday nights after all.

I felt jilted, rejected, but I decided she was right. I was happier in fantasy. I lay on the damp bed, weary of my burning body, my burning mind. I breathed into the pillow that I wished I were dead, over and over, until I fell asleep.

When I woke in the early evening, the fever had broken and I felt better. And angry. And energized by the cool, thin sheen that clung to my skin as I got out of bed. I cursed my death wish and told myself that if I could only live in fantasy, then I would be a master of fantasy, silent and solitary, and the hell with the world I was supposed to know. As I made this vow, my legs felt like cellophane, and I steadied myself against the wall. Looking down at the night table, I saw one of my grandmother's statues, brought there by my mother. It was St. Bartholomew, namesake of my grammar school. Bartholomew had been flayed alive, and the robed replica held a huge knife in one hand, his skin draped over his arm like a suit. Another turtle without a shell.

Hubert's Freak Museum
and Congress of Strange People

Nicky stood in front of Hubert's in his tux, the big Amusement Center sign above him. His wavy black hair tumbled nonchalantly onto his forehead, both the natural way of a child's curl and the cultivated swagger of a juvenile delinquent. As I approached, he started walking backward, away from me, as if in a relay race, expecting the baton. "Let's go," he said. "The Automat gets crowded around now." We changed our bills for nickels and chose sandwiches from the bank of steel-framed windows. Nicky knocked hard on the glass door of an empty slot and, a moment later, the ham sandwich appeared. Until then, I'd never known that people worked behind the wall. I thought the food arrived automatically, as the name said. Nicky told me about living around the corner with Jeanie, and how he never saw Fred.

"You see more of him than I do," he said. "It would bother me, but he isn't really my father." When I asked about his real father, he said, "Jeanie hinted he's a big guy in city government. She'll tell me some day. Want some pie?"

"I don't think so."

"Me neither, let's get going. Let's see some freaks!"

As we walked down Forty-Second, I asked about Hubert's posters, especially Spider Boy, a head with eight furry legs sticking out of it. "We get new ones all the time," he said. "And some take off. We just lost The Half-Girl, but there's talk we might be getting Baby Alpine, a huge fat guy from Coney Island." He stopped at Nedick's.

"A cup of Lipton's with lemon," he ordered. "To go."

"Out of Lipton," the woman behind the counter said.

"Shit!" Nicky said. "Just give me what you have then." Nicky took the paper cup with its dangling tag and said, "Maybe he won't notice."

"Who?"

"You'll see."

The main floor of Hubert's looked like all gaming parlors on Times Square: a dozen skee-ball alleys; flashing pinball machines, their vertical glass cases displaying toothy panthers, rockets, or police cars; a row of splintered twenty-twos aimed at battered ducks; pokerino; six-foot statues of cowboys facing semicircular holsters just waiting for someone to step into them and draw. Employees walked the loud floor rattling change in canvas aprons slung across their hips. Glass booths sold counterfeit identification of all kinds, and the walls hung with stuffed pandas, plastic back scratchers, Chinese handcuffs, and combs like switchblades. On the other side of the room, an admission booth guarded a steep flight of stairs. The grand, bold-faced sign above it read: HUBERT'S FREAK MUSEUM AND CONGRESS OF STRANGE PEOPLE. Below, in small letters: Professor Heckler's Marvelous Trained Flea Circus. Posters announced Serpentina the Snake; Bobby, the Boy with the Revolving Head, and Yvonne: Famous European Waterheaded Girl. Yvonne's picture showed a hydrocephalic woman, and a bright circle promised, "Born Alive—Born to Live." Nicky pointed to a sign, "The Hidden Secrets of Sex, as displayed by the French Academy of Medicine, Paris." "I tend the exhibits," he said.

The heavy woman in the booth greeted Nicky. On the deep stairs an odor drifted toward us, ammonia, sweat, and perfume. At the bottom, old fuzzy mirrors stretched our shapes thin, fat, and tall. More posters pasted the walls with coming attractions, yellowed and long out of date. Glass tanks holding mice, thick snakes, and tarantulas lined the hallway, the signs above them announcing, "Man-eating Pythons!" and "Giant Rats, Straight from the Sewers of Paris!" For a penny, a machine let you look into cast-iron binoculars at images of General Grant and Tony Curtis painted on the head of a pin.

We walked past a row of small chest-high platforms, each act announced by a folding sandwich board on its linoleum floor. Large banners like those outside served as backdrops. "Where is everyone?" I asked.

"Oh, we'll have to come at showtime. But let's see who's around." Nicky took me straight to The Great Waldo, an old man in a three-piece suit with a long, warty nose and slicked down hair. He dozed on a metal chair. "Hey, Waldo," Nicky whispered across the velvet rope, "Wake up." Waldo rose from his chair and scanned the air behind us, looking for a crowd.

"Why wake me?" he said softly, taking out a pocket watch. "There's still time."

"I brought you a cup of tea." Nicky waved the Nedick's cup.

"You're a good boy, Nicky."

"Swallow a mouse for my cousin. He's a talent scout for Paramount Pictures."

Waldo smiled and said, "You sure?"

"He is!" Nicky said. "He could tell them about you! He could make you great."

"Can't you read?" Waldo said, pointing to his signboard. "I'm already great." He trudged over to a cage of white mice, picked one up by the neck, and held it in front of me so I could see its twitching nose. Then he took a feather duster and brushed the rodent in fussy, exaggerated strokes. He lifted it into his mouth, as if savoring it, making chewing motions with his jaw and cheeks, so it seemed he crunched the frail bones. Suddenly, he threw back his head and swallowed. He stared at me, as if to quell any suspicions. "You know where the mouse is now? In my stomach. I ate it." He whistled a little tune as he bent down and took a blue dish from the floor. Holding the plate in front of his vest, he said, "Here it comes, out to the world!" and he retched. The mouse spilled from his lips, fur wet and tiny red eyes dazed, cowering on the bright disk.

"Bravo!" Nicky yelled, and we clapped as Waldo dropped the dank mouse into the cage from quite a height. "Thanks, Waldo," I said, and Nicky handed him the cup. As we walked away, Waldo bellowed, louder than I thought possible, "Nicky, this is not the brisk tea! You know I like it brisk!"

Nicky said, "He's not a bad guy. He'll smoke cigars with his eyes if you ask him. All the others are fakes or real freaks of nature, made that way. 'The Defectives,' we call them. I was kidding you about shaking hands with Sealo, he's just deformed is all." We passed Sealo's empty stage, his poster showing a boy with no arms, just hands that dropped from his shoulders, the fingers fused. Albert/Alberta, half-man and half-woman, rushed by. Nicky said, "He's really into it, pretends he's from Paris. On Monday and Tuesday he plays Coney Island and calls himself Ray/Roberta. He goes upstate and he's Leo/Leola. Down south he's Esther/Lester. When's he's off, Jim from the shooting gallery upstairs takes his place."

We reached my favorite freak, Spider Boy, who turned out to be a teenager with withered legs and very strong arms. He wore an athletic T-shirt that showed off his muscular chest. Two tiny, wrinkled, hairless legs dangled from his gym shorts as he swung back and forth on a trapeze and somersaulted around his little square, just for us.

"He's a total idiot," Nicky said out loud. "Spent a lot of time in a mental hospital. He lives here, stays here when the place closes, probably still swinging."

The outside poster of the Dog-Faced Boy showed a terrier head on a human body, but here was a kid with long hair dyed black and white combed over his face, which was also painted black and white. A transistor radio played the all-news station very loud. From the neck down he wore a fur costume, ending in fanged slippers. When he heard us coming, he turned in his chair, put a toothpick in his mouth, and said, "Bow Wow Wow." The newsman on WINS cautioned how plastic bags, which were getting popular, could cause suffocation. Dog Face rummaged among his possessions, and when we looked over, he had put a plastic bag over his head, sucking the clear membrane to his lips.

"Let's go to my place," Nicky said. "I'm sick of these losers."

"What about the hidden secrets of sex?"

"I already dusted them this week," he said, as we passed The Elephant Skin Lady, whose skin looked like mine during my night with Shelley, raw and flaky.

On the street it was as if we were mice spit out by Waldo, blinking against the light. The cavelike atmosphere of Hubert's lingered with me, knowing that the freaks paced their linoleum squares for the rest of the afternoon, day after day. And that Spider Boy hoisted himself through the dim hall all night long. I would be late getting back to the mailroom, but I couldn't resist seeing Nicky's apartment in the Dixie Hotel. I felt privileged to be walking through a lobby without a package under my arm. The hotel cut through the entire block, from Forty-Second to Forty-Third, and the lobby had a bustling impersonality, unlike our vestibule with its sour milk box. When we reached Nicky's floor, I was surprised by the peeling wallpaper and worn rugs. Some of the tenants had pasted newspaper clippings and postcards onto the blistered brown paint of their apartment doors. Nicky rushed to 10-D, deftly turning the keys in three locks. We went straight to his small room, where he sat at a rolled-top desk. The shelves above him were filled with huge coconuts painted with faces and with what looked like real teeth inserted into their smiles and grimaces. A fan, hi-fi, and television perched at different corners, and Nicky put on a record by the Blues Project, pointing out a long flute solo.

"That was a pretty one," Jeanie said, leaning into the door of his room. I was still embarrassed about almost falling when I bent to kiss her at Richards' funeral. Her heavy makeup seemed out of place in the apartment's drowsy light. "So you're at Paramount," she said. "That must be exciting. Do you meet any stars?" She held a bottle of beer.

"I took an envelope to Sidney Poitier last week. I think it was a script, and yesterday Carroll Baker came up."

"How about Steve McQueen?"

I remembered an article in *Paramount World*. "He's filming *Nevada Smith* on the West Coast," I said.

"Isn't George Peppard in a new movie?"

"He was in *The Carpetbaggers*, but I haven't seen him. Tony Perkins came by last week." Nicky thumbed through an orange crate of records, and Jeanie walked to the open window, put her hands on the sill, and looked down, the light making her thin skirt transparent.

"John's gonna tell Paramount about Waldo," Nicky said, startling me.

Jeanie turned to us. "Really? That would help that poor son of a bitch." I was shocked at the ease of Nicky's lie and how it had found its way out of Hubert's basement. At the same time I liked the feeling that I could change his life. Jeanie teased Nicky, saying, "It's my birthday next week, Nicky, what're you gonna get me?"

"Thirty-fifth?" he asked.

"No, I'll be thirty-four." He put three records on his desk.

"What do you want?"

"To get the hell out of here!" she said, laughing. A baby cried. "Oh, it's Pepe," she said. "He's hungry again."

"He's always hungry," Nicky said.

"Almost sixteen pounds now," she said. "That's big for a three-month old. See you guys."

Nicky unrolled the wooden shutter over his desk and showed me a long piece of what looked like brown clay wrapped in foil. He chipped at it with a penknife, scooped up a handful of shavings, and said, "We can't do this here." We left the apartment and walked the long hall to the stairs, the thick metal door slamming with a vacuumlike force as we stood in the humid stairwell, which smelled like an overheated men's room. Nicky jammed some hash in a pipe and passed it. After a few puffs he opened the door and looked both ways before prancing down the hall in exaggerated steps, like leaping from rock to rock across a stream. I laughed, but he made an angry face. Was he deranged? Was I? The sorrowful sounds of daytime television leaked toward us from the frames of the steel doors. It seemed like a Hubert's in the sky, and I expected more freaks to pop out of their cages. Nicky had left his door wedged open with a matchbook. A calendar hung from one of the desk's ledges, a big X through each day. I envied the errands written there: pick up shirts, dinner dates, days off. A small Infant of Prague, dressed in satin robes and king's hat, held the world in its hand. I was curious about its many petticoats, and Nicky lifted the doll from its base, pointed to a dime, and said, "If you keep a coin here, you'll never go broke." The hash made him more compulsive, and he smoothed the statue's slips. He stroked a pen with a picture of a woman inside who stripped when he tilted it. He put on a record of Bach's organ music, playing it faintly. Neither of us moved, and Nicky sat at his desk while I inspected the coconut heads, which seemed to turn from three-dimensional objects into newspaper photos, Wire photos, composed of thousands of minuscule dots. A huge slamming sound caromed off the apartment door. "McBride!" Nicky said, and ran to the peephole. He hurried back and shoved the pipe into his desk. I kept asking, "Who's McBride?" but he didn't answer. Then we tiptoed to the door and listened. Voices moved to the elevator.

"I bet he smelled it," Nicky said.

"Really?" I said, and then asked again, "Who?"

"Mr. McBride. The manager. He's always after me, after me for a long time. He hates me. If he smelled it, he'll turn us in."

"Turn us in to who?"

"The cops, that's who!"

I suddenly realized how long I'd been away from the office. I looked at Nicky, whom I hardly knew, and concentrated on his face, his black curls, and I asked myself, "What are you doing here in this drug-laden and coconut-head-lined room?" What once seemed absurd now seemed ruinous. Why wasn't I interested in the executives, as my aunt suggested, and how come I got a kick out of Colombo of the stockroom, Kay of petty cash, and Charlie the porter, whose tales about the executives' private lives he constructed from crumpled doodles in their wastebaskets. Nicky changed into a sport coat and tie, saying, "I want to square this away, come on."

We walked down a long hall off the lobby, and Nicky told me to wait outside while he entered an office. I heard him say, "Mr. McBride, has a package arrived for my mother? She's expecting something important. I think it's from the mayor." He spoke in a voice I hadn't heard before, earnest, mature, concerned.

"There's no package, Nicky, and I don't want any more dope in the stairwell or you'll be out on the street."

I was still thinking about his new voice when two businessmen walked toward me, and I fought the desire to run. They went straight into the office, and McBride greeted them, "Hey, cobra and the mongoose!" As Nicky came out, McBride called, "Remember what I said, Bertel."

When we reached the edge of the lobby, Nicky turned and yelled in another voice, this one gravely and deep, so deep that I couldn't believe it came from his throat, "I hate your guts!" He placed the emphasis on *hate* and *guts*, so it had a singsong, maniacal effect. Looking at him, I saw that he was furious, that he meant it. I recognized Fred in this quick, rabid anger that came and went. Then Nicky ran. I walked after him as fast as I could without running, my hands stiff at my sides like flippers. Just like—I realized with horror as I tried to keep my composure and escape at the same time—just like—Sealo!

It was after two o'clock, and I had left at noon. I hurried along the street, thankful that Beardsley was in charge. Nicky walked with me to Paramount. "That business with McBride is really bothering me," he said. "The world is full of bullies like him, real jackasses." He faced me. "We need a common phrase," he said. "Something that will unite us and turn away assholes at the same time. Fend off trouble."

"What trouble?"

"You know, a guy harassing you, a homo, a bum . . . If we're together, it would be really funny if we cursed him at the same time, in harmony!"

"You mean just for the fun of it?"

"Yeah, for fun, but for protection too. It would be like spraying a can of mace and taking off."

"How about, 'Get the fuck outta here?'" I said.

"Too common. How about, 'That faggot eats it?'"

"No. 'Eat it raw!'"

"That's high school. Listen. 'Suck my dick in Macy's window!'" Nicky said.

"Too long. Isn't 'Fuck you' good enough? If we said it together, it could be pretty funny." We had reached Cigars of the World and stood in front of its display of lighters.

"It needs something more," Nicky said.

I remembered the authoritative parrot at Close Quarters. "I know. 'Fuck you, half-ass!' It has a kind of rhyme to it."

Nicky made counting motions with his index finger and, on three, we yelled, "Fuck you, half-ass!" over and over until we got it in one voice.

"We'll have to do it at Hubert's," Nicky said. "We get some obnoxious tourists."

"What exactly do you do there?"

"I'm learning all aspects of the business, and not just the freak business. Sometimes I take tickets when the fat lady's on break, I make deposits, sweep up, but sometimes I check the books, type letters, you name it. Hey, I'll take you to the Flea Circus. Don't worry, Professor Heckler's a friend. Those harnesses on the fleas are made from wire so thin you can hardly see it. It came from Roebling, the guy who put the cables on the Brooklyn Bridge." As I opened the brass doors and waved good-bye, he yelled, "You won't believe the stuff I'm learning!"

The mailroom was in an uproar. Beardsley, still at a long lunch, would never know of my absence. Yardsticks spilled across the floor, flailing everywhere. I recognized them from the publicity campaign

"Harlow Fever," for the new movie about the life of Jean Harlow. The advertising department had ordered yardsticks etched with silhouetted mountain peaks, the Paramount logo, and painted to resemble thermometers, red ink soaring past large black numbers reading "103 degrees," showing how Carroll Baker's performance could make an audience's temperature rise. Inscribed, "The Lusty Film Story of the Banned Book," the small print along the edges noted the simultaneous publication of Jean Harlow's novel *Today is Tonight*. Ruben carved one with a long switchblade, and the next minute a wobbling yardstick protruded from his fly as he called out, "Measure this, Evelyn!"

I grabbed a yardstick and stood it near the coatrack to bring home to my mother. Frankie hovered near the pneumatic tubes, which zoomed heavy capsules containing letters to the receptionists' desks above. It was not a good place to stand, as every so often a receptionist would drop the container back down, where it bounded into a deep trough of rags. Frankie worked for the Fleet Messenger Service and wore glasses so large and thick they looked like they came from a novelty shop. His head bobbed when he spoke, and he smiled constantly, as if expecting you to get a joke he'd just told. He was well known in our mailroom for what Gates called "getting stuck"—he would sway from side to side, holding his black straw fedora in both hands, just below his waist, and couldn't stop swaying. When this happened, we were under orders from Gates to yell, "Okay, Frankie!" which roused him on his way. Frankie could also get trapped in a phrase, repeating it uncontrollably. He did this once while talking to me about race-horses, saying, "Some run good in the rain. Called mudders. Mudders don't mind the mud. The rain don't bother them. They like the rain. Called mudders." Beardsley walked by and said, "Enough, Frankie," and he immediately stopped, smiled, and pulled a stick of gum from his pocket, offering it.

Beardsley looked down on Frankie and other runners from small messenger companies like Fleet, since most of them were mental cases or alcoholics. All were unskilled and knew nothing but the routes through the city that they followed again and again. When Frankie started swaying by the trough, Ruben walked over, holding a yardstick in each hand, and said, "Almost forty, and he still doesn't know how to wipe his ass." He pointed to the long strip of toilet paper hanging from his waist like a tail and took him by the arm to the men's room.

Ruben brought Frankie back, and Frankie gave me a clipping of a comic strip from the *News*. It was one panel of a series and made no sense. The fencing continued, and wooden fragments spun through the air, creating more action than at Hubert's but with a similar cast. Frankie looked around, the same constant smile on his face, and I handed him a yardstick from the box. I urged it toward him, but he just swayed. Ruben made the sound of an alarm clock in his ear, and Frankie took the yardstick, saying, "Thank you! Oh thank you very much! Thanks! Thanks a lot!" I yelled, "You're welcome!" which stopped him, and he turned brightly and said, "Now I can see how much I weigh."

It is shocking to have a man look openly into your face and say such a thing. It is a greater shock when you are a boy. Frankie's face, lit for a second with the thrill of a gift and, more, with how to use it, was pure. I was becoming an expert at interpreting tone, for in that room I had heard tones of irony, ridicule, hatred, disgust, self-disgust, envy, and despair. I had already been scoffed at for taking a mocking remark to heart. Frankie's statement was shocking in that it forced me to return to my former way of believing what was said, and yet I found it unbelievable. Touched and sorry, I said, "No, Frankie. It shows how tall you are."

"Oh," he said, holding the yardstick upright at his side and standing at attention, "I'm taller."

I presented the yardstick to my mother in the kitchen and pointed out the degrees, the quotes from Jean Harlow's book. She smiled and went back to the stove. While I was changing, I heard her call, "Dinner's ready!" in a voice clear and full. I was stunned, and she ran to my room, hugging me and saying, "Oh, Johnny, it worked!"

"I heard you!" I said. "That's great!"

"I wonder what did it," she said immediately, counting on her fingers. "Probably your going to church, but also those exercises. And the diet." She was thoughtful. Maybe science was stronger than faith. "I'm sticking with everything," she said, and ran down to tell Linda. Weeks of silence, and her first words called me to dinner.

What's It All About?

Gates posted me in the lobby to escort Michael Caine to the office of Paramount's president. So I wouldn't miss him, Gates folded a still from *Zulu* that showed Caine in uniform, holding a bloody officer across his lap. Screenplays for his new film, *Alfie*, had arrived for distribution to the executives, and I read one in the mailroom, immediately enthralled by Alfie's way with women. Romantic one minute and dismissive the next. And yet they loved him. Although Alfie was supposed to be a figure of loneliness and desolation, he became my model of independence, calm, and wit. He was as unconventional as the beats but had moved beyond nonconformity.

I loved the way he addressed the camera, speaking directly to the audience. I couldn't wait to meet Alfie in person, the man who said, "I've been doing things all me life I'm not supposed to."

I had brushed into a handful of celebrities in Paramount's halls. I walked at Gloria Swanson's side, eyeing the golden sash around her waist, embroidered with a huge *S*. Marty Allen opened the door at 50 Sutton Place, and took the package of halvah and bottle of Chianti. He was half of the Allen and Rossi comedy team, which Paramount hoped to be the next Martin and Lewis, the Italian straight man and the Jewish clown. My aunt's boss gave me the prayer book Richard Burton used in *Beckett*, as well as a six-foot spear John Wayne flung in *Hatari*.

119

Jane Fonda had stopped me outside an office and asked for a light, which I didn't have. She twirled her cigarette an inch from my face in a way that made me carry a book of matches for the next six months. Her hot pink skirt pulled across thighs I had memorized from *Cat Ballou*, a movie playing down the street, its theme song by Nat King Cole and Stubby Kaye blaring over and over onto Broadway: "Cat Ballou, Cat Ball-ou-ou-ou!"

I had pored over the outside lobby photos of Cat in tight jeans, pointing a pistol. Now she stood before me, looking both strong and needy, waving her unlit cigarette. I told her I'd ask Mike, the executive receptionist, and I ran to his desk, but he wouldn't stop what he was doing, which was blowing dust off a ceramic poodle. The little dog changed blue or pink, forecasting weather, but it had turned a malfunctioning gray. Slowly, Mike handed me a book of matches from Toots Shorr's and continued his huffing. When I returned, Jane Fonda was back in the office, vanished in a literal puff of smoke.

But meeting Michael Caine was altogether different.

When I read the script, I conjured my own image of Alfie, and now I stared at the face of the actor in *Zulu* and tried to picture him in his chauffeur uniform, gently helping a pretty woman into his Rolls. I stood in the lobby across from the elevator starter, an old man who read the paper at his podium. It was late morning, and few people entered the building. Caine was due at eleven, and I was fifteen minutes early. I walked outside and looked across Broadway. Bond Clothes advertised two-trouser suits, and smoke rings blew from lips of the huge billboard for Camels. The late morning light illuminated every chink and fractured bulb, and I began to sweat and returned to the cool marble.

Tall and blonde, wearing a pale linen suit, Michael Caine looked unlike anyone I'd seen. His eyes were sky blue, and he brought the sky into the dim lobby with him. Although I was tall he was taller, and broad, generating light. I introduced myself and stood very straight by the elevator, wanting to talk. I was staring at his knit tie, which matched his eyes, when the elevator operator flung open the brass gate.

"Mr. Caine," I said, as the elevator rose. "I read the script of your new movie."

"Which movie is that?" he said, bemused.

"*Alfie*."

120

"Oh, yes. I've got two others in the works as well."

"I liked the way Alfie talks to the camera. I hadn't seen that before."

"Thank you."

We reached our floor and Benny, the elevator operator, gave me a funny look when we got off, as if I had exceeded my station.

I waved to the receptionist as we walked past. Paramount's president, George Weltner, had a big corner office, and I left Michael Caine with his secretary. We didn't shake hands, though I stalled for a second in front of him. He thanked me, nodding in a friendly way.

I returned to the mailroom, excited by having met both a man's man and a ladies' man. A refined, polished version of Fred. I felt we had made a connection. I had always carried a handkerchief, just like Alfie. I sat at the table and didn't mention my errand, which gave me a secret strength. I recalled our five minutes together, calling him Alfie. Then I started calling myself Alfie.

I hoped Gates would send me up to nine again, but instead I drew a long, crosstown trip. Still, I walked with a new aplomb. I picked up a phrase that Alfie used a few times as he talked to the camera. When he gave advice, he ended it with, "in this life." He said, "It don't do to be dependent on anyone *in this life*," and "Don't let yourself get attached to nobody *in this life*." I tried unsuccessfully to work the phrase into one of my exchanges with the secretaries.

When I returned, Gates sent me back to Weltner's, and I took the stairs two by two instead of waiting for the elevator. Weltner's secretary told me to bring Mr. Caine to Joe Wolfe's office on the twenty-seventh floor, which delighted me because it involved two elevators. The first stopped on the twenty-second, and then you switched to a small car that reached the uppermost floors.

As we walked down the hall, I said, "You know, Mr. Caine, I liked a lot of things Alfie says in that movie. Do you really think men are more sensitive than women?"

"I don't know," he said. "The character makes statements to justify his actions. They're not true or false, really." We were at the twenty-second floor, waiting for the extension elevator. Michael Caine spoke to me more seriously than anyone had spoken to me before, more earnestly than any teacher. There were no operators at this level, and I pressed the button.

As we rode up, I asked, "Do you think Alfie was mean to those women, or do you think he was protecting himself? They all seemed to want something from him."

"Oh, Alfie's rotten," he said, smiling. "But he can't be too rotten, or no one would like him."

"He got a lot of girls," I said. I knew it was a non sequitur as soon as I said it, and I wanted to hammer my thigh with my fist for letting the dialogue drop from the heights of art into my own squirming little life.

We approached the screening room, and he stopped and said, "I just heard a saying. 'A man who knows many women, knows no women. But a man who knows one woman well, knows all women.'"

"Thank you," I said, because I didn't know what else to say.

I had grabbed a pen on my rush from the mailroom, to get his autograph, even though we were strictly forbidden to bother the stars in this way. Now I saw that in my haste I had taken a red pen, inappropriate for signing. But I really didn't care, I felt that such a request might spoil our relationship anyway.

What I really wanted was a tie like his, a plain, narrow knit.

It rained all afternoon, and I raced through my last errand with time to spare so I could shop at Rogers Peet for the tie. I avoided Tie City, since Fred scolded me about the ninety-nine-cent ties. I was ready to pay more than triple that amount. I loved the ads for Rogers Peet, which showed cartoons of tests they put their ties through, and I liked their slogan, "Clothes for Young Men and Men Who Never Grow Old." I was nervous about entering the store alone, and I wiped the rain from my face with my handkerchief, seeing the racks of ties and charging straight for them before a salesman could approach.

The knit ties hung beautifully, thin strips of tiny, glowing coils, crocheted perfectly to their squared-off ends. I decided a shade of red would go with my madras jacket and would "pick up" its muted crimson lines, a phrase I'd heard Fred use. There were a variety of reds, and I lifted a deep ruby, rubbing the fabric between my fingers. Then I stepped back. I couldn't believe what happened: the dye came off, a sticky, bloody scarlet. I lifted another, burgundy, and this too smeared my skin. Same with vermilion. I was dumbfounded that these ties, some of which cost five dollars, would lose their color from the simple fact that my hands were slightly damp from the rain. I looked around, almost ready to welcome a salesman, when I noticed that the pocket of my white shirt was stained with red globules and that the pen I had placed there earlier had exploded, leaking down my chest. The ink had gotten onto my hands and now on several ties. I walked quickly out the door and into the rain.

On the train that night, I told Linda about Michael Caine and folded the cover of the script to show her the first page: ALFIE.

She said, "That's a bad name for a film. A LIFE." She had misread the title. "Whose life?"

"It's *Alfie*, not *A Life*," I said.

"A lot of people will read it the way I did. *A Life*."

When I reached for the strap, my jacket opened, exposing my shirt. "What happened to you?" Linda asked, lifting it to get a better look.

"My pen leaked."

"Your pen leaked? It looks like blood," she said, and laughed.

I rode home, paging through the script, reading the parts where Alfie spoke to the camera, my jacket buttoned tight to hide the garish splotch.

Blistering Heights

Fred called and mentioned having a cookout, the barbecue he'd promised the first time I looked at the city from his terrace. I thrilled to the
picture of Fred, Madeline, Shelley, and me standing on the roof before
a fuming grill, smoke wafting across the skyline as we sipped wine and
watched cabs curve through Central Park. I vowed not to drink
so much.

"Tell your mother I'll bring the steaks," he said. "From Manero's."

"You mean here?"

"Sure, I think I should spend a little time with your mom, and it'll
be a family affair. Invite Linda. Around noon on Saturday. Remember,
I'll bring the steaks."

I hated Fred visiting. When I was younger, I never got to know him
during those afternoons, because he just made small talk with my
mother and aunt. There was always one major argument. With him in
my house I couldn't try on my new self, and when he left I'd have no
sense of him, no sense of the east side, no new expressions to use or
restaurants to name. I was afraid that my obsession with Linda would
be apparent. I remembered asking as a child at Christmastime, "Can
Santa see my thoughts?" Now I felt my thoughts about Linda ruled my
every glance, and I felt sheepish, certain my strong and twisted yearn-
ing was scrawled across my face. I dreaded the weekend instead of

looking forward to it. I told my mother, and she sighed, "A cookout? We don't have any coals. We'll have to clean the grill. Is it still in the basement? Why didn't you let me talk to him?" After dinner my mother said, "Go downstairs and tell Linda."

Linda sat in my grandmother's old chair in the dining room, next to a big white bag from Horn & Hardart imprinted with its new slogan, *It's Not Fancy, but It's Good*.

"A cookout? Just because he's crazy or drunk, we have to be crazy with him?" I heard my mother coming down the stairs. "Did you hear the latest?" Linda asked her.

"Maybe it will be fun," my mother said. "We might as well enjoy it, and I think I know where I put the grill. But it could use a thorough scrubbing." I looked over at my grandmother's bedroom. Her bed was covered with a white sheet, and two large ovals of flat dough speckled with flour rested on it, drying. I asked my mother if she was making ravioli. She used to prepare complicated dishes with my grandmother years back, when my father was home.

"I thought it would be good for me to start cooking again, and I know how you and Linda love ravioli."

"Fred will be glad too," I said.

"Always Fred," Linda said, sighing dramatically.

I picked up the *Journal-American*. A survey showed that the city's police and fire departments were almost entirely white. "That's not right," I said. "Everyone should get an equal chance."

"Don't be naïve," Linda said. "That's how it's always been." She opened *The Tablet*, a Catholic paper, to the Legion of Decency's movie ratings. "They condemned *The Amorous Adventures of Moll Flanders*," she said. That was Paramount's new movie.

"Well," I said, "things will be different when my generation takes over."

"We'll see," she said.

"That's how people stay poor," I said. "They can't get hired."

"It's right in the Bible," Linda said. "'The poor you will always have with you.' Those are Jesus' words."

That night I listened to Long John, and the *Journal-American's* story entered the discussion. Callers on both sides argued, and then I heard someone quote that exact phrase from the Bible: "Jesus said, 'the poor you will always have with you.'" I waited for a response—I was sweating as I held the receiver. *I* was the caller to WOR! Although it seemed like someone else, I was the one who spoke those words, standing in my underwear in the humid dining room, joining those lonely losers who dialed in the night. To summon the courage I had said to myself, "And then he called the radio station at 2 A.M.," and I watched my finger spin the metal rotary, and I became calm.

A rabbi was on the panel, and he spoke for a while about that quote, interpreting it, putting it into context. He mentioned that Jesus' statement "It would be easier for a rich man to pass through the eye of a needle than to enter the kingdom of heaven" actually referred to a street called "The Eye of the Needle" that was quite wide. I said, "I see," and I said, "Yes." He concluded by revealing that the Red Sea parted by Moses was really The Reed Sea, a few inches of water thick with seaweed, and that crossing it was no miracle. Another guest interrupted his monologue while I hung on. He was a barber, always introduced by Nebel as "the tonsorial artist from Brooklyn," who usually just made wisecracks. He cut the rabbi off and said, "Caller, he's giving you a lot of background, but it's an economic fact, the poor *will* always be with us." At that the rabbi said simply, "Maybe, but why do they always have to be the same ones?" I put the receiver in the cradle, pleased with myself for getting an answer to what troubled me, even if I had to take my aunt's side of the argument to do so. I had called the radio station like all the lost souls. I said to myself, "He began to specialize in freaks of all kinds."

On Saturday morning I went to the basement to get ready for the barbecue. When Linda heard the legs of the grill banging along the outside stairs to the porch, she called me. She sat at the terrazzo table, pouring hot milk into hot coffee. She placed a cracked, yellow oversized cup in front of me, the cup my grandmother had used to soak her teeth, and pointed to a steno pad. "I've listed the executives at Paramount since I've been there." She pushed the notebook toward me. "Protestants, Jewish, Italian. Each time someone gets in charge, he brings his own." I looked at the columns where she had neatly listed the names. "The Italians are in now," she said. "Too bad you don't want a job right away. Remember blood is thicker than water."

"Last night you said there will always be poor people."

"That's right, it's in the Bible."

"I have a question. Why do they always have to be the same ones?"

She did a double take. "They're not the same ones, what are you talking about?"

"I don't mean the same people, I mean the same groups, like the blacks, the Puerto Ricans."

"That's ridiculous," she said. "Your grandfather made a good home here, and he couldn't even speak English. He did all right for a foreigner." My mother was already on the porch, wiping down the grill and listening through the open window.

"He knows Papa fell off a roof, Linda, right?"

"He knows. And what does that have to do with it?"

"Maybe he was one of the poor ones," I said.

"He was not!" Linda said. "You're full of foolish ideas."

"We need charcoal," my mother said.

"We need a lot of things," Linda said. "We better get going."

My retort had not gone the way I'd hoped. Linda walked to her bedroom, and I heard her slamming drawers. A few minutes later, she and my mother left for the A&P.

"In case we're not back when Fred arrives, give him a cup of coffee," my mother said, and she dragged the wire shopping cart to the front steps, where Linda waited. I ran to my room and tried to distract myself, turning the radio on and off, leafing through Fred's books. But I couldn't fight it, the desire to invade Linda's apartment.

In that idle hour I had the chance to do what I had fantasized about day after day. I would open her dresser drawers and lift out at leisure the things she had shown me. Each week, I saw dozens of hopeful actresses in tight skirts streaming through Paramount's polished doors; prostitutes in lingerie leaning against Eighth Avenue storefronts; an occasional leather-clad mistress strolling the aisles of the porn bookstores with a riding crop under her arm. But no one aroused me more than Linda, and it was always her face that brought me to the shuddering point. Her stern way, her restrictions guarding a lascivious nature provoked me, a taut electric fence restraining wild and wandering impulses. I'd get feverish thinking of her dressing in the morning, recalling her saying, "These are the things I put on every day." I kept Shelley out of my imagining. She was too real. Sex with her was practice for my fantasies, and not the other way around. And now images of Jeanie unfurled, since I had glimpsed the shadow of her pubic hair against the alley light. But Linda brought me down the stairs, through her apartment, into her room, and before her dresser, where I opened each drawer.

I smoothed my palm over the folded slips, then raised them by their straps. I snapped her crumpled bras into the air, hooking them and shaking them out. Each drawer was lined with shiny white paper, which slid toward the corners if I pulled too vigorously at the clothes. A black bra came to life in my hands, and after inspecting its lace I put it on over my T-shirt and watched myself in the mirror, hefting my hands under the cups: I was standing behind Linda and crushing her soft breasts through the stiff cones. I was Linda and I was myself. And I was a third person watching the two of us, as she leaned into my chest and I pressed against her. I made her bend over the dresser, when I suddenly saw myself in the mirror and I tore the bra off, realizing I was Albert/Alberta, Roberta/Ray, Leo/Leola, Esther/Lester—a man and a woman on my own little stage! How sick was I getting? Still, I continued tugging the wooden knobs, knobs my mother had painted with tiny skylines and then screwed back so badly that the drawers angled out crookedly. I skipped the skirts and sweaters, fearing my mother and aunt's return, worrying whether I'd get everything in place. The half-slips, tossed about, were an easy target, and I placed one on the bed, lifting the brocade hem over my aunt's willing body as she lay across the quilt. I brought a handful of panties to my face, a festive turmoil of white, pink, yellow, and black, and inhaled their soapy fragrance. Ironed blouses filled the long bottom drawer. At this point even the most ordinary square of cotton shimmered with heat, and when I lifted the stack, I saw newspaper lining the bottom—not a page, but dozens of folded papers and clippings. I thought they were obituaries or notices of family members from the local *Star-Journal*, but then I recognized the article from the Profumo scandal. And from other papers as well, detailed accounts from the *London Times* and the *Daily Mail*, stamped with the logo of the Out of Town Newspapers stand on Broadway. These stories were specific, telling how the girls in underwear drew lines in lipstick across the men's buttocks so their strokes would have a target area, how the men reached orgasm by this alone. The writer gave details about the width of the straps, the birch rods, the flails. I was wasting time, but I couldn't stop reading. Other articles, unrelated to Profumo, gave accounts of judicial canings in South Africa, blacks tied to ladders and whipped with lengths of rhinoceros hide, whites fastened to punishment benches and beaten with oil-soaked canes. Under the papers were two books, an ancient cloth edition of *The Illustrated History of the Rod* and a paperback with a green cover, called *Blistering Heights*, by Jane Boston. I knew this kind of cover: understated but pornographic. It had been thumbed through so much that its pages were wrinkled and warped. I read randomly:

"He threw Ellen over his lap and began to spank her, harder and harder. She kicked her legs so high that her sex was exposed," and "It was time for her punishment enema. He told her to remove her pajamas and lie across the bed."

How many minutes had gone by? I stuffed the book back and covered it with the papers. The thought of Linda saving these stories ruined my fantasy. Some of the flogging stories were not overtly sexual, and this dimension of Linda's life cascaded onto my dreamworld and stopped it from being a dream. I stood in front of her dresser trying to regain my excitement, and then I saw the hamper. The airshaft ran from basement to roof, but shelves had been built on Linda's floor for storage, and small doors added. I had watched her turn the tiny metal latch that opened this cabinet when I lay on her bed and she tossed the semen-soaked panties in with the rest of her clothing.

I was heading toward the old laundry when my worry about time sent me to the bathroom. I scooped petroleum jelly from the giant jar Linda used at the dining-room table to remove makeup with cotton balls. She whipped me, I whipped her, and I was out of breath when the front door opened and my uncle yelled, "Olga! Linda!" I tried to clean up by spinning a long length of toilet paper, but the Vaseline just smeared oil stains onto the tissue, hinting what it would do to my khakis. I ran hot water, and as I waited for it to rise through the pipes, I heard a rush of shopping bags as Fred walked by, shouting, "Anyone home? Jonathan John! Amicus curiae!" I splashed lukewarm water on my groin, but it just beaded. Afraid to stain the towels, I unrolled foot after foot of toilet paper, stuffed it into the front of my shorts, and hoisted my pants. I opened the door, calling to Fred. The toilet choked as the nest of oil-stained paper floated to the brim and stayed there for a few long seconds before plunging down.

I found Fred upstairs, where he flung two shopping bags onto the kitchen table. He wore a Burberry trench coat and smelled of smoke, an honest, open fragrance compared to my previous dank minutes.

He heaved brick-shaped white packages into the refrigerator. "I got filets," he said. "Hey, what smells so good?"

"My mother made ravioli."

"No!" he said, with real delight. I told him she was out with Linda, but he ran through the rooms anyway, as if looking for her. I began to swab the algae off our big fish tank in the dining room, so he could see my life. Fred stared at my wrist in the tepid water, a few tiger barbs nipping harmlessly at my fingers. The front door slammed; they were home. Fred, who had seemed so eager for my mother, was now absorbed in inspecting her hobbies, and he scrutinized the boxes of feathers, the large needles and oversized spools of thread, the stacks of jigsaw puzzles. Holding a square of cotton batting, he looked over at me swiping the sponge through the bubbling tank and said, "God save your soul." Which was what I wanted *him* to do.

Downstairs, Fred swept into the kitchen, announcing, "I smell ravioli!" as I walked in the wake of his aftershave, the belts of his topcoat flying into the odor of boiled milk, salve, tomato sauce, and ammonia. My mother stirred a big pot. Linda sat at the table, rubbing the familiar pumice stone over her callused heel, which she then smoothed with an ointment. She had changed into a sundress, and I wondered if she wore anything I had handled. She stood and knocked her cheek against Fred's lips in a grudging kiss and went back to her heel. Fred threw his topcoat over a chair. He wore the black knit shirt and gray pants. He pulled a narrow box from one of the bags and offered it to Linda. "Italian toothpaste," he said. "From Parma. Look at the contents, flavored with anise," he said. Linda laid it down on the table mournfully; she had seen the price. "I stopped by Bloomingdale's," he said. "Olga, these are for you." He reached into the bag and brought out a bouquet of carnations and a large bundle of dried mushrooms.

"Oh, Fred," my mother said, very pleased, laying the flowers down and bringing the mushrooms to her nose.

"Imported," he said.

"Pepsodent is good enough for me," Linda said, getting up and moving the statue of Romulus and Remus so she could reach the radio dial. The Saturday opera flowed out. Fred looked hurt for a second, then puzzled, both expressions merging into annoyance.

My mother put her arm around Fred as they walked down the hall. "It's so nice of you to take John around," she said. "And I have a surprise for you." Earlier in the week my mother had traded twenty books of plaid stamps for a blender. I did the errand after work, taking the train to Jamaica. She had given me eight for myself, and I chose an X-PANDO Chest Expander, two handles linked by five long springs. The cashier took the thick, wrinkled books and wrapped the blender. My prize, in a box a yard long, was too large for any bag. The drawing on its outside showed a weight lifter with a handlebar mustache pulling the great springs in front of his booming pectorals. The bold-faced words X-PANDO stretched across its length. Passengers on the E train craned to read the words as I tried to hide the logo with my forearm on the long ride home.

Now my uncle, aunt, and mother peered into the blender, into the lime juice, ice, and white rum my mother had bought at Sheridan's Liquors. Something was wrong with each pitcherful—too watery, too thick, too sweet. As they drank, each personality went its separate way. My mother started worrying about the ravioli, the coals, and the steaks, and she went downstairs, tightening her apron. Linda turned up her nose at Fred's criticisms and followed my mother. I drank two quick ones and whispered to Fred, "Did you see the name of the rum? Fighting Cock! Get it?"

"Never mind the name," he said, and stared at the bottle with its ugly label. "You have to use Bacardi, and this blender's a piece of junk." He looked at me seriously. "Buy the best and cry once," he said.

"Which reminds me," he continued, "I went to a great place last night, Uncle's, on Second Avenue. Willie Shoemaker was at the bar— you know, the jockey? You should have seen his boots." He bent and traced his finger along his ankle. "Calf leather. Hand-tooled. Beautiful hand-tooled boots." I didn't ask what that meant, although I would look it up.

"What nonsense are you telling him now?" Linda said from the doorway, holding a tray of drinks, each filled to the top, green sludge slipping down the stems. "I had these in Havana on vacation. I know how they're supposed to turn out," she said, and looked at me with a knowing eye.

Fred took a sip and smiled. "I have to hand it to you." He passed me a glass and said, "Let's get the coals started and see how Olga's doing with the sauce." Linda followed us, very pleased.

Fred stood next to my mother, watching her use the long rolling pin with the squares cut into it, which left a checkerboard grid on the sheet of spinach-filled dough. I went outside and lit the grill. A few minutes later Fred joined me and made a sour face when he sipped his drink.

"I told Linda these were good, but they're shit. Cheap rum. Cheap machine." He shrugged, walked to the side of the porch, and dumped his daiquiri over the railing before he went inside. While the coals smoldered, I looked into the empty kitchen. Three open bottles of Schmidt's beer stood on the terrazzo table. In the dining room my mother dialed the doctor's office, asking if he thought she should drink. The steaks rested near the sink. I couldn't resist the beer, as my throat constricted from the sourness of the daiquiris, and the brown bottles promised crisp relief. I ran in and tipped a bottle high. When I slammed it down quickly, afraid that my mother would arrive, a burst of foam rose up the long neck and flowed onto the table. Fred walked in and blotted the beer with a napkin. "Go ahead and finish it under the porch," he said. "And here." He took the cigarette out of his mouth, put it into mine, and fished a pack of firecrackers from his pants pocket. "Left over from the Fourth," he said. I wished I had been with Fred on the Fourth, and as the smoke leaked into my eyes on my way down the stairs, I suddenly felt like Alfie, and I advised myself just to take what I could get in this life.

I sat grinning in a metal chair flecked with rust and peeling paint and rocked. I put the beer on the table next to me, pushing aside terra-cotta flowerpots, watering cans, trowels, and claws. I sucked on the cigarette without inhaling, trying to make smoke rings. Then I exhaled upward. I sealed my top and bottom lips in the middle and blew smoke out the sides. Things Fred did for a laugh. I continued to sip. When I finished, I scraped off the label and placed the bottle on the table. I balanced one of the firecrackers on its lip. Then I lit it, not more than an inch from my face. The splintering explosion, echoed by the porch roof, brought everyone running. They leaned over the railing while I sat there, stunned. "Just a bottle," Fred said, as he walked halfway down the stairs and peered at me rocking in the rusty chair. I was drunk and I had almost blown my face apart. The glass shattered everywhere but, miraculously, not a shard touched me.

I heard mewing sounds and looked under some old boxes, listened at the basement door, and finally found the source in a dish barrel off to the side of the porch. Jammed with rakes, brooms, shovels, hoses, and hoes, it did not seem the place a cat would choose to give birth, but there they were, looking up at me: an orange mother and her four kittens, splashed and sticky with lime daiquiri, Fred's discard, which the mother was licking off the tiny bodies.

The ravioli turned out fine, although my mother insisted they weren't right. We ate the pasta with a bottle of homemade burgundy Linda brought from the wine rack in the coal bin. Then I put the steaks on, standing in the smoke. In the corner of the porch, Fred spoke to Linda in a low tone about college being a waste of time and how a fortune could be made in the city. He waved his wineglass in the air and, when he finished his long story, my aunt said, "Bullshit," and they both walked by me into the house.

Fred wanted his filet almost raw. Once, at Gallagher's, he ordered a "blue" porterhouse, and a few minutes later the chef was at our table, offering his hand. "Allow me to congratulate you," he said. "That's how steak should be cooked." Fred beamed around the restaurant at everyone looking at him and returned the hearty grip.

Over dinner Fred described the club he had gone to the night before, and Linda put the platter of beef in the center of the table. My mother brought in baked potatoes and a bowl of corn. "Wayne Newton comes in, and *boom*! A hundred-dollar bill to the hat-check girl."

"How do you know it was a hundred?" Linda asked.

"She told me. It was Ceil, I know her for years. So I tell her, 'Ceil, send him a thank-you note with one of the waiters.' Ten minutes later Newton's in the lounge asking, 'Who sent the note? Who sent me the note?' Ceil says she did and *boom*! Another hundred! 'No one's ever sent me a note before,' he says." Fred laughed. Linda sneered and my mother looked down.

"How lucky for her," my mother said.

"It was crazy last night," Fred said. "A black guy was doing paintings in the corner, a kook in a beret. They say they'll be giving them away as door prizes. Still lifes, but wild, like a bowl floating in the middle of a room, no table under it or anything. I'll see if I can get one."

Unable to help herself, Linda asked, "Were there any other stars there?"

"Tony Bennett. He sang a few songs when people recognized him. I was with Vito, up front." He turned to me, "You met him, John, at Richards' wake. When Tony finished, Vito raises one finger, says, *Tony*, and Tony runs right over and sits down. Just one finger, and quietly, almost a whisper, *Tony*." Fred raised his index finger as if he were doing the summoning. In that moment he was back at the club, surrounded by the fashionable and powerful, but it was Fred, not Vito, who became the central figure in the room with the lifting of one finger, which the famous singer heeded. We were all silent as we looked into Fred's eyes, which were frightening, moist, and steely. He knew who he was and what power he could command, and yet, for all of his power, he would be beneficent.

Tony.

Linda broke the spell by saying she had read that Liz Taylor was in town, and an argument began over the number of her love affairs. Fred became irritated at Linda's denial of his stratospheric estimate, and the discussion ended with Fred saying, "You act like a big girl who's never had it."

"How do you know what I've had?" Linda asked, as my mother brought her a large bowl of greens. Since Linda never cooked, her job was to toss the salad. She poured oil and vinegar, stirred, and lifted, and after a minute she yanked a greasy green paper napkin used to line the bowl to absorb moisture. She raised it delicately in her tongs and reached over to Fred, placing the oily ball in the middle of his plate. He said, "You loony," and with this gesture their argument ended.

After dinner Fred watched Linda do the dishes while I closed down the grill. My mother was on the porch, leaning against the railing. Clotheslines strung from the tenement pulleys crossed each narrow yard, above homemade fences of chicken wire, old doors, and window frames. "I can't wait till winter," my mother said. "I get so sleepy in the heat, and then maybe your father will be home more."

"I don't know about that," I said. "He mentioned having to go to Canada after this."

"Did I show you the collage I'm doing? I'm using his postcards."

Linda came out and said, "Oh, there you are!" Fred was right behind her, but seeing me and my mother, he slipped back. My mother turned and asked, "Will the fig tree have fruit next year, do you think? This summer was a disappointment."

"I think it will. It looks strong now," I said.

She put her arm around my waist, and I walked her toward the kitchen. When she passed the aluminum door, she paused, touching the screen with her fingertips. "Your father said he'd fix these holes," she said. Suddenly I felt like crying. I ducked my head so Fred wouldn't see my eyes, but he didn't notice, he was shooing a fly toward the open porch door, where it circled right back, almost hitting him in the face.

In the living room, we drank coffee and watched Jackie Gleason. When a skit featured the bombastic Reginald Van Gleason III, Linda said, "There's Fred." She asked if anyone wanted ice water, and when she left, Fred followed her. Leaning in my chair, I could see straight through the apartment. Fred talked to Linda, whose mouth tightened, then she went to her dresser and opened her purse. He put the bills in his pocket. At the end of the show, Fred said, "I forgot something," jumping from his chair. He returned with a small shopping bag. He brought a bright watch to my mother, knelt by her armchair, and said, "Olga, this is for you." He strapped the band to her wrist. The gold face gleamed.

"For when I go to the ball," she said, smiling. "Thank you." The gift seemed to perk her up, but her smile was forced, a strained cheer. Linda looked at hers with disgust. She felt she was paying for the watches.

"John!" Fred called suddenly, "I better be going. Walk me to the avenue."

"I'll come along," Linda said. "I could use some air after all that food."

I was surprised that Linda was going with us. I wouldn't have any time to hear Fred as I walked Major. Fred and Linda chatted while I halted and sped up, at the mercy of our strong and untrained dog. Major and I zigzagged ahead and behind for the mile to Elmhurst Avenue, where we waited for Fred to catch a taxi. No cabs passed. It started to get chilly, and Linda shivered. Fred said to her, "How about a nightcap?" and he nodded toward Grady's pub on the corner. For fifteen minutes I yanked the dog from mailbox to lamppost, then Linda came out and handed me two packets of beer nuts. Twenty minutes later, Fred delivered a bag of chips. After an hour they stood in Grady's doorway, arm in arm, smiling. Fred yelled, "Jonathan John, amicus curiae!" He held something over his arm and smiled. Letting go of Linda, he raised a gray satin windbreaker so I could see it. The jacket, from a New Jersey high school, Essex Catholic, had been altered by its previous owner, a fellow patron, who had peeled away a few letters, so the back now read, SEX A HOLIC. "I got it for twenty bucks!" Fred said, laughing. "It's yours."

He held the leash as I put it on. It was huge and felt like a parachute dropped on me.

"He can't wear that to work," Linda said.

"Of course not," Fred said. "It's for knocking around in. You both start for home. I'm going soon."

"Grady phoned him a cab," Linda said.

Fred pointed at me and said, "I'll call you."

"He's actually a not unintelligent fellow," Linda said.

"Fred?"

"No, not Fred! Grady!" She wobbled in her tan tennis sneakers as if she wore heels. "You have to watch Fred every minute," she said. "That's why I came along." She straightened, as if she had done something righteous, but then she listed off the curb. I grabbed her by the elbow and set her on the sidewalk. She drifted into the avenue, almost nicked by a cab. I looked at her quickly, puzzled, and saw she had closed her eyes. Major, all muscle, strained ahead despite the choke collar. As I walked to Judge Street in my new jacket, with Major tugging me home and Linda continually lapsing into the street, I couldn't help thinking of her secret life, the life clipped and stored under her clothes, the life behind her trancelike face.

Fate

Nicky spun the dial on his huge Zenith TransOceanic, the band's needle roving across its tin map of the United States. It was the exact model I had been saving for. "Goddamn it!" he said, "I can get almost every country in Europe, but I can't get New Mexico." His uncle lived in Taos, and Nicky talked about him with great respect for his small paintings of cowboys and indians. "He just didn't get any attention for his art around here. Downtown, it's all junk. Uptown, snooty stuff no one understands. He did these coconuts." I admired the coconuts, pressing the tip of my finger against the molars of a fierce mouth and praising the raised eyebrows on a very high-spirited face. As Nicky twirled the radio knob, his phone rang. It was the manager of Hubert's. Fred had told me to leave the room when someone got a phone call, and I closed the door and waited outside, thinking that the only calls I got were from Fred. I had spoken to my father twice since he left. Each time he told me how busy he was but also how much fun he was having, describing the antics of Donlon, a new salesman, who rescued dull evenings at bars by rallying patrons into games of charades, which he said he was getting good at. He seemed content away from home, and I was content without him.

Pepe's cries wafted from a few rooms away, and I heard Nicky agreeing to a change in his schedule with great vigor. It was another tone of voice, and I recognized it immediately—the tone of a man's man. I examined the paintings in the hall, some of which I had seen in the arcades, mostly trompe l'oeil. I looked at a man strapped to an electric chair, but when I closed one eye, a stork carried an infant. A rabbit changed into a duck, and a gypsy fortune-teller in her high-backed armchair transformed into a skull. I'd reached the end of the hall, blinking one eye and then the other, when I saw Jeanie holding her baby against her open blouse. "The phone woke him," she said. "Always hungry." I peeked down and saw a fat face, eyes closed, sucking her nipple.

"He's cute," I said.

"Thanks," she said, and she cuddled him. "On lunch hour?"

"Yeah. Nicky got a phone call." I turned to the pictures to avoid staring.

"John?"

"Yes?"

"Have you ever tasted breast milk?"

I shook my head.

Jeanie walked to the dining-room table and placed a pacifier in Pepe's mouth. She laid him on the couch, surrounding him with cushions. Her blouse was still open, and she cradled her arms in front of her as if she still held the baby. When she was a foot away, she told me to open my mouth. She aimed a breast toward me, and I bent low, but milk streamed across my shirt and tie. "Kneel down," she said. I got to my knees and she squeezed her breast again. The squirting milk surprised me by its force, and I moved to catch it. Warm liquid shot across my forehead and into my eyes. "Did you get any?" she asked.

"Not much," I said, standing up, and wiping the milk away with my fingers. Jeanie walked into the kitchen and brought back a towel and a juice glass. I brushed the cloth over my lapels and shirt, while she eased out an inch of milk. She lifted Pepe and I drank. "It's good," I said.

"Pepe loves to nurse," she said, looking down at the baby. "All boys do. They never get over it. Have a seat." I looked at the *Daily News* on the table, opened to the comic strips and crosswords. "Ever do 'The Jumble'?" she asked.

"I'm not too good at puzzles," I said, trying to take my eyes away from Jeanie's breast, an object of lust that had changed into something else.

140

Nicky came in. "New schedule at Hubert's. I have to work weekends."

"That's too bad," Jeanie said.

"Not really. I've been wanting to meet the Human Canary. Come on," he said to me, walking to his room. When I said good-bye to Jeanie, she winked. Did Jeanie see me differently near that hallway, where a wink changed everything?

On Forty-Third Street Nicky said, "I have a plan to get McBride. That ball breaker accused me of throwing bottles out the window. Everyone knows it's Oskin upstairs, but he wrote a letter saying he'd get us kicked out." He got angrier and angrier, railing at McBride's weight, taking an inventory of his dress, focusing on his tie tacks: an eyeball, a middle finger, a slide rule . . .

"Maybe he just has a weird sense of humor," I said.

"A sick sense of humor. He looks like an undertaker in that shiny black suit. And those jowls like a bulldog. Ever seen him sneaking around?"

"I don't think so."

"That's because he's good at it. He acts like he's on a big case, but he's really a peeping tom, I swear. He came into the apartment once when Jeanie was in the shower. 'Did you call me?' he asked. 'Did you call for me?'"

"He just walked in?"

"He has keys. Another time I was in the basement, doing laundry, and I saw him in the alley, climbing a ladder and staring into the hotel next door!"

"Are you sure he wasn't working on something?"

"What are you, a hick? He's sick, him and his assistant, Mr. Lane. He's the house detective, but he's the same. They're called 'voyeurs.'"

We reached Tenth Avenue, and Nicky led me into a shop he called "Sextons and Bishops." Priests' silk vestments, cassocks, and surplices hung from armoires. The shiny wooden floor creaked as we passed tall statues of saints through an odor of polish and must. Trays of rosary beads and scapulas filled the shop, and deep marble holy-water fonts were tagged with prices. Sunlight from the street angled into the room, forming towers of dust motes that stirred as we walked down a flight of stairs. The basement room was lined with bookshelves holding fireworks of all kinds: bottle rockets; roman candles; scarlet whistling chasers; and mats, soft planks of eighty packs of firecrackers, their fuses tied together, each covered with an eight-by-ten-inch full-color label. Nicky rummaged in a wooden barrel containing bottle rockets and sky rockets with fat fuses and spindly wooden legs and held one up critically, pointing to the tipsy, uneven tripod. The sight of the daring explosives touched some part of my boyhood, and I felt the desire to insert a firecracker into an unusual place and turn my back on it, running.

"What can I do you for?" A skinny man entered the room wearing a green janitor's outfit and carrying a cardboard box that smelled of onions. He sat at a card table. Lodged above his head, between two asbestos-covered pipes, a transistor radio played WNEW, and I recognized "The Make-Believe Ballroom," but the host, William B. Williams, in a playful mood, called himself Guillermo B. Guillermos. The man lifted four hot dogs from the box and laid them out on the table. He pushed chili back onto the dogs where it had dribbled over the sides, and then he brought one sideways to his mouth. "They're stingy with the onions," he said. "I tried to save a buck going to Trolley's."

"Didn't old man Trolley sell the business a few months back?" Nicky asked.

"Sheets the bit out of me," the man said, angling the bun toward his lips.

Avoiding the sky-illuminating contraptions, the tight packages that projected fountains, stars, and flags into the firmament, Nicky picked through cherry bombs and ashcans, dense capsules that ravaged and tore. Holding up depth charges, he said, "Stay lit under water. Great for flushing down toilets, blows the pipes apart." He jumped at the sight of red explosives shaped like sticks of dynamite. "These," he said, "are M-80s, and these are what I'm gonna tape to McBride's office window."

He explained his plan to blow up the pane of glass, gauged to explode just as McBride relaxed in his apartment after work. His voice got louder when I thought it should be getting softer. "The glass will blow right across the hall. He'll shit in his pants." He made a guttural sound I hadn't heard for a long time, the sound we coughed up as little boys to create the noise of dropped bombs.

Nicky paid, and when we were halfway up the stairs, the man called to us. "Hey, you guys looking for some clean pussy?" He waited a second, watching us stare.

Then he said, "No such thing!" and laughed.

Nicky and I glanced at each other. In perfect harmony, as we had practiced, we roared, "Fuck you, half-ass!" and took off through the silky vestments.

We stopped for pizza and sat in a greasy booth. "I'll show you real naked women," Nicky said. He made a barker's voice. "Real live naked women!" Nicky saw that his pleas to help him destroy McBride's window began to irritate me, so he started offering things. First he tried to pay for my lunch, but I threw my bills down quickly. He ordered two coffees without asking if I wanted one.

"Where are these naked women?" I asked.

"Right here, in the city. But there's one drawback. I said they were live, but they have what some might consider a major flaw. They're dead."

"Come on!"

"Hey, squack is squack! Want some pie?" He called for two slices of coconut custard and told me about his friend in the city morgue who would open the drawers for us. Many were prostitutes who had died of syphilis. "Beautiful girls," Nicky said, "but I warn you, covered with sores." When I didn't respond enthusiastically, he said he knew Rosebud, an acrobat with Barnum and Bailey. We'd stand around the women's dressing room on the pretext of seeing her.

"No thanks," I said.

"Hey, how'd you like to become a priest?" He knew a defrocked bishop who worked on the Staten Island Ferry, and who performed ordinations for twenty-five dollars. Nicky would pay.

"You can marry your friends when they want to fuck a girl," he said. "This guy performs the ceremony as soon as he's out of Battery Park. When we reach Staten Island, you're Father John."

"That's bullshit," I said.

"You think so? Then go right to St. Pat's and ask. But don't tell them it happened to you, or they might do something weird, like keep you there. Hey, you like the Yankees, don't you?"

"Yeah."

"If you don't want to be a priest, free of charge, which I don't understand, how'd you like a real Yankees uniform?"

My face told him to go on.

The pie arrived, the top of each slice beaded with liquid, so Nicky gently blotted them with his napkin. He explained how the outfit belonged to Chip, a freak burned over his whole body who worked at Hubert's, billed as Mr. Potato Chip. He wanted to commit suicide in center field at Yankee Stadium and planned to dash to the monuments and blow his brains out, but a guard tackled him.

"How'd you wind up with the uniform?" I asked.

"I cleaned out his locker. Know how Chip died? He got caught in another fire, one that burned down his whole apartment building. Funny thing was, he was always scared of flames. He used to drive us crazy at the museum, asking everyone, over and over, 'Do you smell smoke? Is something burning?' At first I thought it was part of his act, but he was serious. I can't remember the number or guarantee the size. He was a lot shorter than you. You'll have to take it to a tailor."

I declined, and I knew what would be next, the offer of a beautiful girl. It came when the waitress refilled our cups.

"Look, all you have to do is walk down the hall with me. It'll take two seconds. I just need a second pair of eyes. For that, I'll even fix you up with my special girlfriend, and you don't have to worry about it. I'm not the jealous type."

"Is this Anna?" He had described many girls to me, all of them special, but Anna was his favorite, an honor student who had already appeared in TV Guide as a model for mascara.

"You'd love her. Especially you. She's read all the Kerouac novels, and you know that book of poetry you're looking for, Mexico City Blues? She has a copy, paid twenty-two dollars for it in a bookstore in the Village, an out-of-the-way place not many people know about. She'll take you there. And get this, her father owns his own business. Know what it's called? Superior Screw! I'm not kidding! I've been to her house—she has a whole collection of those big-eyed paintings you like. In fact she looks like one herself. I'm telling you, you're made for each other!" Her only imperfection, he said, was her extremely long legs, which made her awkward when she danced. He incorporated a flaw into everything he proposed to give it the ring of truth. "How about me setting the two of you up?"

"I'd rather have that fall to fate," I said.

"Oh, man," he said, disgustedly. "Call *me* fate!" Then he leaned close. "And *fate* says that you're going to help me blast McBride into smithereens."

Dirty Bunnies

Later that day Gates called my name and said, "I have something a little different for you. Do you know who Adolph Zukor is?"

"Zukor on nine," I said. "910."

"That's his office, yes. He founded the company, must be in his nineties now."

"I've never seen him," I said.

"He doesn't come in much anymore," Gates said, "but he's here today, and he needs an escort. I want you to go with him."

"Where?"

"Not sure yet, but he'll be in his limo, and you just have to go along for the ride."

Gates couldn't stop smiling, and I said, "Come on, Mr. Gates," but I knew he was serious.

Adolph Zukor founded Paramount Pictures in 1916, when he was forty-three. That made him ninety-two in 1965 when I stood before Millie, his secretary, who was in her seventies. A large mirror mounted on her desk faced her, and as she spoke she glanced left and right at two smaller mirrors. They were a set, each framed with pink scallop shells and pearls. A case of manicuring instruments covered most of the green blotter in front of her.

"Take Mr. Zukor to the front of the building. When his car arrives, help him in. When you get where you're going, help him out."

"Okay," I said.

"Mr. Zukor has business. Hank will drive. You just watch out for Mr. Zukor." Then she whispered, "See that he doesn't fall. Make sure he holds your arm." I tried to get enthused, thinking I'd see what Mr. Zukor's day was like. He was the first executive I'd spend any time with, and my mother and aunt would want to hear about it.

Mr. Zukor, a tiny, bald man, walked out of his office followed by two singers, Jan and Dean. Zukor wore a black suit, which made him look whiter. I had never seen anyone so white, his skin even paler in contrast to the tanned and golden-haired duo, who had a big hit called "Dead Man's Curve." Mr. Zukor moved very slowly, in half steps, letting one foot catch up with the other. The soles of his shoes never left the floor.

"This is John, Mr. Zukor," Millie yelled. "The mailroom's best boy." He grabbed my wrist and gave it a shake and said good-bye to Jan and Dean. I took his arm and started toward the elevator, but he tugged in the opposite direction. "This way," he said. He had a German accent. I let him lead. He gripped my forearm tightly, and I could tell he was light and that I wouldn't have any trouble catching him if he stumbled. We walked down the hall like bride and groom, him sliding across the floor, and me taking a step and waiting for him. Three or four secretaries passed us as they crossed from one office to another, each saying loudly, "Good afternoon, Mr. Zukor," and smiling at me as people smile at someone with a toddler or a dog. I thought I'd been in all the offices, but he opened a door I hadn't seen before. There was no name on it, and it turned out to be a restroom. It had two stalls and two sinks. Mr. Zukor let go of my arm and backed into a stall, holding its sides. I didn't know whether to stay, but when he didn't say anything, I walked over to the sink and looked in the mirror. I had gotten the Hawaiian god perfectly centered on my knot that morning, and I tightened my tie. After a few minutes I tiptoed over, but Mr. Zukor faced the floor and didn't seem to need me. I went back to the mirror. Finally he called, "You! You! Are you here?"

"Yes, Mr. Zukor," I said, running.

"Help me up."

I pulled him by his hand. His face was red.

"Nothing today," he said, as he shifted and buckled his pants. "No dirty bunnies today."

For the first time all summer the elevator operators did not joke with me about the size of my penis or whether my girlfriend was a virgin. They knew Mr. Zukor. The limousine was right at the door, and I was relieved when the chauffeur, Hank, introduced himself. He wore a full uniform and cap in spite of the heat. "Hello, Mr. Z," Hank said, and Zukor raised a finger.

"I'll ride with you," I said, opening the front door.

"Oh no," Hank said. "Mr. Zukor likes the company."

The car was plush and cool and rode so softly it was like being in a living room. I could see why Alfie easily coaxed girls into the backseat. We were separated from Hank by a Plexiglas panel. I looked out the window with pleasure as we passed the doorways to lobbies I'd entered on errands: The National Screen Building, The Hollywood Reporter, MGM, The Motion Picture Association of America. I wished Fred could see me driving so smoothly through midtown.

"Tell me your name again," Mr. Zukor said.

I told him. "Know how long I've been here, Johnny?" he asked.

"No, Mr. Zukor."

"Since 1916," he said. He had a warm smile. He got a kick out of that date. "You like pictures?"

"Very much."

"I like pictures too. You know what I like about pictures? They're different from anything else."

"Yes, they are," I said.

"They're different from furs, or garments, or the automobile business," he said.

"It must be great to see the whole movie come together," I said, remembering how Linda had described films being shot in pieces and not in the sequence the audience sees it.

"In a regular business, like furs," he said, "if the customer buys a coat and doesn't like it when he gets home, he takes it back. In pictures, if they don't like it when they get home . . ." He shrugged. We stopped at a light, and a man on the sidewalk next to us walked in stiff, exaggerated, mechanical steps, a briefcase at his side. When he passed, I saw an enormous gold key in his back, unwinding slowly.

"Look, Mr. Zukor," I said. "Look at that man!"

Hank's voice came from a speaker. "It's some kind of publicity stunt." He had been listening.

Mr. Zukor didn't budge. "I can't turn my neck that way," he said.

When Mr. Zukor and I arrived at Barneys Clothing Store, three men ran to greet him, and he nodded happily as I moved from his side. One of them, whom I understood to be Barney, took his arm. They walked deeper into the store, but when Mr. Zukor stopped and turned, so did they. He said, "You can wait here, Johnny," and pointed to some chairs near the front.

"Make yourself comfortable," one man returned to say to me.

Mr. Zukor disappeared, so I thumbed through the magazines, all business and sporting journals. Two salesmen chatted near the window, and one looked over, nodded toward my jacket, and spoke as if I wasn't there. "I'll never understand it," he said. "In India, only the poorest people wear madras."

Another salesman helped a customer trying a herringbone sport coat. As the customer turned before a three-sided mirror, the salesman stroked the stiff, pressed back of his jacket, saying, "Just like glass!"

After an hour Hank came in. "Not ready yet?" he asked.

"I haven't seen him since we got here," I said.

"He goes in the back for a little schnapps," he said, and sat down next to me. "Should be any minute."

When Mr. Zukor appeared, he was escorted by his old friend.

"All set, Hank," Barney said.

"Give me a hand," Hank said to me. In the back room we picked up shopping bags full of boxes and brought them to the car. We returned for long, heavy cartons that must have contained overcoats. There were shoe boxes and hatboxes. We filled the Cadillac's huge trunk. As Hank slammed the lid and we stood there sweating, I said, "How much stuff can Mr. Zukor wear?"

Hank looked at me as if I were crazy. "It's gifts," he said. "Mr. Z's a generous man." I went inside for Mr. Zukor. On our way out the same salesman pushed a square of fabric toward a customer, rubbing it between his thumb and forefinger. "Butter," he whispered.

In the car Mr. Zukor said, "I'm a little hungry and there's something I've heard about, something I want to try."

"What is it, Mr. Zukor?" I asked.

"Millie told me about a dessert. I forget the name. She says it's very good, so we'll try it together. You try it with me, and Hank too," he said, smiling.

"Thanks," I said.

Mr. Zukor seemed a pleasant man. He enjoyed things, and he spared no expense, that was clear. I wondered where we were going and was flattered to be going with him. I pictured those little glass cafés along Lexington Avenue and their flaming desserts.

"She says there is a layer of cake, and then a layer of ice cream, and then a layer of cake. The cake is very, very thin, she says, very thin." He put his thumb and forefinger together, raised them to his eye, and squinted.

"A pastry?"

"Maybe like a pastry, I don't know." We drove for a while and then he said, "It must be like a pastry, because you pick it up. Yes," he laughed, "without a fork."

Hank's voice boomed from the speaker, "It's called an ice-cream sandwich!"

"That's it," Mr. Zukor said to me. "A sandwich, with ice cream in the middle." He sat back with satisfaction. Hank double-parked at Woolworth's and brought three ice-cream sandwiches, which we ate on our way up Broadway.

"Very good," Mr. Zukor said.

"Very good," I agreed, as the long car twirled through traffic, but I felt disappointed and I didn't know why. I felt disappointed even as I ate ice cream in a limousine. I wanted to defend my maligned sport coat. I wanted to walk out on Mr. Zukor and his pent-up dirty bunnies. I tried looking down at myself from above, as I did when I crumpled into my aunt's comforter, but there was no real outrage, just resignation, and I did not disappear into the third person but stayed my old self, licking the waffle's edges before the ice cream further streaked my wilted madras, and I said, "It's great to have all three flavors in one."

Still, I couldn't wait to tell my aunt about the trip. It was almost five, and Beardsley and I were the only messengers without an assignment. At this hour we were just killing time; it was too close to quitting to be sent out. I was sitting on the table reading fillers in the *Daily News* when Beardsley walked over and began whispering about his evening with Evelyn.

"She broke up with her boyfriend," he said. "She's attracted to my scar. Most women are." He shrugged. "Some of them see it as a fencing scar. I fucked her last night, wanna hear about it?"

"It's okay," I said.

He gave me a thorough description, grinning the whole time, sweat from the day's errands accentuating the ruddy seam. I grinned a Miss Subways grin, false and hopeful the moment would end. Then I noticed that each time he added a sentence about Evelyn, his eyes moved to my crotch. Another filthy sentence, another glance. His face drew nearer as he talked, so he was almost in my ear. Gates noticed and sent Beardsley for stamps, a make-work assignment. "I'll tell you the good parts later," he said, walking out.

Gates was short twenty copies of *Variety*. He looked at the clock, ten to five, and asked me to hurry. I walked to a big newsstand on Forty-Second, and as I struggled with the pile of papers under my arm, I saw Jeanie watching me. She stood in front of The Nutt Hutt, pushing Pepe back and forth in a carriage, and at first I didn't recognize her in the motley parade. She held out a bag of cashews and asked what I was doing. I showed her the copies of *Variety*. She looked at the front page, and her eyes widened. "I've never seen this before," she said, giving it back. "I'll walk you to work," she said, and we rushed against the tide of pimps and dealers whistling and popping out of doorways, saying, "Smoke?" and "Jewelry for the lady?"

I turned into Paramount. "Why don't you come for lunch next week?" she asked. "Yeah, come up at noon next Monday," she said, wheeling the stroller around.

"I can't," I lied. "I have an appointment."

"You do?" she said. "Let's make it Tuesday then."

I dropped off the papers and raced to my aunt's office, thrilled and frightened of my lunch with Jeanie. I wanted someone else to meet her, my double, and I wanted to watch them together.

On the way to the subway, I told Linda about my trip with Zukor. "I thought he might be taking us someplace special," I said.

"You thought Adolph Zukor was going to sit around with a chauffeur and a mailroom boy? Wait a few years, and I'm sure you'll get the chance. He might be dead by then, but there'll be someone else if you play your cards right. What are you doing tonight?"

"Watching the Mets, then read a little."

"Reading what?"

"A book of poetry."

"I suppose you think that'll prepare you to talk with Mr. Zukor? Remember what McBain said when I told him you were interested in poetry. He said, 'Tell him to stay away from that sickening poetry.'" We approached the subway newsstand where Linda bought her paper every night. It had a new display of buttons with witty slogans. When I laughed at one that said, "No More Mr. Nice Guy," Linda yanked it off the cardboard. "How much?" she asked.

"Fifty cents."

"Here's a quarter," she said. The man shrugged, and we descended the stairs. I felt a rushing affection for Linda in that moment with the silly button, for her sashaying dress and secret life. Over the summer I had become an expert at passing her bathroom at night just as she rose from the tub, listening at the hinge to drops falling into the water and then the hushed, almost inaudible strokes of the towel. I had also wandered downstairs when I heard steps from the basement, to watch her sort lingerie on the bed. I had brushed against her as we stepped onto the train, and I thought she brushed back.

When I got home, my mother stood in the center of the kitchen in her apron. She was usually busy, and it was strange to see her without a cleaver or a ladle in her hand. She had been waiting for me and was obviously nervous. "I've called Fred," she said. "I asked him to have a talk with you. It's your father's job, but what can I do. I went to borrow another book and found your folder. He's going to talk with you this weekend. On Sunday, for dinner."

I wanted to see Fred, but I was embarrassed to see him under these circumstances. My mother had returned the folder to the bookcase, and I reviewed the clippings. Matronly women in girdles smoothed their palms against their hips. White bras so bland I concentrated on the dark cleft between the two breasts, the only sign of flesh. I had been nibbling on the edge of sexual information, scavenging and scrounging. I knew Fred hadn't told my mother about Shelley and, as I looked into the bathroom mirror and wiped soot from my cheeks, I puzzled over what Fred would tell me on the weekend. A few years earlier, before he left on a trip, my father put a book under my pillow entitled, *Listen, Son*, published by the Maryknoll fathers, and I used all my wits to decipher the abstractions and mysterious praises about the body, known in those pages as the temple of the Holy Ghost.

Believe It or Not

I woke up on Saturday to my mother singing in Pig Latin. At first I thought she was on the phone, but when I entered the kitchen, she leaned against the stove, reciting from a marbled composition book. It was a hot morning, and she lifted a chunk of lasagna from the frying pan. "I'm learning a language," she said, smiling. She put a fork and napkin on the table.

"Why?" I asked. "You already know Italian."

"Yes, but Dr. Abbott recommended it, and it's fun." She slid the heavy plate in front of me, stepped back, tapped her feet, and began a little song. "Ear-way-in-yay-e-thay-oney-may! Ear-way-in-yay-e thay-oney-may!" She laughed with delight as she repeated the line.

"What's that?" I asked. I couldn't help laughing myself.

" 'We're in the Money' in Pig Latin. Soon I'll know the whole thing. If I can get Tom Peck involved, I could work up a routine for the Monsignor Little Club. I'm going over to see him now." She walked down the stairs, humming.

I sat at the kitchen table and leafed absentmindedly through a *Times* article on Harlem's illegitimate children and my mother's poetry anthology. W. H. Auden's poems seemed similar to Alfie's asides. I loved his voice, at once more private and more public. Then I wrote my own poem, addressing the sky and asking the moon to help abandoned children. I put down my pen with great satisfaction at having righted the universe on the old steno pad. I looked again at Auden, whose words seemed whispered, surrounded and buffered by white space, yet entirely confident. Like Alfie's, spoken directly to me.

I called my best friend, Cooney, whom I hadn't seen much as his father, the police commissioner, forced him to work at the 110th Precinct seven days a week. Mr. Cooney had big plans for Mark to follow in his footsteps, but in searing mid-August his father granted him weekends off. At the same time Fred cut my dates with him shorter and shorter. He seemed distracted, and I felt like a burden. One Saturday I met him at his apartment, sat on the terrace while he talked on the phone, shaved, and showered. Another time we had breakfast at Flamingo's and that was it. I loitered for the rest of the day, stopping in churches, bookstores, and museums, finding myself more and more at home in Manhattan. Now my time with Fred had been reduced to Sunday night, the idle stretch meant only for recovery, the glamour of the weekend over. And for dinner, a late one at that.

Cooney asked me to take him to Times Square, and we went on the day before I would meet Fred. I had a feeling our trip would be a disaster, and it was. He wanted only one thing, a dirty magazine of quality, which I promised. I would call for him at ten. I drank a glass of milk by our second-floor window, staring down at the long clotheslines and homemade fences. On the one real fence between the Sheehans and the Costigans, two cats howled, twined together. If my mother had been home, she would have filled a tall glass, leaving the faucet running. Then she would have dashed from sink to window, whirling hopeless spirals of water at the cats thirty feet away. I liked the feeling of being alone, my mother gone and Linda running errands as she did every Saturday. It was almost like Fred's. Then I thought a door closed downstairs, maybe the wind or perhaps Linda hadn't left after all. I heated what was left of my mother's coffee and headed for the *Times* at the bottom of the stairs, when I heard another noise. I paused. Something in Linda's apartment, perhaps a breeze through the basement, the cellar door open. I grabbed the paper and leaned on the newel post. Again, this time a clear whack, like someone hitting a wet rag against a wall. Then once more, slightly different, a snapping towel. I tiptoed toward Linda's door and opened it. The sound again. Was she home?

As I drew closer, the sound came clear and clean. I measured my steps, going quietly through the kitchen, the dining room, the volume increasing. I turned into her bedroom and saw Linda lying on her stomach, across the width of the bed, facing the wall. Her broad white buttocks in full view, flushed in places. She had pulled her skirt and slip to her waist and pushed her panties below her knees. A strand of beads circled the back of her neck, at the start of her upswept hair. Her pumps stood next to the bed. My eyes shifted from the reinforced heels of her stockings to the clasp on the necklace. They were easier to look at than what I wanted to see most: her smooth backside. She raised a long wooden stick I recognized as one of my grandmother's sauce spoons and slapped it hard against her left cheek so it shook. Then she hit the right, wobbling it. A Paramount yardstick leaned against the wall, perhaps she had tried it as well. Again and again her arm reached around awkwardly and swatted, as she rubbed her pelvis against the comforter, bucking a little. As I backed away, she sighed, and I thought for a moment she sensed me, but I kept walking, relieved when another self-involved gasp came from the bedroom, then another . . . She had moved into a new stage, and I glided up the stairs, into the bathroom, where I opened the window to the airshaft leading to Linda's room. The methodical strokes echoed upward, with an occasional deep breath. I was desperate to hear my aunt in a way I had never heard her before, but to keep my ear to the air shaft, I had to stand in the claw-footed tub, one shoe pressed against its steeply sloping end, the other on the squeaking rubber mat, air bubbles gushing through the perforated rubber. Glancing at my wrist, I saw the time: almost eleven! I was late! I zipped up as best I could, grabbed my baseball glove, and stepped quickly down the stairs.

Cooney's mother was yelling into the phone when I entered their dining room. Old postcards, pens, ledgers, and matchbooks from stacked, half-emptied drawers covered the table. The Cooneys were being audited, and Mrs. Cooney shuffled through the pile with her free hand. She took her position as wife of the police commissioner very seriously, touting her superiority to the rest of the block. I left without her seeing me and waited against the wrought-iron fence in front of the attached tenements. Their doorway faced Queens Boulevard's simmering cars, drivers shouting at the women in short-shorts who lounged on the tall stoops, which formed a kind of cement bleachers. Sometimes one of the girls jumped into a car and would be dropped back later. Sometimes the same car came for her regularly, and she'd disappear for a week or two. Sometimes they married, and their children toddled the same steep steps.

Mrs. Cooney wouldn't let Mark into Manhattan without his father, so he lied that we were going to play baseball. I was flopping my stiff and outgrown mitt against my side, when a deep voice called from the next stoop, "What's the capital of New Hampshire?"

"I don't know," I said.

"It's Concord," the voice said. "You don't know shit. What's the capital of Idaho?"

"Boise."

The voice belonged to Mr. Quinn, who squatted in front of his door. He worked in the Great Bear Transmission shop on the corner. His yellow shirt with the bear cub on the pocket was smudged with the kind of grime that comes from rolling under tables and getting stomped with the gritty soles of work boots. His face bore the same marks, his lip split and bloodied. Mr. Quinn had six children, who usually swung along the railings, but there was no sign of them today.

"Alaska?"

"Fairbanks."

"No, you nitwit, it's Juneau. What an asshole." He shook his head and grinned down at the slate step. "How about Montana?"

Cooney finally walked out, followed by his mother pushing his ninety-year-old grandfather, who was strapped into a wheelchair, grimly staring ahead, his jaw clenched by age. A few years back Mrs. Cooney had a tumor removed from her forehead, and the surgery left one eyebrow raised, so that she appeared in a continual state of questioning. She asked about my mother and if we were moving. We had no plans, and I told her so.

"It's getting terrible here," she said, tilting her head toward Mr. Quinn, who was biting his fingernails and then holding his crimped hand away from his face, examining it. "What riffraff. Just this morning he fought with the postman." The mailman's leather bag had been stolen from his cart while he sipped coffee in the luncheonette. The mailman accused Quinn and there was a fight.

"Worse, who knows where our mail is?" she whispered. "And when I'm expecting receipts!" Her eyebrow looked more inquisitive than ever. The grandfather began to drool, and Mrs. Cooney lifted a small box of DiNobili cigars from the old man's shirt pocket, shook out a gnarled black twig, and placed it between his lips. He was allowed six a day, and when he finished them, he jammed the inch-long, tar-soaked butts into the bowl of his pipe and lit up. At this the families on the stoops groaned, knowing the putrid odor would drift their way. As Mark and I walked down the block, Quinn yelled after us, "Helena! Helena, you fucking know-nothings! What're they teaching you?"

We went straight to Ripley's Believe It or Not Odditorium, where we were greeted by a statue of an aborigine, a self-portrait. The sculptor had placed his own toenails, fingernails, and hair in the clay. We spent an hour in the Chamber of Tortures, lingering at the Iron Maiden, an upright casket closed partially on a half-clothed, heavily made-up, sexy mannequin, spikes entering her eyes, throat, and breast. Before leaving, we watched a wooden wheel that rotated by itself, a vertical carousel of steel balls tipping and causing it to spin. A sign read, "Perpetual Motion?" As we continued down Forty-Second, Cooney ecstatically browsed the filmy storefronts displaying glossies wrapped in plastic and Styrofoam blocks stuck full of switchblades. I had described the magazines in Fred's apartment in detail, and we both hoped to find our own copies of *Smoothies*, but I couldn't get Cooney to go any further than the entranceways. "I don't want my father to find out," he kept saying.

At the window of a secondhand magazine shop so dingy and dusty we had to bob up and down at the glass door to see if it was open, Cooney agreed to walk in. He explained that we wouldn't be noticed there, that our business would be welcome; he had seen magazines in the window that promised explicit pictures. A man stood at the cash register watching cartoons on a small television. The place smelled like our basement after the sewer pipe burst over a bin of *National Geographics*. Stacks of magazines, wrinkled and damp, spread across the floors and were piled on wooden crates that served as shelves. We went through issue after issue.

"Any *Smoothies* yet?" Cooney asked in a loud whisper.

159

"Not yet." I felt pressured to come up with something good. Cooney walked over. "I don't think they have any *Smoothies* here," he said, irritated.

"Well," I said, "you didn't want to go in the other places."

"If we can't find them shaved, do you think we could at least find some with pubic hair?"

"Pubic hair is easy," I said, and began to flip more desperately through the stiff pages. Five minutes later, I showed Cooney a completely naked woman wearing a rain hat, the thin plastic kind my aunt kept in a little triangle case in her purse. The model was about to unfurl a black umbrella as she stepped over a puddle. We studied it closely, asking ourselves the same question. Was that pubic hair or just part of the umbrella?

Two dollars.

As we argued about who'd approach the cashier, Cooney ran out the door. Tucking my glove under my arm, I put the magazine down and opened my wallet. The man said, "Is that the one you want?"

"Yes," I said. The cover, which I hadn't looked at until then, showed a stocky woman in a garter belt and panties bent over a couch with her rear in the air. It was called *Buttman*.

"Are you sure?"

"Yep."

Looking straight into my eyes, he swiped the magazine off the counter and onto the floor. "Go out and play in the sunshine," he said.

Out in the sunshine, Cooney asked, "Where is it?"

"I looked at it again. It wasn't pubic hair. It was really part of the umbrella. Let's go to Hubert's." I hoped to redeem my status, as Cooney looked back longingly at the reeking porn shop.

I talked the acts up as we walked along the faded banners in front of Hubert's. Zoma the Sadist, a half-naked black woman wielding a dagger and crouching over a half-naked, bleeding white woman. The Feejee Mermaid and Otis the Frog Boy. Cooney noted they looked fake, but against all reason I said they were real.

We passed the shooting gallery and pinball machines, and I almost hoped Ricky would appear to pitch the place. Saturday's crowd was different, mostly out-of-towners, pointing and giggling. "This is what my father would call a tourist trap," Cooney sneered.

"The whole name is Hubert's Freak Museum and Congress of Strange People," I said, hoping to add gravity to this worn-out world.

"And we're strange for coming here," Cooney said. "Let's go home." It was his father's tone. I wondered if it were true, that my warped summer had warped me. We were turning away from the fat lady in Hubert's ticket booth when the barker, a black man in a black suit with a leopard-skin vest and matching African chieftain's hat, introduced himself as a prince. He walked a rabbit on a leash, tugging it by a diamond collar.

"You boys are over eighteen, right?"

"Sure," Cooney lied.

"Then let me show you some items from my private collection." He winked. We followed him into a storage room of unplugged Skee-Ball lanes, broken twenty-two rifles, and fat rolls of coupons. He pulled an index card from his vest. He reached in again and held up a pencil. He brought out a small black telescope wrapped and stapled in clear plastic and placed it on the cracked glass of a pinball machine.

The Prince picked up the index card and held it by its corners, between the thumb and forefinger of each hand. A keyhole was stamped in black ink in the center.

"This is not an ordinary card," he said, "because we compressed photos into the paper, reduced and pressurized as on microfilm, into the black image." He pointed to the keyhole. "You take this home, go someplace private like the bathroom, and rest this card in a saucer of water for half a minute. No longer, no less. Then lift it out and hold it to the light." He poked his nose very close to our noses. "You see a woman, naked as an apple."

"How much?" I said.

"Quarter."

I plunged into my chinos, feeling for a coin with my fingertips, but Cooney handed him a dollar. "Give me four," he said, raising his eyebrows toward me. "Are they all different?" Cooney asked.

"Let me see," the Prince said, inspecting the cards with his thumb and tilting them sideways. "Yes, different poses." He took my quarter, frowning at me and pouting out his lower lip. "And just one for you," he said.

We put the cards in our shirt pockets, while the Prince closed the black telescope in his fist and said, "Here is something very special, still untested in the open market. The Colt X-ray." Our eyes jumped to his hand, but he kept it closed, saying, "It's called 'The Colt' due to its size. Small but powerful. You can see the bone in your finger." He held up his pointer with its long yellow nail. "You can see the lead in the center of a pencil." He tapped his pencil on the glass. "And of course, you can see easily through flimsy things, like dresses . . ." He tugged at his leopard vest and smiled. "Two dollars." Cooney yanked out his bills, and the Prince grabbed them. Then he pressed the tube into Mark's palm, forcing Mark's fingers to close around the X-ray machine. "Save it for your household," he said, looking toward the door. "When you can look through your sister's brassiere!" He smiled a conspiratorial smile, and Mark beamed back. "How about you?" he asked. I didn't like the idea of the telescope. I had seen it on the back of a comic book, next to an ad for a monkey in a teacup. Tempted then, I decided it couldn't work.

"That's okay," I said.

"It makes the impossible possible," he said, "and the incredible true."

"No thanks."

The Prince frowned again and whirled us out of the storage room and into the din. Cooney removed the cellophane from the X-ray machine, and I held my index card to the light. I couldn't figure out how the images were hidden in that keyhole, and I pictured the dishes in our cupboard and the saucer I would use. Leaning against the poster of Otis the Frog Boy, Cooney pointed the telescope at his finger. "Holy shit! I can see the bone!" he said. I took it and saw the bone running up the middle of my finger as well. Cooney grabbed it from me, slipped down against the wall, his back against the poster, and pointed it at passing summer dresses. Watching him, I wished I'd bought one. Suddenly he straightened and looked into the tube's other end. I leaned over, and we both saw it at the same time: a tiny feather pasted onto the transparent lens at the far tip. "That guy really took us for a ride," Cooney said. "The place you think's so wonderful is a gyp joint. I wish I could tell my father."

"Don't blame me," I said. "I didn't fall for it."

"The cards might work," Cooney said. "I've read about things like that in *Popular Mechanics*. They just might. Let's go." We got on the train to Queens, depressed and annoyed with each other. The cars were almost empty. Who'd be leaving Manhattan to spend a Saturday in Queens? Cooney started criticizing the trip. I said, "Because of you, we had to carry these stupid gloves around. No wonder they wouldn't sell me that magazine."

"I thought you said you put it back?"

"I made that up. What the guy really said was, 'Tell your friend to stick to baseball.'"

"Bull!"

I slapped Cooney's forehead with my mitt, and we wrestled in the empty car. He pinned me to the long plastic orange seat, lying on top of me and pressing the heel of his glove into my adam's apple, until I reddened and he withdrew it. I sat across from him, angry that he couldn't see what I loved about Times Square. It was as if Times Square didn't exist in Queens. At the Elmhurst Avenue stop we went into Admiration Cigar, where school kids bought candy during the week. Cooney couldn't find Pixie Stix, straws filled with sour powder. He asked Mr. G, the gray-haired owner, whose eyeglasses were held together by brown pipe cleaners. He raised his finger in the air. "Pea shooters!" he said with an accent. "Pea shooters!"

"They're not peashooters, Mr. G," I said. "They're straws, made of paper."

"Pea shooters!" Mr. G said again. Mr. G spoke only in expletives and never left his seat behind the counter. Outside, we leaned against a parked car. Cooney said his father hated Mr. G and had told him a few words to say whenever Mr. G gave us a hard time. I looked over at the front window, half of which was filled with junk. Mr. G's handwritten sign read, "For Sale. Few Items. Bert Cage."

"I'll show you," Cooney said.

We went back and lingered by the comics, always forbidden. Another scrawled sign read, "Do Not Open." Cooney rustled a magazine called *Sick*, shaking it until Mr. G called over, "Not, sir!" Knowing Mr. G watched, Cooney bent it back and dramatically whipped through the pages by their corners.

"Not, sir!" Mr. G yelled this time. "You are skating on tin ice!"

"Did you hear that?" Cooney said. "*Tin* ice! I don't think I'd fall through *tin* ice, Mr. G!"

"Out!" Mr. G ordered.

Cooney looked over and said, "Oh, gefilte fish!"

"What, sir?" Mr. G asked.

"Gefilte fish and oy yoi yoi yoi matzo balls!"

Mr. G rose from his seat and headed toward Cooney, the first time we had seen him from the waist down. He wore black shorts.

"What gefilte fish? Why?" he asked.

We walked out and Mr. G trailed us, asking again and again, "Gefilte fish? Why?" Mr. G yelled often, but this was different. Half a block away, Cooney laughed and said, "It worked! Don't ask me how!" I looked back. Mr. G still stood on his doorstep. I had no idea what Cooney had said, but I knew he had touched Mr. G with syllables I couldn't look up, a curse whose power overshadowed the nonsense spiels on Forty-Second Street.

Cooney's father was at work, and his mother had left a note on the kitchen table saying she had taken his grandfather to the doctor for a checkup. Cooney filled a plate with water and patted his index card into it. He turned on a lamp, and we watched the clock's second hand. "Did he say a minute?" Cooney asked.

"No, half a minute. Take it out."

"I think he said a minute," Cooney said.

"I don't think so, Mark," I said. "Take it out, you can always put it back."

"He said, 'no more, no less.'"

Cooney pulled the dripping rectangle from the water and gently wafted it over the saucer, shaking free the last drops. Then he raised the card to the light and we leaned to it. Ink ran down the card, and Cooney held it so tightly that it came apart in his fingers. "I knew it was a minute, you jackass" he said.

"It would have been worse if you left it for a minute," I said.

"You took us there."

"It's not my fault—I bought one too."

"That shows how stupid you are, you bring me and then you fall for this garbage. You know," he said, "I have stuff in this house that beats anything we've seen today. Let's go to my father's room." We walked the stairs to a small den, with a single bed, armchair, armoire, and a

164

dresser. It looked onto the street. A subway map was tacked to the wall, the kind given out free at the token booths, as well as a framed drawing of two stick figures made of nuts and bolts, a female pursued by a male, the caption of her words reading, "Not without a washer!" The closet held his suits and old patrolman's uniforms. A tumbler on the nightstand had a coaster attached to its base, a miniature jock strap with printing on the waistband that read, "For Your High Balls." Cooney brought out a box of shoulder holsters, and we looked for a gun. He mentioned that his father read *Playboy* and wore a diamond ring.

These seemed more like flourishes by the mailroom boys than acts of a man's man. My own father was harder to place in the world of men. His dresser held only a bottle of bay rum and a safety razor. When he was home, he stayed in his white shirt and tie from morning till night. In the evening he raised his tumbler to my mother, softly shaking the ice and saying, "Olga," when he wanted a refill. When he left, there was not much difference in the household.

Cooney pulled a paperback from the nightstand drawer and nodded at me knowingly. "You took me all the way to Times Square, and what did we get? Nothing. Ten minutes in my father's room and wham!" We sat next to each other on the bed and leafed through *My Brother Was An Only Child*, a book by Jack Douglas with an introduction by Jack Paar. "Jack Paar is that really filthy guy who's on late."

"This is just a joke book, Cooney," I said. "Where're the *Playboys*?"

"Wait," he said, staring at a blank page with the boldface title, FOR MEN ONLY. At the bottom it said, "Hold lighted match behind this page." Cooney brought a handful of stick matches from the kitchen, and we struck them again and again on the rough slate windowsill. Then we saw something, a slowly forming brown silhouette. "See!" Cooney said, "This paper has it, the image inside, like I read about!" It looked like a pair of legs, the start of a groin, and we craned against each other until the paper flamed. I smacked it to the ground and we both blew on it furiously, thin black ash falling to the rug and tiny gray cinders parachuting through the air. When the fire was out, Cooney looked at me and said, "There really was a woman on that page!" Before I could answer, he said he heard you could get a call girl to the house by dialing PEACHES backward, and he lifted the heavy black phone, but a car pulled up. Mark's father stepped from a limousine, his crew cut closely shaved, making him seem taller and broader. Looking toward the sky, he said to the driver, "Full moon. Harlem'll be jumping tonight."

The room smelled of smoke. Cooney placed the book in the night-stand, and carried a handful of charred paper downstairs, where he knocked it into the toilet bowl. As he wiped the ashes from his palm, he whispered, "Whatever you do, don't tell my father you took me to the underworld today." I was puzzling over this when Mr. Cooney arrived. We stood in the kitchen while he read a note from his wife, crumpled it, and, when he raised the lid of the trash can to throw it away, he said, "Mark! What the hell is this?"

"What?" Cooney asked.

"All this." Mr. Cooney dipped his hand into the garbage and stirred stacks of envelopes and bundles of magazines. He turned the can over and spilled the contents onto the linoleum. It was all the mail that had been stolen in the morning. Lodged into the bottom of the container was a leather mailbag—the postman's sack that Mrs. Cooney mentioned had disappeared, causing the mailman's fight with Quinn. Mr. Cooney waved the big pouch through the air, and the three of us stared at two large holes cut from the soft skin, each in the shape of a footprint. Mr. Cooney walked quickly to his father's bedroom and brought back a pair of bedroom slippers, each fitted with a new leather innersole. The nutty grandfather had escaped somehow early in the day and carved up the sack.

"I told her to keep those straps tight," Mr. Cooney bellowed. "This is a federal offense!" As I left, I heard Mark trying to make conversation with his father, to stave off the anger that might be felt later over the burned book. He said to Mr. Cooney, who was dialing, "I got Mr. G today, Dad. Wait till I tell you."

That evening I heard a new voice on the radio, broadcasting live from The Limelight, a bar in the Village. Jean Shepherd told stories that had shape, like Roy Eldridge's solos, and a great sense of timing. He made wild sounds of explosions, squeals, and cries. He described his friend Flick hurling a rock a miraculous seventy-five yards at a trolley, knocking it out of service, and the lure of a girl named Jeanette Dombroski whose every move caused an undergarment strap to groan.

When I turned off the radio, I could hear my mother rehearsing.

East-lay Ide-say Est-way Ide-say
All-say around-lay ethay own-tay!

She had learned to perform "The Sidewalks of New York" without
missing a beat, not a mistake or hesitation in her glee.

I couldn't wait for the next day, when I would meet Fred on the east
side that now rang so crazily in my ears.

The Facts of Life

On the train to Grand Central I worried about my mother putting Fred on the spot, especially since I hadn't spent the night at his place in weeks. What would he tell me? Madeline had practically moved in with him, and I got the feeling we wouldn't see each other at all once autumn arrived.

I had never cleaned my blue suit and made the mistake of mentioning this to my mother. She reached into the closet and brought out a rusty can of Everblum, a strong solvent she poured onto a rag and wiped over my shoulders before I could object. Its fumes lingered on the subway, and when I got off in midtown, I could still smell the pungent aroma. When we met, Fred asked how things were at home. I answered to get his sympathy.

"Everything's fine. Mom's studying Pig Latin."

"Good God Almighty!" he said. "I wish I had more time to spend with you." He pulled on the collar of his soft blue shirt that had the Brooks Brothers' roll and turned to a group of teenage girls we had passed. "What you really need is someone your own age." To my horror Fred approached them. I couldn't see the girl's face or hear what Fred asked, but she simply said, "No," and turned to her friends. The word had weight and zip at the same time, and I admired it. It made a thud like a bird hitting the windowpane. Fred took a step back and said to me, "You can never tell." I saw the girls staring as we walked away. One held a chocolate ice-cream cone to her mouth, hiding a laugh. I wanted more than anything to be standing with them. To get rid of the hollow feeling, I told myself I preferred older women.

I loved the east side at night, even on a Sunday, with the couples moving from bar to bar, going in and out of restaurants. "Let's have a drink before dinner," Fred said. "There's a great place called P. J. . . ."

"P. J. Clarke's!" I said.

"No!" he said. "Not P. J. Clarke's. Don't interrupt. P. J. O'Hara's. No one knows about it yet. They're both on Third Avenue." Some of the bars we went to were decorated with portraits of hunting dogs, others with guitars, some with model airplanes hanging from the ceiling. Many displayed huge aquariums behind the bar. But P. J. O'Hara's had the plain wood, dark paneling, and red and silver stools of Queens. It was narrow and deep, extending far from the street. At a table in the back, Fred ordered Jack Daniel's for both of us. Over the summer he had allowed ice, but not water. I got used to the burning in my throat and looked forward to the way it made me feel, like I was sitting a few inches above my chair. Fred faced the front, and I looked at a framed newspaper on the wall with the headlines, O'HARA RULES WORLD. I recognized it as coming from a shop on Forty-Eighth called Your Name in Headlines. The text was always the same, and I pointed this out. Fred looked at me thoughtfully, lit a cigarette, and said, "You really like the west side, don't you?" I denied this immediately and tried to explain that was where I had spent my lunch hours, but he held up his hand, saying, "No explanation needed. Everyone has his own taste." We talked for a few minutes about my upcoming year in high school, my last, and what I'd been listening to on the radio. "Try Big Wilson in the mornings. Biggie. He plays the piano on the air. 660." He leaned across the table and said, "Although the DJs play music, they're really all frustrated actors or musicians." I had heard his theories of "frustration" before. Once he had an argument with a handyman fixing a crack in the bathroom ceiling who explained his solution at length. When he left, Fred called him "a frustrated engineer." In a drugstore, impatient with an officious pharmacist, Fred accused him directly: "You're a frustrated doctor—go back to counting pills with a knife."

"How about 'Danny Stiles on your dials?'" I had pulled in some odd stations down at the staticky end of the spectrum and thought Fred would be impressed, but he gave me a strange look and turned serious.

"Your mother called me, wants to make sure you know the facts of life, the birds and the bees. I think I was out of line when I brought Shelley that night. I should have talked to you a little beforehand." Anticipating my worry that I had performed badly, he raised his palm again, saying, "Not that anything went wrong. Still, you need to be around more women, get to know them. Not that I'm an expert, divorced, no kids. A kid not mine but with my name. I'm one to talk."

He called for another drink and reached into his breast pocket, taking out a deck of cards. He shuffled through them and then excused himself to go to the men's room. It was a "French deck," pictures of couplings of all kinds. I had seen these before, but never to inspect so closely and alone. Instead of my memorizing them, they seemed to memorize me, fixing their images to my brain. When Fred returned, he took the cards. "People do all kinds of things together, nothing wrong with it. Even President Kennedy said, 'I'm not through with a woman till I've had her three ways.' He really said that." He put the pack in his jacket. After sorting through the deck, I couldn't stop seeing everyone around us without clothes. I lingered on a heavy blonde, and Fred leaned across and said, "Remember, every woman has a good quality. You can find at least one good feature in every woman." He added, "The main thing is just be natural."

I had heard so much about unnatural acts—in the papers, in school, and in the mailroom—that I guessed Fred was against them as well.

"As for sex, it's simple. Women just lay there while we knock our brains out." Fred ordered a third drink for himself, which brought him to a new subject. "You know Close Quarters? When I have a deal to make, I like to meet my mark there. Gail knows when I'm doing business—I always order a double martini. The mark calls his own, and I make sure we have at least three, and he usually drinks doubles too, to keep up. But I never get drunk, and he gets plowed. Know how? There's just ice water in my glass!" His grin was wide and stayed on his face. "That's a fact of life too! Hey, you know where the word *mark* comes from? Madeline told me." He smiled and examined his fingernails. "From the carnival! When a sucker got screwed at one booth, the carny slapped him on the back, but his hand was covered in chalk. He walked around marked as a chump, so the other carnies could take advantage!"

"My best friend's named Mark. Mark Cooney," I said.

"Yeah? You never want to name anyone that . . ."

I left the table for the men's room. But when I opened the door, I surprised a sitting woman, her arms raised, mouth open in astonishment, her skirt hiked up, so for a split second I saw long legs and a garter belt and I slammed the door. I looked again at the sign, MEN, and I walked back to Fred. He laughed, and we went down the corridor together. He opened the door, smiling, and this time I saw it was a beautiful mannequin, all made up with chiffon and lace. Fred stood by the statue and patted her hair. "This gets the newcomers every time," he said. "Just a joke. You know, this is a good job, done by that guy who did the statue of the aborigine over at Ripley's."

"I thought an aborigine did that, with his real toenails and his own hair."

He smiled and said, "Believe it or not."

In the hall Fred was onto something else. He pointed a finger at me. "You'll get into fights with women, and you should know how to handle yourself." A man left the real men's room and walked past us. "A woman does two things: kicks and scratches. The scratches you can't avoid, but if she goes to kick, lift your leg sideways, like this," and he raised his leg and twisted it. "That way, her shin hits the heavy side of your sole. Try. Go ahead, give me a kick."

I kicked at him gently, and he turned so fast that my shin banged his shoe, as planned. "Again," he said. After a few more tries, I kicked with my left leg for the fun of it, but my uncle spun in a kind of whirl and caught me with his right shoe, delighted. I had never seen him more graceful. "That will come in handy," he said. "Now take that piss."

The urinals held big blocks of ice, and I tried to see how much of a hole I could drill, aiming at one place, but it hardly melted.

When I returned, a flabby, disheveled man had taken the table next to us and chatted with Fred. His pockmarked jowls collapsed around his mushy neck and drooped onto his white shirt collar. He wore sunglasses and stretched far back in his seat so that his legs reached under the chair across from him. "So this is the b-b-boy?" he asked. Fred did not introduce us, which was odd. While the waitress took the man's order, Fred whispered, "This guy was a driver for the mob, hit all over the head with a ball-peen hammer on the docks. Now he's nuts."

"W-w-what's the good w-w-word?" the man said to me. Fred answered as if joking, "We're talking about the facts of life."

The man mumbled into his chin. "Like my old m-man told me. They got a h-hot-dog roll between their legs and we g-g-gotta put the frank there."

"We're just leaving, Santo," Fred said, still smiling.

"F-f-fuck a nigger in the ass," Santo said as we got up. "Fuck a b-b-blind nigger in the ass." He wasn't looking at us but was penciling block letters on the cardboard side of a yellow legal pad. "Yeah," he said, as we walked away, "Fuck a blind n-n-nigger in the ass. That's a voyage into the dark un-un-un-unknown."

Fred gave the bartender five dollars on the way out and told him to take care of Santo. "A very sad case," Fred said to me and the bartender.

The bartender pointed at a baroque cuckoo clock and said, "He tries to order twelve shots every midnight, so he can down each one as the bird chirps. It would kill him."

"Very sad," Fred said, shaking his head. I shook my head too.

"And by closing time," the bartender said, "he's pissed off so many people, someone usually gives him a smash in the crash."

We ate at Il Vagabondo, an Italian restaurant with an indoor bocce court, and sat at a table alongside the dusty lane, watching old men toss the balls and argue. We carried our drinks into the back room, past rushing waiters and busboys. Fred opened a door that led to an alley. Two guys loaded a truck with foul-smelling cans of grease. "Another fact of life," Fred said, "is that they make soap out of that," and he climbed two sets of stairs that led to a ladder. We stood on the gravel roof, overlooking Sixty-Second Street, the branches blowing in the first of the prefall breeze, the leaves tough and weathered. "This is the street where I was born," Fred said, "and so was every one else in our family. Those streetlights were there when I was a kid." He pointed to the short green posts holding gas lamps. He clinked his glass against mine. "To a new generation. Now you see where the old folks came from." We started down the ladder when he said, "Oh, two more facts of life. One, always go first when you're with a woman and you climb a ladder. Otherwise, you see up her dress. Know the Doubleday bookstore on Fifth and Fifty-Third? There's a spiral staircase right in the front window. Take a look next time you're there, take a look at the creeps just staring up women's dresses." I pictured my aunt on the stool, and how Fred would scorn me if he knew. "Fact number two," he said. "If you get in a fight on the roof and you start using poles, pick the short one against the long one. On a roof the long one's hard to manage, gets blown around by the wind."

We finished the night at The Flick, an ice-cream parlor on Second Avenue filled with old movie stills. We were served by women in outfits like Playboy bunnies.

"Do you have any questions?" he asked. "Anything?"

"I think you've covered everything, Fred," I said.

"Great," he said. "I was a little nervous at first, but I think it was worth it, and I feel good about helping you out. One thing," he whispered, looking at me directly. "I went through a lot of philosophy— you know, you've seen my books. I worried for years about what I do, but one day it hit me: I'm not really a good man. Not 'good' in the way the world sees it, know what I mean? That was a big relief. So now I go off and I make some dough, but it's never enough, and it's not a way to live really."

He slapped his palm against the tablecloth so heavily that the spoon flipped out of my sundae. "But why should I feel blue? Next time, I'll take you to Madeline's favorite French restaurant, for French food." He paused. "Is everything clear, is there anything else you want to ask? Anything at all?"

I couldn't resist. I said, "Fred, what's a French fuck?"

"A French fuck? I never heard of it. French fuck? Where d'you get that? Not French tickler?"

"No, a guy in the mailroom said it."

"Never heard of it. You should watch out who you talk to."

We took a cab to Fred's and sped down Third Avenue, making every light. Fred stuck a bill in my pocket to pay for my ride home after he got out. I began to nod off as the cab tore through the green. I felt as if we were on a runway, gliding above the avenue then lifting over the city. We were high in the darkness, looking down on the ribbons of taillights and headlights, the theatre marquees, the lit skyscraper windows, and I saw down into one cab. There, in the backseat, a teenager rode with his uncle. The boy's head was tossed against the cushion, his mouth open. Did he faint or pass out? Just tired? Whatever the reason, he was unconscious, but when his uncle kissed him good-bye, he woke up.

Daisy Mae

Jeanie took a long time to answer the buzzer, and I thought she had forgotten our date. When she opened the door, her plain dress and sandals made her life-size, and not the blonde who seized my heart in the funeral home, the blasé vamp bending over a windowsill, or the lost beach goer in tight shorts eliciting whoops from guys in doorways. I handed her the tiny bag of candy I'd bought at Loft's, a quarter pound of chocolate turtles.

"How sweet," she said, holding the door open with one hand, shifting the cigarette from the other to her mouth, and taking the bag. I followed her into the kitchen. Nicky's long chunk of hash dominated the Formica table, and she caught me staring. "This time you won't have to smoke it in the stairwell," she said.

"You know?"

"I bought it for Nicky to begin with. I figure better here than on the street. Fred used to get me a ton of it. I understand you see a lot of him." She leaned against the sink, and I watched the strip of flypaper hanging from the window frame, pushed by the exhaust fan, and wondered if the breeze prolonged the twitching lives.

"I was seeing him almost every weekend, but he's busy now."

"Sounds familiar." She opened the refrigerator and took out a white paper bag and two cans.

"Do you work near here?"

"Not since I had Pepe, and even before that, I didn't have a real job. Joe doesn't want me to, even though I'd like to do something."

"Who's Joe?"

"Joe. My husband. Pepe's father. Didn't Nicky tell you about him either? He owns the arcade upstairs from Hubert's. That's how we met. I did the books there. I'm a bookkeeper, took courses at city college." She unrolled wax paper from two salami grinders and slid them onto paper plates. "We'll eat first," she said.

"First?"

We ate in silence. I noticed a Band-Aid as she lifted her sandwich, and I asked, "What happened to your hand?"

"This?" she asked, holding up a withered pinkie that I hadn't seen before. "Or this?" and she pointed to the plastic strip. "I was born with this, and I cut myself here last night opening a canned ham." Not waiting for an answer, she asked, "Are you going to college or straight into business?"

"I think college, but I have another year."

"Nicky too, but he wants to keep working for Big Joe." Suddenly Joe was "big," and I asked myself what I was doing in this kitchen with his wife, the ex-wife of my uncle, the mother of my cousin. Then I looked from above: The part in my hair still crooked. My gawky frame in faded madras, trying to fit into the city but sticking out like the wrong piece of a jigsaw puzzle. I said to myself, "He sat in a kitchen with a pretty woman . . ." It didn't work. I wanted to leave.

"Nicky's smart," I said.

"Big Joe's a genius. Made that arcade out of a hole in the wall, revamped Hubert's, the flea circus, really helped make it the crossroads of the world." She opened a pack of Kools and filled a hash pipe, her own, with a carved ivory hand cupping the bowl. We passed it back and forth, and then she stood up. "Let's go."

"Where?"

She didn't answer because she was holding a lungful of hash, and I followed her out of the apartment. I had assumed the baby was sleeping, and I paused. "Pepe's with a friend," she said. We walked down the hall, and Jeanie shook a ring of keys at another door. A zebra rug covered the floor, and an enormous turtle shell hung on the wall. Three white leather couches filled the room, and a combination coffee table and aquarium stood in the center, fat goldfish pecking the gravel. "This is Big Joe's. I wanted us to have a change of scene." I liked Jeanie, but I couldn't forget Big Joe. I hated the name, and I made an inventory of the employees at the arcade, the ones likely to be ordered to beat me up, or worse. Most probable was the three-hundred-pound Boyd, who was teaching Nicky to throw knives.

"Sit down," Jeanie said, and she took a chair across from me. She put her hands on her knees and rocked. Her whole manner changed, and she seemed like a flirtatious schoolgirl and not the serious older woman I dreamt about. "I've known you for quite a while," she said. "When I visited your grandmother once with Fred, you put an ant into your mouth, you were that little, and I had to get it out with my finger. Fred and I laughed how you followed me around for the rest of the day, taking my finger and putting it in your mouth. And then, last spring, you almost fell on me!"

I was horrified at my sucking her finger and that she noticed my awkwardness at the wake. It was like watching a film about yourself you didn't know was being shot. "But what do you remember about me?" she asked. "How would you describe me to your friends?"

"I know you're good to Pepe and to Nicky."

"Do you think I'm pretty?"

"Yes," I said, "very pretty."

"You're blushing!" She stood in front of me, smoothing out her dress. "Do you think I have a nice body?"

"Uh-huh."

"Of course with this dress on, it's hard to tell," she said, looking down, suddenly troubled. Then she brightened. "But you've seen me in shorts. Hey! Let's have something to drink, some ice tea." When she returned from the kitchen, I was bent over the aquarium, my face about a foot from the floor. The fish came to the top, hoping to be fed.

"My uncle raises angelfish," I said.

She put the drinks down hard on the glass surface, and the fish scattered. She sat next to me on the couch, reached over, and pulled a large book from the end table, a photo album. The cover said, in large letters, Frankel's Modeling Agency. "I want you to see some pictures," she said.

She spread the album across her lap, and our shoulders touched. She opened the first page, an eight-by-ten glossy of herself in a cowgirl's outfit, hat, boots, and vest. She held a pistol to her lips, which formed an *O*, as if she were blowing smoke off the tip of the barrel. "That's funny," I said.

"Is it? What's so funny?" She closed the book, keeping her finger in place and turning angrily toward me. "Tell me what you find funny about it."

"I mean, the gun. It doesn't look like you."

"Maybe not," she said thoughtfully. "It's supposed to be the Cat Ballou look."

There were several other cowgirl poses, where she leaned against saddles on fences and on piles of hay. In another sequence she modeled an evening gown. "See how the back is cut away," she said, moving her finger between the shoulder blades. She wore toreador outfits, cheerleader skirts, and bikinis. "I still haven't lost all the weight from the baby, but nursing has made my bust bigger. Not bad, huh?"

"No, you look great," I said. I took a sip of tea.

She closed the book. "Well, I'm thinking of trying to get into show business, and so I had these taken at the Frankel Agency—you probably heard of them. You're supposed to have a set made, and then you send them around."

"I see," I said.

"But you know all this," she said. "Anyway, I thought maybe you could get someone to take a look at them across the street." I thought hard. What was "across the street," and why would I be the one to show them? Across the street from the Dixie was the back entrances to theaters and, down the block, the Times.

"Across the street?"

"Yeah," she said, annoyed. "Don't play dumb. At Paramount."

I was astounded. How had my fantasy about Jeanie gone wrong? Because she had her own parallel fantasy, and now they collided. I felt stupidly betrayed by her reason for inviting me, angry at my naïveté, and bewildered by hers. "Oh," I said, "I don't know anyone involved in this stuff."

"Nicky says you know everyone."

"I know them to say good morning to, but that's about it."

"Well, that's more than I know, and I'm dying to do something. Don't you think I'm as pretty as those girls that come up for parts?

180

Nicky told me that you saw at least fifty girls come up one day to see about a part, and they weren't that hot."

"Yes, but I saw them when I was delivering Selznick's mail. I don't know how those things work."

"You find me attractive, though, don't you?" She leaned off the couch a little.

"Yes, it's not that."

"Tell me one thing—don't you think I'm prettier than Carroll Baker? And better built? She has no chest at all!"

I agreed.

"Don't you think my name could be on one of those stupid yard-sticks that Nicky brought home? Don't you think a lot of boys would like to pull their puds over me on the picture screen?" She paused. "That's what it comes down to, isn't it?"

"I guess so," I said. I had never heard the word *pud*. She was facing me and talking right into my mouth.

"Nicky says he sees you chatting to executives when he's in the lobby and you're getting off the elevator. True or false?"

"True, but it's about the Yankees or the heat, small talk like that."

"Then that's the perfect time for you to tell them about me, about a friend of yours." She lit a Kool. "Look," she said, exhaling, "don't you think I have a chance? That's all I want, a shot."

"I understand," I said. "I know what you mean, but I'm a nobody. I just deliver the mail."

"You know I'm attractive enough. All I need is the connection, and I'm asking you to do me that favor."

"I really can't, Jeanie."

"Well," she said, "there is another way, if you were willing."

"What?" I said.

"Linda."

"Linda?" I said. "Linda's a secretary—she doesn't know anything about making movies."

"Her boss must." She sat up stiffly and spoke as if trying out for a part. "I'm aware she never cared much for me."

"Her boss is the purchasing agent. He buys the drapes for the offices, the desks, the paper, that kind of thing."

"Bullshit!" she said. "She could get someone to look at my portfolio. You're making everything impossible so you don't have to do it."

"I'm not, Jeanie."

"I wonder how Linda would feel if she knew you were here."

"Why are you bringing Linda into this?" I said.

"You want to know why?" she said loudly, pointing at me. "Because I'm getting out of here if I have to climb on your back to do it." When I just stared, she lowered her voice. "I thought you liked me. I thought we could have a relationship. And that it could be fun. You do like me, right?"

"Sure."

"Then why won't you do this one thing? You have no idea what I'm going through," she said, putting out her cigarette. "No one has ever given me even the simplest break."

I tried to think who I could show the photos to.

"Listen," I said, "let me think about it. Let me see what I can do." Just saying these words gave me the feeling I could do something.

Jeanie simply said, "Thank you" and kissed me, a long kiss that pushed my head against the deep leather. "You know what Big Joe says about me?" she asked, looking into my eyes. "He says my body seethes sex." Then she leaned against me again, and I smelled her hair, perfume, and chlorine. Neither of us spoke, and it was quiet except for the bubbling of the aquarium's filter and the passing police sirens. After a few minutes I pointed to the tank. "Some of these have tail rot," I said.

When my lunch hour was over, Jeanie walked me out, saying, "We'll do it again soon, when we don't have business, just for a good time."

"Yes," I said, stepping onto the elevator. As the doors closed, she yelled, "Oh," and reached in, banging the panels. She gave me an envelope of photos. As I went down, I thought I would have to hide them in the mailroom, from my aunt on the way home, and in my house. I looked at the brown paper. "John/Paramount Pictures" was printed across the front in a childish hand.

I did nothing with the photos except look at them and masturbate. Worse, Nicky arranged for me to meet Big Joe on his return from Los Angeles and I couldn't get out of it. He kept insisting on how much fun it would be, a wild Friday night, which they often had together when Joe came home from a trip. I asked if Jeanie would be there—I didn't want to see her so soon. Nicky assured me it was just guys. He described a possible itinerary: a drink at the Rainbow Room, where

Soupy Sales might put in an appearance. Then down to Little Italy to Umberto's Clam House. Nicky couldn't believe I hadn't been to Mulberry Street. "The little Italian men have clubs behind storefronts where they play checkers. You can get great necklaces, horns warding off the evil eye in silver or red plastic, and cheap! At Umberto's they take the squid and conch, put it on your plate, then dunk a hard biscuit in boiling water and flop it on the dish. Hey, the sauce is fiery. You have to choose: medium or hot. The first time Jeanie had it, Joe had to take her for a walk around the block."

"How can there be medium and hot?" I asked. "There has to be something else, like mild, right? You can't go straight to medium."

"What? And then we might go to The Flick, an ice-cream place with women who are half-naked."

"Oh, yeah, I've been there."

"You've been there?" Nicky was disappointed but went on quickly. "So we end up at the Red Garter, a silly place, but I bet Joe gets us a couple of beers to round out the night—how does that sound?" Any worries I had about Joe faded with Nicky's words. I wanted to wear a horn around my neck and take in the town.

Nicky and I were meeting Joe at the Top of the Sixes at 5:30, and I waited in Nicky's room for him to get dressed. There was a new coconut head in his collection. It had a tomahawk sticking out of its skull. The opened box lay on the excelsior-strewn floor. Nicky chattered incessantly as he wet his hair, changed his pants, and refilled the hash pipe. I splashed on some of his Clubman aftershave. It was 6:00. "Won't we be late?" I asked. "We have to get uptown."

"Nah, he's never on time," Nicky said.

In the elevator Nicky sang, "Cara Mia," trying his best to imitate Jay and the Americans.

"If you like that stuff," I said, "why don't you go to the opera?"

As we walked through the lobby, Nicky said, "Oh, yes, and there's the matter of this," and he pulled the M-80s out of his jacket. They were taped neatly to a piece of cardboard, braided into a fuse over a foot long. Strips of duct tape dangled, ready to be pressed to the glass.

"You're kidding," I said.

"It'll only take a minute," he said, and he trotted down the narrow hall that right-angled from the lobby, while I dragged behind. Nicky approached the office door, which was held open by a wooden wedge.

He looked in and smiled, meaning that the desk was empty as he planned and McBride relaxed in the adjoining room. I sulked along the opposite wall, kicking my heel against it. The door was very old, its huge window of frosted glass stenciled with "Wm. Patrick McBride, Mgr." Nicky taped the contraption dead center, saying, "This is a nice, slow fuse," and he lit it.

As we walked away, he said, "I only wish I could see his fat ass jumping out of his armchair when it blows." We neared the lobby, the honking cabs getting louder. I couldn't wait to be on the street, in a crowd, and the minute we were, Nicky said, "Now that wasn't so bad, was it?"

We stood outside, poised to listen. As Nicky combed his hair, how could it be that we saw, coming up the street, Mr. McBride himself? We ducked behind the chairs of a closed shoeshine stand while he turned and headed for his office, swinging a grease-stained paper bag. We followed him into the lobby, watching him loll down that narrow hall, almost filling it. The device was sure to go off any second, and I felt like calling out or running alongside, anything to get him to pause. Then I would compliment him on his tie tack, his yellow shirt, try to make him feel good as I spared his life, hoping he would forgive me. Nicky and I stiffened as he approached the door, neither of us speaking. I choked on silence, watching him walk as I had never watched a man before. He's taking his final steps, I thought, and everything about him seemed lovable, fragile, as he placed one foot in front of the other on this ordinary evening. I thought—this guy will be dead and I'm not doing anything about it.

I despised Nicky. I despised myself. And I loved McBride, who was to die.

The two seconds it took McBride to pass the loaded door were heavy and slow, and he was no more than four steps inside when the whole window blew, jarring the door off its top hinge, the shock seeming to quake the walls. But more, it looked like a comic book's description of a blast, a jagged yellow zigzag obliterating everything in a black slash of smoke. All of my silence was released in it.

Nicky ran.

McBride peeked out and ducked back.

"Jesus Christ," Nicky said on the corner. We were both shaking. "That could have blown him across the hall. I'm going upstairs for a minute." He walked away in a little tap dance. Then I saw he had wet himself, and he skipped lightly to keep his pants from touching his skin. I felt dizzy, warm, and when I wiped my upper lip, blood covered my finger. I slipped the handkerchief from my back pocket, alternately holding my head high and blowing my nose to the ground. On the corner I stared at my reflection in Jake's Wig Emporium. The dusk couldn't come fast enough, and I wanted to lose myself in the smoky Times Square fog. When the bleeding stopped, I wiped my face clean. I felt someone leaning next to me. It was the Dixie Hotel's house detective, Mr. Lane. Nicky had pointed him out, another peeping tom. Now he watched the office workers make their way home. A woman in a very short skirt passed, and Lane turned to me and said, "How'd you like to live across the street from a gal like her?"

At that minute Mr. Lane's peeping tomism seemed the most innocent of vices.

Nicky never came back.

Jeanie's pictures were getting the worse for wear. Sometimes I thought I loved her, a woman who never had a chance, since she'd grown up in Hell's Kitchen, becoming a mother so young. I thought Fred must have treated her badly, and I wanted to make up for it. Other times, I wished I'd never see her again. When I fantasized about her, I smelled smoke, the menthol of her Kools. As I got off the subway in the morning, I walked dreamily through the fragrance of just-lit cigarettes. I decided there was only one executive I could show the photos to: Jim Treadway. A friend of my aunt, he worked in advertising, but he was also a regular guy who joked around with the messengers. He hung a signed glossy of Raquel Welch above his desk. Naked, she sat with her knees pulled up to her breasts, all skin but none of it revealing. I thought I could appeal to the side of him that had framed the photograph and ask his opinion. Then I'd report this as Paramount's decision. But there was the danger he'd tell Linda. I thought of just asking him to write a rejection on Paramount stationery and then realized I could write it myself. Even to my eye, the pictures were absurd. I had seen some of the portfolios dropped off by models. A résumé and clippings were always attached to the stills. One slow afternoon, I paged through *Variety*. Warner Brothers ran an ad announcing auditions for a film version of the *Li'l Abner* comic strip. I wrote down the address and time and called Jeanie from the telegraph office when Tommy went to lunch. I told her about Warner Brothers, but she seemed grieved. "I'm not talking about this on the phone," she said. "Come on up. It's 10-D, you know."

"I can't just leave," I said.

"Next time they send you out, walk over." She hung up.

Gates sent me on the most hated trip, to the newspapers far downtown, the *World-Telegram*, *Journal-American*, and some minor weeklies, errands that took the whole afternoon. I ran from place to place and made it back a half-hour early. I called Jeanie and she said to meet her outside the Automat. I had hoped she'd greet me as part of our secret relationship, but she was grim. Pepe slept in the stroller. "I don't care about Warner Brothers," she said. "What was the response at Paramount?"

"Paramount isn't interested," I said. "I checked with a few executives, but Warner Brothers might be. They're looking now. They're having auditions at this address." I gave her the information, which I had written on a Paramount pad. At the top it said, *From the Desk of Fred LeRoy*, the retired stockroom manager. "It's next week. See the time?" I couldn't believe how easily this came to me, and it came easily because I told myself I wasn't lying: Paramount wasn't interested and Warner Brothers was looking. The illusion that this was privileged information seemed a slight deception. I convinced myself, and I knew I'd convinced Jeanie too when she slapped the paper with the back of her fingernails and put it hurriedly into her purse. "Thanks," she said, grabbing me around the neck with two hands and kissing my oily forehead. I walked to the mailroom, relieved and disappointed. I had hoped she'd make another date. The trip had taken three hours, and I was right on time. I gave Gates the signed slips and sat down. Ruben showed me his new, pointy wing tips that added inches to his height. He'd fastened horseshoe taps to the heels so they clicked harshly, and he was bouncing up and down when Gates called me again. This was unusual, since we were sent out round robin and I'd been the last to return.

"You just got a call," he said. "Jeanie left a message. She wants you to meet her in fifteen minutes at the Orange Julius."

"Can I go, Mr. Gates?" I asked. "Just this once?"

"Okay," he said, turning to his carfare box. "This once."

Jeanie sat alone at the counter, smoking. There was nothing but froth at the bottom of her glass. She had changed clothes and wore a bright yellow scarf around her neck. I stood next to her, but she stared straight ahead. "Jeanie," I said, tilting my head toward her.

"One question," she said, spinning on the revolving stool as if knowing I was there all along. "Is this thing from Warner Brothers on the level? Are they really looking?"

"They are, Jeanie. I know they are. I wouldn't have given you that date if they weren't."

"Really?" she asked. "And think before you answer. You better not be shitting me." She tapped her withered pinkie against the empty glass.

"Really, Jeanie. Go find out."

"I will," she said. "But I'm a little nervous."

"Don't be," I said, as if I had experience in these matters. "You'll do fine."

"I thought I'd read the comic strip first," she said, "just to get an idea of what they might be looking for. There's Daisy Mae, of course, but a lot of other girls too."

"That's a good idea," I said. "I think you'll do well."

"You know," she said, "I think I will too." And she smiled.

"I have to go," I said. "Please don't call me at work again. You'll get me in trouble."

"I know," she said. "Are you mad at me?"

"No, I just wish you luck at Warner Brothers," I said. My lie had given me strength, and my voice sounded like Nicky's. "I have to go."

She just stared.

"Bye," I said, pausing.

"Okay. Bye," she said, getting up, but then she sat back down.

The next day Jeanie walked into the mailroom at nine. Only Gates was there, but everyone would be arriving soon. I rushed from the table and spoke to her outside the telegraph office, Tommy Tinston looking up from his headphones. Gates watched. He had the same expression as when he pretended not to notice a commotion and then he sent everyone out on make-work errands. I tried to shield Jeanie from his view by turning my back to him.

"Remember yesterday, when I saw you at the Julius?" she asked.

"Yes."

"Well, I just wanted to see you again, to see if you were goofing on me. I thought you were fucking me over, and if you were, I had Joe's gun with me. I wanted to tell you."

Her words did not upset me. I worried that someone would over-hear them, a worry that postponed real fear.

"Let's go out here, where we can talk," I said, leading her from the mailroom. It was a rainy morning, already hot, and Jeanie wore a flimsy, transparent raincoat over a halter top and short-shorts. Her damp hair stuck to her forehead and cheeks, so it looked as if she walked behind a shower curtain. The smelly plastic crinkled when I held her arm. I dreaded Beardsley turning the corner. I opened the door to the porter's room, right outside the time clock. It was empty, and we sat on metal chairs surrounded by barrels of mops, stacked dollies, hand trucks, and rows of brown uniforms on wire hangers. The room reeked of grease, cardboard, sweat, and pine disinfectant. "What's wrong?" I asked.

"I almost hurt you," she said.

"Why?"

"I could have killed you with that gun."

"What did I do?"

"Nothing. Nothing at all, but I hear voices," she said, shaking her head, "and one told me to do it. It's horrible. She tells me to do terrible things, and I can't stop listening. I'm afraid I'm going to hurt Pepe. She told me to shoot you if you goofed on me again."

"But I wasn't goofing on you."

"I didn't think you were, but I can't stop listening. She's a female cop, a policewoman who grew up around here. She knows everything about me." She started to cry.

"I'm sorry," I said. "But remember, there really isn't any cop. She knows all about you because she is you."

"What?" She looked at me, horrified, her face clenched. "I'm not a cop! The cop's in here!" She pointed to her temple.

"It must be terrible," I said. I got up and stood over her, my hand on her back. "Are you going to a doctor?"

"I'm beginning again. I couldn't have treatments when I was preg-nant, so that'll be good."

"Yes," I said.

"Anyway," she said, drying her face with a tissue, "I wanted to tell you."

"Don't worry," I said. "It's okay."

I walked her down the empty hall to the elevator.

"I hope you feel better," I said as the elevator arrived. Tony stopped the car evenly and leaned out, looking left and right. Seeing it was me, he said, "Going down," drawing out the last word and singing it in a long falsetto to make me laugh.

"It's really bad," she said, backing into the car.

As I walked away, I could hear Tony's voice trailing downward, continuing the high pitch in a song by Frankie Valli, "Walk Like a Man." I hoped he wouldn't stop the car between floors to finish the song, as he often did when he had a pretty girl alone.

Gates called me over when I got back. I had walked past his desk quickly. His manner was different from when he called for a pickup. He pointed to the chair next to him.

"Trouble?" he asked.

"Not really."

"Sure?"

"Yeah, everything's okay."

"Pardon my saying so, but she doesn't seem your type." He put his pipe into his mouth and smiled slightly.

"You might be right," I said.

"You've been seeing her?"

"Just now and then."

"Do you mind some advice? This area's not the best to meet girls, especially women a little older, like her, okay? They'd like to marry a guy like you, to get them out of here, know what I mean?"

I started to defend Jeanie by saying she was married, but caught myself. "I understand," I said.

"She's too old for that," he said, mainly to himself, "but there could be blackmail involved—you never know."

"I don't think so."

"Well, if you do see her again, let me tell you something. When you take off your clothes, fold them neatly into a pile, like you do with laundry." He put his pipe on the desk and made folding motions with his hands. "See that she keeps hers neatly too."

"Why?" I interrupted, starting to laugh.

"You think it's funny," he said, "but if a girl like that calls you for rape, you can point to the clothes. Neat, folded clothes show you didn't force her into anything. It shows you planned it out mutually, that you took your time, okay?"

"Okay," I said.

"Watch out for yourself."

"Thanks, Mr. Gates," I said.

At the table I brooded about Jeanie, if she'd return or try to kill me. I didn't want to see Nicky anymore either. I dreaded Jeanie's audition for the part of the fun-loving Daisy Mae.

A Lesson from
the Oneida Colony

Linda was furious that Fred had talked to me about the birds and the bees. My mother reported this when I walked into our dining room early on Saturday. She sat at our table with Tom Peck, who had emptied a box onto the glass top, nostalgic remnants from his dead parents and his youth's lucky charms. He enthusiastically shook a felt bag of piano keys, sorted mah jong tiles, and donned earphones from his father's shortwave. He urged my mother to become a ham-radio operator, and he imitated Morse code by clicking his teeth. My mother showed me a long dowel with a silver rectangle nailed to one end: a sponge wrapped in duct tape. It was Tom's invention, The Arachnid Arrester. "For getting spiders off the ceiling. He's brought one to us," my mother said, waving it, "and one for Linda. Isn't that thoughtful?" Tom said shyly, "My father was really the inventor."

"Linda wants to talk to you," my mother said, and began to arrange loose piano keys into a pattern. "She's across the street."

At my great-aunt Nona's apartment Linda tended the aviary of Nona's son, Dominic, a cabinetmaker and the librarian of the Elmhurst Cage Bird Society. Dom was out of town judging a canary contest, and he had asked Linda to look after his birds, something she enjoyed. Nona, ninety years old, dozed all day in a rocking chair, a rosary in the lap of her black dress. At the far end of the flat, thirty canaries fluttered in a walk-in cage. Dom also raised angelfish, and the air around Nona gurgled with the sound from waist-high tanks as the windows blurred.

When I arrived, Linda turned to me, her arm inside the aviary. "Here he is," she said, "Fred the Second." She was about to remove a new egg and replace it with a plastic one. This was Dom's method until the hen stopped laying. Then he returned the real eggs and took away the fakes, so they all hatched at once and there would be no larger, dominant chick. Linda had a tender efficiency with the canaries. She gently shooed the mother and made the substitution quickly, latching the wire door. She sat on the edge of the daybed in a light summer dress, the fresh egg cupped in her palm.

Two canaries trilled vigorously from opposite ends of a branch. A hen in the middle looked side to side, choosing. I lifted a heavy maroon drape, fuzzy with feathers and chaff, to examine Dom's library, all bird books: *The Norwich Canary, The Popular Budgie, Adventures with Talking Birds.*

"We only have a few weeks left," she said.

"I know," I said. "I'm going to miss the city."

"Well, you might meet some nice girls this year at Mater Christi, and now you can take them to midtown, show them around. Do you ever see the one you brought to the prom, the one from Corona Avenue, the policeman's daughter?"

"Not really. That was just for the dance."

"There's time. I was wild about Mac, but after him, no one interested me again. I still remember the day I found out he was seeing someone else. Our engagement had been set. I still have the dowry in the basement. It was a Saturday, like today, and I went to the movies. I sat there all day—I couldn't tell you what I saw. It was like I died, like I was at the bottom of a pool. And then a week later Jimmy from the Island said he wanted to marry me. Imagine!"

"Why didn't you?"

"He was a real *cufoni*. You know, from southern Italy. When I met his mother, she served octopus and ravioli filled with an awful cheese. Our family wouldn't have approved." She laughed, but there was pain

192

in her smile, as if she had done the right thing and it hurt. Or she had done the wrong thing and it hurt.

"But you liked him, right?"

"A little. As much as you can like someone once you've been crushed. By the way if you do leave next year, I have a lot of dish towels and sheets in that chest, things you can take."

"Thanks," I said, "but I still don't know what I'm doing. Even if I get in somewhere, it'll cost a lot."

"Maybe Fred's right for once," she said.

"Right? About what?"

"About leaving. Maybe you'll get a good job," she said, turning her profile toward me. "And remember, I might be getting a place in Manhattan. If I did, you could live with me." She winced when she said this, a grimace I recognized in myself when I guessed an answer.

"I thought you said I should go away to school."

"Think about it, that's all." She rolled the little egg in her hand. "So Fred talked to you about the facts of life. I'd love to hear his idea of the birds and the bees," she said.

"I knew most of it," I said, leaning against the doorframe. Her wrist and forearm were stained white from the bucket of disinfectant she had sloshed over the aviary floor. The smell of bleach mixed with the fennel fragrance of the birdseed and the sour odor from the tanks.

"Did he educate you or just tell stories of his conquests?"

"He didn't talk much about himself. Mom put him on the spot. I wish she hadn't asked him. It was embarrassing."

"It shouldn't be," she said flatly. "It's straightforward enough. How far did Mr. Big Shot go?"

"It was fine, we talked about everything."

"Everything? The same way you told me you knew everything?" She stroked her thigh as if she stroked a cat. "You only had to ask, you didn't have to go to Fred. As if my brother could solve the mysteries of the universe . . ." Linda got up and delicately placed the egg on a cotton nest in a bell jar.

"I know more than you think," I said. She smirked and sat back on the single bed, crossing her legs. Minute feathers stirred on the black ticking.

"The truth is, you wouldn't know the first thing to do with a woman."

"I would and I have," I said. These words had a strange, patriotic ring.

"Oh, really?" She paused. "Well, there's no need for us to fight. My objection is to Fred's barging in, just when I was doing my best to bring you along."

I said, "He didn't barge in, Mom arranged it," but she ignored me.

"It's hard to know where to stop, where to draw the line. Remember when I showed you my things? I've thought about that a lot."

"Me too."

"You were ready. I could tell by the way you exploded." I hugged myself by the elbows. "Still, it wasn't fair of me, was it?"

"It was all right."

"No, it was almost dishonest." There was a flurry in the cage, loud squawking, and a small burst of yellow feathers. Two long males faced each other, low on the perch, opening their mouths and spreading their wings menacingly.

"What's going on?" I asked, bending toward the bars.

"That happens all the time," she said. "I only did it to educate you."

"I know," I said.

"It's important to get this at home, like learning to have a glass of wine. Come here for a minute," she said, and she held out her hand.

When I walked over, she squeezed my fingers. "Let's hope you don't get another fever," she said. Then she lifted herself an inch off the bed and tugged at her panties, a kaleidoscope of thighs, knees, and ankles, until the silk pink triangle was beside her. She pulled the hem of her dress to her waist and I peered at the brown hair hardly visible between her closed thighs. "Do you see?" she asked, looking down at herself. "Can you see the place you put it?"

I saw everything and nothing.

I was still thinking that I had "exploded."

I thought: the place *I* put it?

"What's the matter, can't you see?"

"Not really," I said.

"Not really?"

A phrase from a camp song about a lost bear crazily occurred to me, *He's walking near and far. He's walking near and far . . .*

She looked at me as if I were ridiculous, an expression that seemed ridiculous itself.

"I'm only doing this once," she said, "so tell me if you can't see."
She pulled her thighs slightly apart.

"I'm not sure," I said, bowing a little.

She glanced around the room. "Get the flashlight," she said, motioning with her chin, keeping her hands between her legs as if she'd lose her place. "On the end table." I brought the slender aluminum tube Dom used to find eggs at night, and she said, "You'll have to kneel." I aimed the light, and she shifted, pulling at the pink skin and gyrating her index finger. "See now? That's just for a woman's pleasure. It has no other purpose—I read that." The room filled with silence and breathing. "Now you know," she said, covering up. I stood and thumbed the flashlight's switch off and on, off and on. The noisy birds and bubbling tanks resumed. She grabbed her panties in her fist and said, "Let's get dressed," though I was fully clothed and she had removed only her underpants. As she stepped into them, she said, "We know each other like no one else in this crazy family." There was satisfaction in her voice, the voice she used congratulating me on figuring the correct tip. She pulled a slat on the venetian blind and looked through it. "The sun's coming out. I'll make some tea." I followed her to Nona's end of the house, where I used the bathroom, the closed john door just a few feet from the stove, where Linda stood over a pan of boiling water, and I came almost as soon as I held myself, not an explosion but a spigot simply opened and shut.

When we returned to the cage with our cups, I was thinking about her saying, "Let's get dressed," as if I had entered a fantasy of her own. She asked again if I had any questions, and questions poured out of me. My voice clear, unwavering, a voice phoning a radio station, asking if a woman could get pregnant if she was nursing, if a woman had to climax to get pregnant, did stockings keep a woman's legs warm in winter . . . Linda mentioned the Oneida colony, upstate, where she and her friend, Kitty, had gone on vacation for silverware, and how she bought a historical pamphlet there that told of older women initiating boys into sex at puberty. She thought this wise, repeating that it was like learning to drink. I asked if women wanted sex as much as men. "Yes, I'd say so," she said, and she strummed the bars with a fingernail.

As we talked, I felt she was right, that we really knew each other, could almost say we loved each other, and this new dialogue made me confident enough to ask my plaguing question. "Linda, I have something that's been bothering me. No one can answer it," I said cheerfully.

"What is it?"

"What do they mean by 'unnatural acts?'"

"Unnatural acts? Unnatural acts?" she repeated, indignant, then angry. "How would I know? How would I know anything like that? What do you think I am?"

"I'm sorry," I said, but she cut me off.

"You don't know when to stop," she said. "You've changed." She looked at me with disgust. "I'm getting some honey."

While she was in the kitchen, I picked up a radio on the bureau. Linda returned carrying a jar by its lid, saying, "This was all I could find. Dom has nothing in this house. I don't know what Nona eats around here." She saw me fiddling with the turquoise radio in the shape of a satellite.

"That's one of Fred's," she said. "Junk. He disappeared like I told you he would, didn't he? Like the Beatle wigs he promised everyone a while back, leaving all the kids on the street asking about them, storming around me every time I walked to the subway."

"He told me he'd be busy in the fall. It's not his fault." Linda pushed a spoon deep into the jar, scraping the bottom.

"Busy trying to keep his head above water. Loaded one minute and broke the next. He's a philanderer—there's a word for you. He didn't want to lay roofs or type for a living like the rest of us."

Fred's flaunting of our domestic world still encouraged me. At the same time, I loved Thoreau's simple life as well as Kerouac's hell-bent drive. Linda seemed to me more like Thoreau, sitting in her cousin's den, tending the dusty aviary for a little quiet. But then there was her sexual side, idling. When I went to leave, Linda grabbed my hand. "It's your choice. Fred, who disappears, or me, who has your best interests at heart. Think about it." We walked slowly past the tanks of angelfish. "Don't be alone so much," she said. "It's not good. What are you doing today?"

"I might go to the Village."

"Again? For what?"

"A poetry reading." That meant listening to anyone with a beard standing under a tree in Washington Square reading pages yanked from a knapsack.

"You need to be well rounded," she said. "Why not take up golf, like McBain?"

"Maybe," I said.

"I'll pay for the lessons."

"Thanks, Linda," I said, although the only green around us was Calvary Cemetery. In the back of the apartment, our voices roused Nona, who lifted her eyelids with great difficulty. "Linda," she strained, "the nephew's working?"

"Yes, Nona. With me, in the city."

"How tall now?"

"Five eleven, Nona," I said.

"Remember the song we used to sing, Linda, the song about work?"

"I'm not sure, Nona," Linda said.

"You know it, the work song," she said impatiently. And she began to sing.

> *Where do you work-a, John?*
> *On the Delaware Lackawan.*
> *What do you do-a, John?*
> *I push-a, push-a, push.*
> *What do you push-a, John?*
> *I push, I push a truck.*
> *Where do you push-a, John?*
> *On the Delaware Lackawan.*
>
> *Where do you work, Marie?*
> *In the telephone company.*
> *What do you do, Marie?*
> *I push-a, push-a, push.*
> *What do you push-a, Marie?*
> *I push, I push-a the plug.*
> *Where do you push, Marie?*
> *The telephone company.*

Listening to her sing was amazing, like hearing a bird talk, the tune clear and bright, unlike her usual sighing and groaning. We applauded, and Linda accompanied me to the stairs. At the top of the landing she held my elbow, her eyes moist, and she whispered, "The summer will disappear, Fred's disappeared, but I'll always be here." Her words had both power and frailty—she spoke with confidence but seemed about to break down. I couldn't help thinking of my Brooklyn catechism's definition of God, that He always was and always will be, and Linda's presence took on an eternal dimension.

Mickey Mantle's Autograph

Fred's call at the end of August promised a light lunch, a farewell to summer. His upbeat voice got me enthused all over again about being with him, but I knew it would be our last time together. He was already encouraging me toward my senior year of high school and college after that, plans he'd scorned earlier. I was to meet him on Saturday, in front of Yorkville's Jaeger House, where I had once eaten with Linda.

I left in midmorning to see a film on Jackson Pollock at the Metropolitan Museum of Art. I had read about Pollock in a magazine. I liked the strength of his face and the passion of his paintings. He was the same in the movie, masculine and artistic, talking with a cigarette in his mouth about the canvases exploding around him. In the final scene the director placed his camera under a glass panel, so the audience gazed up as Pollock flung his brush, saying, "This might look random, but it's not." He spattered paint until he covered the transparent surface and the screen went black.

It was hot, but I walked to Yorkville, energized by abstract art, where emotions seemed hurled into recognition. I arrived early, sat on a shady park bench near Gracie Mansion, and read my new book, Ford Maddox Ford's *The Good Soldier*. At a quarter to one I approached the Jaeger House, recalling my lunch with Linda and how our waiter ended his opening recitation by saying, "These are the schnitzels."

Fred came down Eighty-Fifth Street with the same crisp, out-of-my-way stride. His bald head gleamed above his tan poplin suit and black knit shirt. I hoped I'd done the right thing by wearing my suit.

"Jonathan John," he said, shaking my hand and kissing me.

He suggested Rickadella's. I remembered a little filler-sized story I'd read about a patron shot six times in the chest there. I mentioned this to Fred, who frowned. "Yes," he said. "I do recall that." He seemed to consider it more than I liked, and I hoped his mind wasn't on danger but on how sharp I was, how I knew something about almost every place in the city. I still wanted to impress him, holding a slight dream that he might want me to join him in some way. He swung toward me, pointing a finger. "Hey! You used a memory trick to bring that back, right? One of the memory tricks I told you about. At Richards' funeral, remember? See, your old uncle taught you something!"

We sat at the bar. Fred knew the bartender and ordered coffees, along with little plates of hard-boiled eggs, pickled pig's feet, sausage, and bags of chips. The eggs came from a glass jar labeled, "Boneless Chicken Dinner." Fred put money in the jukebox to drown out the only other patrons, an arguing couple, choosing the bombastic voice of Jimmy Roselli. Each time a song ended, the couple's words rang loud and clear. The woman said, "It goes deeper than that . . . " The man replied, "Go ahead, keep comparing me to Mike." Fred pushed his plate aside and lit a Winston.

"Don't you smoke Chesterfields anymore?" I asked.

"No, I'm trying to cut back." He held the cigarette in front of him. "These look uncircumcised after nonfilters." An exterminator arrived, wearing a black T-shirt that said, *Licensed Killers*. He began spraying the wainscoting and joists. "I hope you guys won't mind the smell," the bartender said.

"That's a funny word, *exterminator*," I said. "I wonder where it comes from?"

Fred looked at me. "Come from? Where does it come from? Where do any words come from?" he asked loudly, so the bartender could hear him, and he laughed. But before he laughed, he exhaled a long sound, "Ahhhhh . . . ," which he did throughout the day—a new tic, accompanying an observation of which he was particularly proud, so he supplied his own applause. I had placed my book on the bar so it wouldn't skew the shape of my jacket, and it caught Fred's eye.

"I like the title," he said. "*The Good Soldier*. Who wrote it?"

When I told him, he turned on me, almost angry. "Ford Maddox Ford? What kind of a name is that? Sounds made-up, fake."

"I think he did change his name," I said. I had learned that in the foreword.

"So I'm right?" Fred asked. He smiled again and wagged his finger jokingly. "I could tell right away." The bartender read the *News* at the end of the bar, but Fred blared in his direction as he addressed me. "You never heard *Ford* Henry *Ford*, did you? Or *Ford* Whitey *Ford*? It's bullshit." He blew a smoke ring toward the ceiling.

"How's Madeline?" I asked.

"Fine. She's fine, thank you," Fred said.

"I've been getting *The New Yorker*," I said.

"She appreciated your note. Look," he said, "I'm sorry I've been out of touch, but things have gotten hectic around here. I'm trying like hell to hold onto that apartment, and I just don't have the time like I used to. Or the money either, to be frank." He looked at me to see if I was disappointed in him.

The couple's argument accelerated, and the woman ran out the door. The man placed some bills on their table and walked slowly after her.

"Now I won't have to waste any more coins on the jukebox," Fred said. The bartender refilled our cups and went into the back room.

"Find any new places lately, restaurants?" I asked.

"One opened last week. A not unpleasant place." He pulled a matchbook out of his pocket and showed me the cover, "Beyond the C." "It's way over there, near Avenue C." He struggled to look at the address. "My eyes are getting weak," he said in a small voice. Then he roared, "But I've got a new book called, *Throw Away Your Glasses*. The guy who wrote it cured a cross-eyed girl by having her sit on a swing at night, where she focused on one star, twisting and untwisting. I'm doing eye exercises. Three times a day. I pretend my nose is a pencil, and I write my name in the air with it." He bobbed his head, happy to have the inside information. "Of course," he said, looking around, "I do it in private. I hate glasses. The doctor who wrote this book calls them 'eye crutches.'" Our conversation lagged, and I felt, for once, that

I was with my uncle and not with the man about town I admired. Had he lost his enthusiasm for me, or had I stopped relishing his every word? He spoke in clichés and made pronouncements like "You can't change people," shaking his head profoundly.

I was bursting with the Pollock movie, which I thought might excite him since he liked the artist at Uncle's. I said, "I saw a movie this morning."

"A movie in the morning?" he interrupted.

"At the museum," I said.

"A movie at the museum?"

"Yeah," I said.

"Movies at the museum in the morning—that's wild, I tell you."

"Yeah, about an artist. He drips paint on the canvas, really splashes it around." I mixed some skepticism in with my admiration.

"That junk! They say a chimp could do it."

"I don't think so, Fred, there's a plan to what he does."

"Bullshit!" he said, grinning an openmouthed grin, the grin that couldn't comprehend how stupid I was, the grin he wore when he told me about Jeanie showing him their baby when he had been away for a year. "In fact, they're getting a chimp to do it. And you'll see, people will pay big. God have mercy on us for what they'll sell next." He raised his eyes to the ceiling. "Hey, did I tell you what Warga did last night, right here? Murphy, the Irishman, breaks a broom over the back of his neck. And then Warga says he can drive a nail into the bar with his palm. The bartender, Steve—not this guy, the night guy—comes up with a nail, and Warga stands it on the wood. The crowd surrounds him, it's packed. Warga raises his hand and then stops. He pauses. He asks Steve for a handkerchief, one of those Hav-a-Hanks on the wall. He unfolds it, he's so dramatic, Warga, and everyone's quiet—not a sound really, except for two Italians at the end of the bar. They're having an argument, who's a better singer, Sinatra or Roselli. Did you know they're both from Hoboken? So now Warga's got the nail standing up, the handkerchief over it like a tent. He makes everyone stand aside. He raises his right hand high and slams it down! Boom!"

I waited.

"Don't you wanna know what happened?"

"Yes, I do," I said. "What happened?"

"Jesus, I have to ask?" He shook his head, annoyed. "The nail goes right through his hand and blood zooms up to the ceiling! It's here somewhere." He walked back and forth, staring at the beams. "Yes, here," he said, and pointed. We looked at the brownish, Pollock-like splatter and sat down.

"I've been thinking," he said, "maybe you should try to contact your father. Ask him to call you more."

"I don't really have anything to say to him, Fred. He's been home a couple of months all year and writes stupid postcards once in a while."

"He's still your dad," he said. "You'll miss him when he's gone, though you don't realize it." He walked around the bar, got the coffee himself, and filled our cups. "I know. I lost my father. You heard how he died, right?"

"Yes," I said, "falling off the sugar refinery."

"That's right," he said. "I was at school, and the principal called me to his office. I never got in trouble, I was a good student. I knew something was the matter. When I walked in, he was standing behind his desk. He had an awful look on his face. He said, "Hello, Fred. Sit down. No, stand up. No, maybe you should sit down. Or stand if you want. Your father was crushed to death in Jersey today, falling onto a load of pig iron."

"That's terrible," I said.

"What an asshole," Fred said. "But that's what I remember. Sit down. No. Stand up. Sit down." It was the first time Fred had expressed any sense of loss or vulnerability. I looked at his reflection in the long mirror, his head bent over his plate.

We were sitting in silence when the bar's front door flew open, hitting the wall hard and shaking its window. Then the room filled with quick, explosive bursts. I thought only of the shooting earlier in the summer, but before I could turn, Fred knocked me off the stool. As I crashed to the floor, my thin chest trilled in time with the stuttering explosions, and I crawled and scrambled toward the back room, shaking off the shield of Fred's weight. The clamor ended as I reached the open kitchen door on my hands and knees, where I looked up at the bartender's vast apron. He held a pickle in one hand and a paper plate in the other.

"What's going on?" the bartender asked, chewing.

"Shots," I said, as I pointed to the front where Fred stood, dusting off his pants. The bartender walked to the vestibule and opened the door. Little curlicues of blown-up paper littered the floor, the remains of a pack of firecrackers.

"Those weren't shots," the bartender said. "It's kids, with stuff left over from the Fourth."

"Just firecrackers, John," Fred said. "Imagine that."

"The first time we went out together, I thought there were shots, remember? At Gail's? I knocked the coffee cups over?"

"Yes, I do," he said, putting his arm around me as he steered me to the bar, where he paid. "And now I'm just as jumpy."

We walked through the park, taking the exit by the Plaza Hotel, when I saw a theater, the Paris Art, playing *Ladybug, Ladybug*, a movie I hadn't heard of, which made me want to see it. Pointing to the marquee, I said, "I wonder if that's any good?"

"That movie?" Fred said enthusiastically. "You want to see it?

"Sometime," I said.

"What's wrong with now?" At the ticket booth Fred said, "Look, it starts soon." I loved seeing Fred at the booth of the Paris Art. A man's man talking to the ticket taker of an offbeat movie, a pale girl with straight brown hair. He paid. I looked forward to talking about it afterward, probably in Flamingo's, and I hoped he wouldn't be put off by it as he was by Pollock. Fred turned and handed me a ticket.

"Here," he said. "I'll meet you in an hour and a half. Gets over at five. And here's some change for Mason Dots."

"Okay," I said, laughing, as I watched Fred run toward the steps of the Plaza, steps I often climbed as a messenger. He was glad to have the time to himself. And a relief came over me too. I could watch the film though my own eyes. It was the first time I'd gone to a theater alone, and I thought of Linda sitting in the dark after her breakup with Mac, saying she didn't know what she saw, probably wiping her eyes, oblivious. "Like at the bottom of a pool," she had said. The ticket taker stood with her arms folded at the tiny candy counter, ruining my feeling of independence; she had seen Fred dump me. Posters touted a coming feature, showing a deranged woman in a nightgown wielding a sharp ax that was the hand of a clock, and the face of the huge vandalized timepiece hung crookedly behind her.

I counted five patrons: two couples and an old lady dragging a box of books by a rope. *Ladybug, Ladybug* ended with children being dismissed from class due to the sounding of an air-raid siren. A little girl walked home alone and, as she crossed the town dump, a passenger plane flew overhead and she panicked, thinking it might drop a bomb. She looked toward the sky, terrified, and then she ran to an old refrigerator, climbed into it, and slammed the door after her.

Fred was waiting, and I shielded my eyes.

"How was it?"

I started the plot when he interrupted. "Kookie!" he said, pointing to the old lady who had just gotten the box of books through the door and was on her way down the street, pulling the frayed cord. "I'll walk you to the train on Fifty-Third." I loved the side streets of the east side, especially the blocks with window boxes of geraniums, tidy restaurants, and florists placed unexpectedly among the brownstones. On the empty street a small boy came toward us, struggling with a big aquarium. He lowered it to his knee every few steps to get a better grip. Watery gravel sloshed along its bottom. Fred stood right in front of him and took the aquarium from his creased hands, saying to me, "It's heavy." The boy, wearing a sweaty white T-shirt and shorts, looked at Fred.

"Are you gonna help me, mister?"

"Where're you going?"

The boy pointed to the end of the block. Halfway there, Fred handed me the tank. Under the blurry water, a turtle bounced along the bottom.

"Is that your son?" the boy asked.

"No," Fred answered.

I found myself lifting my knee as the boy had done.

"What happened to your son?" the boy continued. "Did he die?"

"I never had a son," Fred said. "No one died." Fred took the tank.

We followed the boy into the side entrance of a brownstone, down the steps to a basement apartment. Fred put the aquarium on a dresser in the dark dining room, and the boy thanked us. As we walked toward the steel front door, a man's voice screamed, furious, "Who's there? Who the fuck is it?" Fred dashed into the bright street and I followed, both of us laughing. I had never seen him duck a confrontation, but he was all smiles. "At least we got the tank home in one piece."

"That was nice of you."

"Jesus, his old man might have been a nut. You read about good Samaritans getting sued or even killed." He lit a cigarette, nervous. "What do you think he meant about my son dying? Strange."

On Fifty-Third and Fifth, Fred guided me up the stairs of a church and put a quarter into my hand to light a candle. He pointed to the front altar and its bank of votives. "I'm meeting someone here," he said, as he walked with me. The dark church relieved the outside heat, the fragrance of melting wax giving the feeling of night. I knelt, stretching the long wick toward a cup, thinking of Linda, my mother, Fred, and myself. Fred stood behind me as the candles flickered, each one burning with someone's hope.

I heard Fred's friend arrive and turned to see a little man so drenched in sweat he looked hosed down. He wore a shiny white short-sleeve shirt, not cotton but the kind Fred told me never to buy. He dropped two full shopping bags and began to talk loudly and quickly. Fred talked back just as loudly. The man insisted he told the truth. A minute later he changed it to the God's honest truth. Fred tapped my shoulder and led me to the side of the altar. We stood near a rack of pamphlets. One was titled, "The Foolishness of God."

"I have to get busy," he said. "It means a little money." As he spoke, a worker in paint-splashed overalls used a power drill to fasten a thick holy-water font that had come loose. It was hard to hear, and fine bits of marble soared through the air. Fred sneezed twice, tiny sudden sneezes that he muted by quickly turning his head to his armpit.

He looked over at the worker on his knees. "Imagine breathing that stuff? Well, the E train's right across the street. You know." I felt bad about arguing with him earlier about the dripped paintings. We had walked together to this point, and I was grateful for that. His friend fidgeted near the font, his feet very close to the worker, and then he dipped both hands into the water and pushed his wet fingers through his hair, sighing with relief. Fred saw me staring and said, "We got a crazy thing going." The friend took the shopping bags into a front pew and sat down. "That stuff is Yankee printed matter. Yearbooks, scorecards. This guy is good at Yankee signatures, learned them from the Louisville Slugger ad right in those pages! There's the bat and all the autographs around it, just for the picking. People pay a lot for Mickey Mantle, and he does the *M*s just right." He was delighted with the simplicity of the scheme. He took a big breath. Facing the altar, Fred kissed me and walked slowly up the aisle. I watched him leave, and the little fellow, the forger, hurry to follow, pulling the weighty bags with him. Fred didn't slow down but kept his strict posture, proud, as if he had just given away a bride.

I took the bus instead of the subway so I could look out the window. No one shared the seat with me, and I put my book down. I guessed what collectors would pay for the fake signatures, whether Van Forkenberry was involved. I loved the languor of the bus, its frequent stops, the arriving and departing passengers, and I watched Fifth Avenue pass—the going-out-of-business electronic shops, Tie City, Tee Pee Town.

An elderly woman, seated diagonally across the aisle and one row ahead of me, pulled the cord for her stop. When the bus braked, she struggled to stand. I thought about helping, but each time I rose she seemed just about to make it. Finally she wobbled to her feet, holding onto the backrest. She had walked a step or two when I noticed a leather glove—a thin, brown glove—on her seat. I called, "Ma'am! Ma'am!" and when she turned, I said, "You forgot your glove" and pointed. She took a few steps toward me, confused, clutching her purse worriedly and patting her pockets. I gestured again toward her vacant seat, smiling with good intentions. As I did, the glove moved. The lovely, wrinkled, fine brown leather slid over to the seat next to hers and out of my sight. The old lady watched, then stared sternly before rushing off. I was mystified, until a small black man leaned over and looked at me. He was short, and the back of the seat had made him invisible. He had rested his hand on her side, all I had seen of him, and our eyes met, mine and the eyes of the man whose hand I had mistaken for a glove. I couldn't bear my error, my forced good will, and at the next stop I jumped out the rear exit, running down the steps to the subway.

The Merry Go Round

I hadn't seen Nicky since the night he blew up McBride's door. I avoided Hubert's, but I found Jeanie all over the city: looking in a dress shop, crossing Madison Avenue, entering St. Pat's. Each time I got close, it wasn't her, and I walked away with my pulse hammering.

One day, delivering a hot-pink rush envelope to Linda, I heard her talking in McBain's office. "Stay back," she said when I looked in. "It's very upsetting." She stood by the window and I came right over. A crowd had formed at the Strand Hotel, and three police cars parked crookedly, their lights whirling. A black woman lay on top of the hotel marquee, arms and legs at broken angles, her face staring straight at the sky. Turning away, Linda said, "She looks just like a doll lying there." Police appeared in windows across the way, and we watched them move from floor to floor, leaning out, craning up and down. When I got back to the mailroom, there was a note saying I had had a call, which alarmed me, since my only call all summer was from Jeanie. A minute later the phone rang. "Hello, *cumpari*," Nicky said. We chatted for a minute, and then he apologized, "I'm sorry about that night, I really am. I just couldn't stick around. I'll tell you later." He convinced me to join him for lunch.

When Nicky shook my hand, he said, "How about the Automat, for old times' sake?" We walked to Forty-Second.

"First," he said, "let me tell you about the prostitute who got pushed out the Strand, landed on the marquee." He chopped his palm with the side of his hand. "Cops say she got tossed from the roof." He pointed upward.

"I know," I said. "I saw her from my aunt's office right before you called. All twisted up."

"You saw?" He was annoyed at being scooped. "This neighborhood's getting really bad, man, and that's one reason we moved." Except for some Pinkerton guards playing checkers and a few sleepy vagrants, the Automat was oddly empty for lunch hour, and we took our sandwiches straight to a table.

"You're not at the Dixie anymore?"

"No, didn't I tell you? I guess I haven't seen you in a while. I moved in with a sister on the east side, a half-sister actually. Very nice area, tree-lined streets, not like here."

"Did Jeanie and Joe move out too?"

"Yep, all of us." He stuffed a big roll of ham into his mouth.

"What about that office? Does he still own Hubert's?"

"How'd you know about that office?"

"Jeanie told me about it." I knew I'd made a mistake.

"What are you telling me?" he asked. "That my mother told you about that office? Why?"

"Yes," I said, getting in further, "she showed it to me."

"What the hell were you doing in Big Joe's? Oh, no," he said, pained, flopping his sandwich to his plate. "You fucked my mother? Not you too?" He said this last sentence to himself, head down.

"I didn't do anything with her," I said with great force, amazed how easily I lied when she was involved.

"Oh, forget it," he said. "It surprised me for a minute, that's all, you knowing about that office. A lot of things are bothering me lately. I actually miss it around here. Just look at these bums." He spread his hand toward the Pinkertons, the guy sleeping with his head on the *News*, the mongoloid swabbing the floor.

"Where did Jeanie and Big Joe go?"

"Big Joe is staying at a club downtown, sharing an office with a Jewish radio station. Jeanie is taking acting lessons, something like that. She wants to get into the Village scene, she told me, but she's still around."

"You quit Hubert's?"

"I got so sick of seeing those fucking freaks and the tourists. And I'm uptown now. You starting school soon?"

"Yeah, after Labor Day. Are you going back to Rhodes?"

"No, I'm going to a school in Switzerland. Some relatives chipped in. You should see the place—in the mountains, beautiful. You sleep on sheets they hang outside, in the Alps. They smell like snow." Nicky got coffees for both of us, and he joked with two old ladies as he waited. One pinched his cheek.

"So nothing happened with McBride?" I asked.

"Nothing at all. In fact he was very nice the next time I saw him." I accidentally poured too much cream in my coffee, and Nicky watched it turn light tan.

"I couldn't believe we let him walk right toward it," I said.

"We were in shock," he said. "It was shock that froze us. I can still see him heading for that door now."

"I ran into Lane by the wig place when I was waiting for you."

"Listen, I still feel rotten about springing that on you. I just didn't realize how much it would get to me. By the time I came back you left."

"I wasn't feeling too great myself, you know, and then I had to go home. At least you could be alone."

"At least you could go home," he said.

We left the Automat, and Nicky walked with me to Paramount. We were both quiet, and Nicky stopped at one of the junk-shop windows, pointing out a bronze statue of an exhausted Indian riding an exhausted horse whose nose almost touched the ground. "See that?" he said. "Called *The End of the Trail*. My uncle says it's America's greatest sculpture." A few minutes later we passed the Van Dyke, and he surged to life. "You know Mick, the guy who cooks there?"

"Yeah, with the warts."

"Right. Well, he hooked up with two runaway girls. One is absolutely gorgeous. The other's a dog."

"Where from?"

"From the place they ran away from!" he yelled. "Who knows!" We stood outside Paramount's brass doors, and the noon lunch group was returning and the one o'clocks were leaving. "I've gotta go," I said. "I'll be late. I don't know when I'll see you again."

"I might stop back, but if not, I'll send you a postcard from Switzerland." We shook hands, and I turned away. He pulled me by the elbow. "Wait a minute, I didn't finish about Mick," he said. "I told him, 'Mick,' I said, 'one of those girls is really beautiful.' And you know what he said?"

"What?"

"He said, get this, he said, 'But to be fair, Nicky, to be perfectly fair, I gotta fuck 'em both.'" And he laughed a forced laugh, long and wide. I watched him laugh. I watched him as if I was looking through the wrong end of a telescope and he was far away and getting smaller, in a room in a chalet on the tip of the Alps, a quiet room with shutters, a bed fragrant with pillows smelling of snow. Astounded that I didn't laugh, he laughed twice as hard, bending over and pounding his foot against the hot cement to summon hilarity, but the sound from the soft sole of his Hush Puppy was lost in the roar around him.

On my last day Linda took me to the Blue Ribbon, a German restaurant. I ordered Welsh rarebit, which turned out to be a cheese dish. I thought it had something to do with game, as I had seen Gail put it on the menu at Close Quarters. Linda complimented me on my successful summer and we had coffee and dessert, a treat. There was a triumphant air around her, and she pursed her lips as she spoke.

"You might consider working for Paramount and going to college at night. Plenty of executives went to night school."

"It's still a year away," I said.

"That's true, but I have some news for you. Paramount just took over Tanner, the photo company. We've been buying from them for years, and I know old Mr. Tanner. McBain says they always need people, and when you finish high school, you could have a job."

"Doing what?"

"Selling cameras and film. You'd be a salesman."

"I thought you wanted me to go to college."

"I did, but a chance like this might not come again."

"Do you think I could do it?"

"You'd be great with people. I know. I see a lot of salesmen. And remember," she said, "nobody knows you like I do. You can do it." She continued, "I know men. I went with Mac for four years."

"I don't have to decide now, do I? I have my whole senior year."

"There's time," she said, smiling. "And I'm thinking of getting my own place in Manhattan."

"You are? Where?"

"Just thinking about it, that's all. A long way off, probably."

There was a clear link between the job and her apartment. Like me, she was tired of Queens, the leering men on street corners and the barren weekends limited to church events and errands. If I lived alone with her, would she stop hiding her clipped pages? Would there be no secrets between us?

"Did you see the last copy of *Paramount World*?" she asked, taking it out of her bag and opening it to "Home Office News." She read, "'We will be sorry to see John Skoyles leaving our mailroom and reception desk duties. His agility and willingness to please should carry him far in whatever field he chooses.' Isn't that great? Keep that so they'll remember you when you apply for a job later."

For the first time, the waiter placed the check by my plate. "See," Linda said. "You have the look of a man now, a man taking a woman to lunch." We walked toward Paramount, and she took my elbow, crushing my forearm to her breast. At an excavation site where thick girders emerged from a foundation, Linda said, "Remember, your grandfather was a builder, like them." She tossed her head to the side. "They kill themselves making the city tall, and then the rich move in and look down on them."

Linda continued talking, but I didn't hear her because I saw Jeanie ahead of us, standing in the doorway of a discount electronics store. Even though she had dyed her hair a reddish auburn, there was no mistaking her this time, and I recognized her skimpy blue shorts. A big man in a dark suit stopped to talk to her, bowing down and rising up. He was giving a sermon! I walked on the outside, gazing over Linda's padded shoulder, which seemed to jerk even more quickly than at her usual fast pace. When we drew even, I glanced at Jeanie. A bunch of teens from the suburbs tumbled past us, and I heard her voice. For a split second I thought she addressed me, but then her words became clear. In a matter-of-fact tone, she said, "I'll fuck any, nigger or white." Linda didn't turn—perhaps she didn't hear. She always marched straight ahead as she'd taught me to do, as if stuffed with cotton. I thought that maybe Jeanie was joking, teasing the crowd. I repeated her words to myself. I couldn't believe that she'd say "nigger," that she'd fuck anyone on that littered, sticky street. I looked back, and she still swayed there, bobbing her head out of the doorway, saying the last words I would hear from her.

When I returned from lunch, messengers were crowding the reception desk, and Beardsley said, "It's all set for tonight. We're having an end-of-summer party, and everyone's coming. And it's like a going-away party for you. You've got to be there." Mario, who never left his post, smiled shyly.

"Are you coming?" I asked him.

"No," he said. "Goodbye." I shook his hand. He started to say something but stopped.

"It was good knowing you, Mario," I said, to put him at ease.

He shuffled, looked down. "When you were in the mailroom, did you ever wonder if shit could heat this building?"

Beardsley arched and said, "I think your disgusting thoughts could heat this building."

"You know, I bet sex thoughts, dirty thoughts, could heat a room," Ruben said.

"Oh, yeah," Beardsley said, "once they learn how to harness them."

I told Linda I wouldn't be leaving with her. I called my mother. The party appealed to me. For three months I had sorted my way through the simmering Times Square streets, and I longed to see Forty-Second Street at night. I was ready to dally around town, just to watch everyone rush by as I had done all day. I was nervous about being with Beardsley after hours, but the idea that Carberry would be there gave me consolation. Carberry, another summer employee, was a college student and nephew of Charlton Heston. He read and reread *Inside Africa* and had his sights set on an eventual ambassadorship. He always wore a bush jacket festooned with epaulets, pockets, and belts. Even though he was a little older, I would not be the only schoolboy. I imagined Kerouac joining the party without a second thought. A few secretaries stopped to talk on their way out, and I missed walking to the Metropole with everyone else. I ran into Beardsley on the elevator. He left late every night, because he washed up obsessively in the men's room. Beardsley's face, freshly splashed, gleamed with his bright scar. By the time we got to the club, the droplets along his shirt and collar had dried, but the raw furrow still burnished his cheek. He saw me looking and said, "A dab of Vaseline really makes it shine."

The Metropole's barker, whose one step toward the sidewalk had frightened me away earlier in the summer when I tried to peek from behind the painted line in moments stolen from an uptown trip, now smiled and squeezed my shoulder as he patted me past. The darkness surprised me, and Beardsley moaned and shielded his eyes as we entered. Three girls danced topless along the bar. The marquee said, "Mongo Santa Maria," but it was early, 5:45, and a house band played. Ruben and Carberry slumped in a round booth with two secretaries from advertising, Nancy and Lucia.

"I'm paying for everyone's drinks," Beardsley said, "but they have to drink what I order." Ruben got a Stumplifter, which Beardsley instructed the waiter how to make. My drink was a kindly Seven and Seven. Lucia had been complaining about her size, four feet eight, and that nobody wanted to go out with her.

"Some men like 'em petite," Nancy said. "Right, Beardsley? Don't some men like 'em petite?"

"This place is some dump," Ruben said to me as he looked around and shook his head at the foggy mirror behind the bar, the ruby velveteen wallpaper, and the men in cheap suits twirling on stools.

"They say, 'Good things in small packages.' Did you ever hear that one, Lucia?" Beardsley asked. Lucia looked depressed. "I'll never be like one of them," she said, nodding over to the dancers.

"Looks aren't everything," Beardsley said. Lucia stared at him, his face riven triangularly by its polished scar, and she burst into tears and ran out the door. "Lucia, Lucia," we called, but she was gone. Nancy fumbled in her purse, but Beardsley said, "Go on, I got it." And she left.

"Now we can really watch action," Beardsley said, gazing over at the swaying women on the bar and settling into the deep booth. After another drink we stopped at Ray's Pizza and lined up at the counter with slices hanging from our fingertips. I had had two Seven and Sevens and looked around as the evening settled, the garish lights lovely in the dusk. They had not yet become a glaring, dominant force of the night, when night seems there merely to fill in the gaps between them.

"Let's get on with this wingding," Beardsley said, and he led us to Forty-Third Street, past Paramount's brass doors. I thought of my

Aunt Linda riding home earlier, alone on the E train, and I wished the party hadn't been on the last day. I'd wanted to walk home with her. She had told my mother she was going to miss me.

Beardsley's old landlady was on her way out as we walked up the brownstone's steps. Hunched and toothless, she spoke in a brogue. "You boys behave," she ordered, and then she grabbed Beardsley by the arm. "I'm still waiting for you to replace those vanilla wafers." Beardsley's room was plastered with centerfolds and posters from Paramount, which he had autographed himself. On a photo of Olivia de Havilland trapped in an elevator in *Lady in a Cage*, he had written, "Beardsley, Let me out!" Sophia Loren, lying on a couch in a royal outfit, signed her portrait, "To my King, Your Queen." Beardsley opened the tall refrigerator to show us the quart bottles of Budweiser filling its shelves. Ruben threw himself on the bed, which was covered with bags of chips and pretzels. "I snuck out for supplies this afternoon, when Gates sent me to McGraw-Hill," Beardsley said. I found the communal bathroom. Layers of wet newspapers stuck to the floor. The six sinks were thick with slime, and the shower curtains, soiled and stiff, hung like steel drapes. Two refrigerators hummed in a corner, and on the card table four hot plates were ringed with what looked like boiled-over chicken-noodle soup. A cat box near the urinals writhed with worms. I imagined Beardsley combing his long hair in the mirror each morning, and I combed mine.

We picked up the beer, and Beardsley stuffed Carberry's many pockets with chips and pretzels from the open bags. I stopped by the foyer on the first floor, looking at the white wicker couch and chairs. Clocks of all kinds hung on the walls, and a caged gerbil ran in a wheel. "No," Beardsley said. "It's the old lady's—it's where she waits when someone's out late. We have the lounge."

The lounge turned out to be the basement, a dark space with tiny shoe-box-sized windows at the top of its cement walls. It was a large room, filled with beach furniture. In the center stood an ancient pool table, its base bolstered by stacked magazines and, next to it, a Ping-Pong table that looked as if it had been hacked by a machete. It had a Hubert's aura around it. Beardsley walked in aggressively, a proud host, and turned on huge fluorescent ceiling lights. Roaches and water bugs scattered. Another boarder, Johnny Link, sat at a card table, shuffling cards under a desk lamp. He had been there alone, in the near dark.

"Forget the solitaire, Link, it's party time," Beardsley yelled, dropping two bags onto the pool table.

"It's not solitaire," Link said, clearly annoyed. "Yesterday I invented a card game for three, and today I invented a card game for four."

"Heave ho!" Beardsley called, and threw a beer to him.

We unloaded the six-packs onto the tables and sat around drinking. I couldn't stop staring at Link's eyes: one blue iris and one black. After a few beers he left, and I asked Beardsley about him. "A piece of broomstick went in there last year," he said, touching his own eye socket.

Beardsley left for cigarettes, and Ruben said, "I bet he brings back some girls." I looked over to Carberry to see if this unsettled him as much as it did me, but he was already in an alcoholic haze. His curly hair became wilder in the humid basement, and the pyramid of his pompadour had exploded at its crest, fine hairs blowing free of its stiff wave. He strolled around the room checking the asbestos-covered ceiling pipes for spiders, holding a beer and eating chips from a pocket stained with grease.

Johnny Link stuck his head down into the basement. "She's gone, Beardsley, I'm sure of it," he called.

"Beardsley isn't here," Ruben said. "He'll be right back."

"Well, you guys are welcome, if you want. It's more comfortable."

Upstairs, Link sat in a wicker armchair in the landlady's foyer, leaning over the glass-topped coffee table. He had changed his clothes and wore a lime-green polyester suit, thin white nylon socks, and black loafers. His hair was wet from the shower, and he smelled very sweet. He pointed to some red capsules. "This is chocolate mescaline," he said. "I just cut it with cocoa, hence the name. And here's some speed, which you guys need after a hard day's work." He pointed to a shot glass half full of powder.

"I'm too drunk," I said.

"Friend," he said, lilting toward me, "it'll only make you more aware of where you already are." The blue eye did not focus.

We all snorted, and I became aware I was losing a grip on myself.

Carberry took the gerbil out of its tank and scratched its head.

"Watch me give Lucky some speed," Link said.

"Oh, come on," Ruben said. "Leave it alone."

"You know," Link said, "I'd like to have a little guy like you around, just so I could click my pen on the top of your head." He took a ballpoint from his shirt pocket and tried to bounce it off Ruben's skull.

"Is that the old lady's pet?" I asked.

"Fuck her," Link said. "For what she charges, we should put her through some shit."

Carberry held the gerbil by the tail while it made what looked like efforts to fly. Link licked his finger, dipped it into the pile of methedrine, and dabbed the gerbil's nose gently. Its squeak startled Carberry, who let it drop.

"You dumb shit," Link said.

The gerbil hit the floor and scrambled up Ruben's leg as he fluttered his pants wildly. It ran up his back and over the top of his head, where it took a great leap at a drape, slid to the rug, and dashed between Carberry's legs. Carberry tried to avoid stepping on it and tumbled to the floor, bringing the coffee table and piles of pills and powder with him.

"Christ! Close the doors," Link yelled, and Ruben deftly drew the French doors together, sealing us in. I helped Link slide the heavy glass from the coffee table into its frame and collect his drugs. "Under the sofa," Link said. He pulled it away from the wall, and the gerbil shot past. "Move all the furniture to the middle and watch the lamps, Dickfingers," Link said to Carberry, who was brushing himself off.

"Here, Lucky," Link called. "Here, Lucky."

The gerbil stood on its hind legs against the wall, puzzled. Link moved forward, but the gerbil zipped around the perimeter. "He'll get tired soon," Link said. We stood holding beers as the gerbil kept running in absurd and frantic angles, until Link grabbed a lampshade, slammed it down, and trapped Lucky. But this only gave him a smaller circumference to navigate, which he did faster and faster. Link dipped his hand in then quickly drew it out. "Jesus!" he yelled, and stepped back, shaking his finger. Four heads bent over the lampshade and watched Lucky, who stopped suddenly with a little somersault.

"Put him in the tank and she'll never know what happened," Carberry said.

"Yeah," Link said, holding Lucky's neck between his thumb and index finger and looking into his wide eyes.

We moved the furniture and returned to the lounge. The front door opened, and we heard Beardsley's voice and heavy footfalls as he walked down the stairs followed by two women. Link ran right up to Beardsley and happily described Lucky's fate, ending the story with the words, "Dead as a fuck!" Beardsley smiled politely, put his hand on Link's shoulder, and pushed him aside as he introduced us to Margot and Venus, both dressed in hot pants and bikini tops. Each carried a big purse on her shoulder, and Margot wore fishnet stockings punctured with large holes. Their bodies were so pushed out by their clothes that they looked more costumed than provocative. They towered over us as we sagged in the beach chairs. It was hard to look at them and hard not to look at them too.

"This the party?" Venus asked incredulously.

In answer, Beardsley ran to the pool table and turned up the radio, as if hoping the blare would take away the cellar's cracked and gritty concrete floors, the cobwebbed pipes, the beach furniture, and the trails of broken chips and pretzels around the hacked-up Ping-Pong table. "Have a beer," he said, opening several. Venus, whose blonde hair hung straight over her face and who caught me staring at her, walked over and said, "Let the walls come down for you, man."

The women paired off quickly with Beardsley and Link and went upstairs. Carberry and I were sitting on the pool table, begging Ruben to change the station, when Beardsley yelled from the top of the stairs, "Guys! Yoo-hoo! Get up here fast! Margot's gonna dance!"

Ruben stayed put. "I'm not getting involved in that shit," he said, but Carberry got out of his chaise lounge and shrugged. "What the hell," he said, and we left together.

Beardsley gently shut the door to the landlady's parlor, closing us in. It was the first careful thing I'd seen him do. He drank from a small bottle of gin. Margot, in a far corner, gyrated, head down and eyes closed, to music from a big plastic radio on top of Lucky's tank. Lucky lay headfirst in his water dish, where Link had placed him. Margot wore only panties, and her tiny breasts barely moved as she bobbed around. Without her clothes she seemed smaller and older. Beardsley smiled like an impresario, and Carberry and I looked at each other and then at Margot shifting gears to the music. She rocked back and forth like she rode a horse, her fists in front of her, holding invisible reins. At the end of the song, when the loud bell rang and the disc jockey announced the "WABC Chime Time: 9:01," Beardsley insisted we get on the floor, our backs against the couch. We sat together, shoulder to shoulder, squirming to avoid touching each other as Margot moved alone across the room. While the disc jockey's voice boomed out an ad for Palisades Amusement Park, Beardsley reached over and pulled the glass coffee table against our chests like a tray, and Margot hopped up. She danced six inches from our faces, our eyes level with her shins. I strained away from Carberry.

"Lie down," Beardsley said. It took me a moment to realize he was talking to us. He slid under the table, flushed and serious. Carberry and I wriggled with him, staring through the bottom of the glass at Margot, who continued to dance. Delicately and rhythmically, she slipped off her panties, leaned to the right and the left. She did a short squat thrust and a push-up. I could hear Beardsley giggling or gurgling. Margot knelt on one knee and moved in a slow circle above our three pimply faces. Then she was gone, out the door. We pushed the table away, clumsily, bumping into each other as we got up. I had a sudden panic that I'd lost the key to my house, and I grabbed my pockets until I fingered the metal through the thin cotton. Beardsley broke the tension, saying, "That was on me." An unintended pun, a strange sequel to the Pollock movie. Then he ran after Margot. I noticed how loudly the clocks were ticking, even with the radio on. Carberry and I went to the basement without speaking. Ruben was slumped in the recliner and said, "Let's get out of here and go to the Merry Go Round."

"What about Beardsley?" I asked.

"He gave Margot what was left of his paycheck. He'll be busy for a while."

It was ten o'clock, and I was anxious to get home. "I think I'll just go," I said.

"Let's just have one quiet beer," Ruben said, taking me by the elbow. "The Merry Go Round is decent, and we could use some quiet."

Outside, I said, "I really would like to say good-bye to Beardsley. Who knows when I'll see him again?"

"Then go up to his room," Ruben said. "We'll wait here."

Link chased Venus down the stairs. She was in a huff, and he waved a small brass trophy of a man heaving a shot put. "Any place on Eighth Avenue would give twenty bucks for it," he called, but she went right out the door. There was no one in Beardsley's room, and I was surprised by my disappointment. I felt I owed him something and hoped to buy him a drink. I scrawled a message about the Merry Go Round on a gum wrapper and tucked it into the door jamb. I felt sober as I walked out. Men and women gathered on every stoop to escape the heat, and some boys my age threw a ball against the brick wall. The heavy sodium vapor lights illuminated the whole block. "I left a note," I said to Ruben, and he looked at me, annoyed. Carberry seemed too drunk to care.

The Merry Go Round's bar was an oval in the center of the room—an oval so long that it seemed straight. Carousel horses jutted out from the walls, and a circus-top canopy hung over the bar. It was quiet, with jazz playing on the jukebox and the talk hushed. We were the only whites, and we sat in a booth in the back, talking about the summer. Ruben brought a pitcher of beer. After twenty minutes Beardsley appeared, totally drunk. Ruben was right; I shouldn't have invited him. He couldn't find a chair, so he wheeled over a barstool, at the same time ordering a double shot of bourbon. From the stool he looked down on us, eyes half-closed.

"Margot is the greatest," he said. "You guys don't know what you're missing." White flecks of saliva dotted his lower lip as he tried to get the words out. Ruben got up and we said our good-byes, so Carberry and I sat alone, hovered over by Beardsley, who was falling asleep and tilting on the stool. A black man with gray hair and a light double-breasted suit approached. He put a thin box on the table and said, "I thought one of you gentlemen might be interested in this." He lifted the lid so that a set of steak knives gleamed on red velvet. The regal color caught Carberry's eye, and he immediately asked the price.

"Ten dollars."

"Are they sharp?" I asked.

"Watch," he said, and took a nail and a slender hammer from his inside pocket and drove the point into our table. Then he sawed across the upright nail with one of the knives. As the blade went back and forth, Carberry and I watched, our chins facing each other across the table. The nail came cleanly in half. The man blew on the blade and then replaced it in its slot. "Think of how that can slice a tomato," he said. Bewildered by the comparison, Carberry asked, "Are tomatoes that tough to cut?"

The man said, "Who wants a set?" I thought of Linda giving the guy at the newsstand a quarter for my button, and I said, "How about ten dollars for two sets?" Without hesitating the man agreed, and we took out our bills. I thought what a great gift it would be for my mother, better than the usual half-pound of Barton's Almond Bark I brought home on payday.

Around midnight, Beardsley toppled off the barstool, hit the floor, and wouldn't get up. I dragged the stool to the bar, and Carberry and I tugged at his thick shoulders, but he smiled as if he were going to sleep. We finally got him into a sitting position, and he looked at us and said, "Fuck you both, you two miserable mail boys," and he tried to spit. His failure to project saliva only inspired him, and he continued until he soaked the front of his shirt with an ascot-sized stain. Kneeling next to him, I felt a huge hand on my shoulder. When I turned, the bouncer said tenderly but with power, "Get the animal out of here, darling."

"Just give him a few minutes to sober up," I said, and he nodded. We got Beardsley to his feet and unloaded him into the booth. The bouncer brought a cup of coffee. Carberry and I played a game of pinball, but when we returned, we saw Beardsley had smashed his watch on the table and was sawing a shard of the broken crystal across the veins on his wrists. Carberry grabbed the splinter from his fingers, away from the mild scratches.

"I loved my parents," Beardsley said. "My parents were never without a rubber band thanks to all the rubber bands I stole from the rubber-band factory." Then he whispered, "Take me to my car," and rose up. Carberry and I held him by the armpits.

"You have a car, Beardsley?" I asked, but he kept leading us.

Carberry said, "We can't let him drive like this." He paused. "But I don't want to take him home. The landlady's probably there, coming home to a pile of shit and her dead pet."

"Maybe we can just put him in the back seat," I said.

The Merry Go Round's rear door opened into a dark lot, and Beardsley stood there, wheezing. Vehicles were parked against a fence, their trunks facing us. We walked Beardsley from car to car as he bent over their taillights, patting them, feeling the fins and bumpers. At the rear of a Falcon, he circled the round, red light with his finger and said, "Here."

"We can't put him in the car," I said, but Beardsley bulled ahead, pulling us along the passenger side, and I opened the front door. Inside, the radio played softly and a woman with a beehive hairdo turned toward us from the steering wheel, putting out a cigarette in the ashtray.

"Hi, Beardsley," she said, smiling, and Beardsley thudded in. I stuck my head into the car, farther than I should have, and the woman stared at me questioningly. In that moment I heard Long John on the radio saying, "I have with me tonight three furriers . . ." She started the ignition.

Carberry and I sat at the bar for a final beer. Fatigue, alcohol, and the thrill of sitting in Times Square made me maudlin. I developed a tremendous affection for Carberry, and we wished each other the best in the coming school year. When we finished, we embraced, before tucking our boxes of knives under our arms and leaving.

But we couldn't find the way out. We walked into the men's room, the manager's office, and then tried the handle on a broom closet. The room seemed to have changed since we joined the crowd at the bar. When laughter came our way, I refused to turn toward the voices, but my effort to stay cool made me self-conscious and I dropped my knives. Carberry helped me as I laid the case on the jukebox, fitting the blades into their velvet slots. Finally we saw the exit and, outside, we realized that the bar, like the carousel it was named for, revolved constantly, but so slowly that you didn't know it until you got off.

In the spring I received a letter from Wesleyan, hinting at deficits in my application but suggesting that an interview might compensate. My mother asked Tom Peck to drive me to Connecticut, and Linda wanted to go along. I put my blue suit aside when I discovered *Esquire*'s college issue, where men in madras poised their wing tips on the bumpers of Ferraris. I saw my wilted jacket blending in perfectly with the college crowd and tried to revive it by spraying my mother's plant mister across its orange and brown squares, as I had seen Fred do. I hung it from the shower curtain, where it only seemed to withdraw further into itself, the lapels curling up like autumn leaves and murky drops of dye running from its hem into the bathtub. I had better luck with my tie, the one with the Hawaiian god, which my mother pressed evenly.

Linda had not forgotten that Long John Nebel had put the idea of Wesleyan into my head, and she called Fred. Fred told her that Nebel's friend, Al Sadler, would be there to escort me to the admissions office. I had often heard Mr. Sadler on the show. He had a weak, whining voice that reiterated points Nebel already made, and I remembered exactly how Nebel introduced him. After giving the biographies of the more celebrated guests, Nebel would say, "And among our panelists tonight is Mr. Al Sadler, raconteur and world traveler." His producer would sometimes add, with a chuckle, "And Chinese cuisine maven."

I stepped toward Tom's car, and my aunt gripped me by the shoulders, saying, "You look like college material!" She insisted I ride up front, the unfolded map in my lap.

I expected a campus filled with *Esquire* models, but most walked barefoot, in beards and jeans. It was a beautiful afternoon, unseasonably warm, and students lounged at the roots of ancient oaks, talking and reading. The girls wore tights and had long, straight hair. Tom preferred to wait in the car, while Linda walked with what I thought was great pride but turned out to be scorn for the disheveled students I was falling in love with. I entered the glass doors of the administration building and cringed at my reflection, a parody of the college issue. Fred had told me to recognize Sadler by his bald head, long sideburns, and drooping mustache.

Linda and I sat in a room with other hopefuls, and every time the door opened, we looked up. Linda read the new *Paramount World* and handed me an article reporting that Jan, of Jan and Dean, had sustained serious brain damage when he crashed his Corvette, just like in their song, "Dead Man's Curve." The notice tried to sound upbeat, announcing that Elvis would take his place in the feature *Easy Come Easy Go*, playing a singing, treasure-hunting frogman.

At 9:30, the appointed time, my name was called and I went in alone.

The admissions officer had shaggy hair and wore a blue shirt and chinos like mine. But he didn't look like me. He struck me as handsome, his straight features open and calm. His blue oxford collar was unbuttoned, and he had a commanding air even though he was casual. He was impressed that I wrote poetry and knew the work of their poet-in-residence, Richard Wilbur.

My file lay on the green blotter before him, turned to the five-hundred-word essay I had struggled with in late January. I had delayed filling out the paperwork until a few days before the February deadline, when I cleared our glass-topped table of my mother's wires, spools, and Styrofoam and looked over the brochures and applications. I cut my finger plucking a place in the glass where I had chipped it with a Ping-Pong paddle. Every few minutes I got up and swirled a pencil around the aquarium, chasing a swordtail from the black mollie babies. I leaned back in my chair until it rested against the chest of drawers behind me. At this forty-five-degree angle, I closed my eyes and pretended I was falling backward. After a few seconds of being suspended, I began to swoon, and when I felt completely dizzy, I slammed the chair right with wonderful relief.

I longed for Wesleyan, but my guidance counselor, Brother Ryan, mentioned Fairfield University and Stonehill, the funeral director's recommendation. Brother Ryan said of Stonehill, "Not a place for brain banks, and a lousy sports school, but an oasis from city life." I asked him why he thought I might like it, and he reprimanded me, saying, "I am not a soothsayer!" I didn't apply to Stonehill, because it was recommended by the funeral director, and I couldn't shake the idea that it was a training ground for morticians, a notion confirmed by its name. After leaving Brother Ryan's office, I looked up *soothsayer* and stumbled on *sophistication*. *Sophistication*. The word my mother used to categorize Fred, the quality I prized. I was shocked by *the employment of reasoning that is superficially plausible but actually fallacious*. How was Fred sophisticated in that sense, and why would I want my reasoning to be false? I read further: *worldly-wise, knowing*. There was more: *insouciance*. Not caring what other people thought. So I concluded that my true indifference to what stirred my classmates (the smoking room for seniors, Julie Barrow getting pregnant, the discovery of malt liquor) was really sophistication. And if my line of reasoning was flawed, well, wouldn't that be sophisticated of me as well?

I liked the secular name of Fairfield University, sounding like a state school even though it was run by Jesuits. The catalog listed Billy Taylor, jazz pianist and disc jockey on WLIB, as an advisor, so I applied there as well as to nearby Queens College, though the idea of coming home each night made me squirm, because I wanted to be free of Linda as I was free of Fred. What I really wanted was to be free of the boy who desired Linda so badly and who watched himself from above.

I had no trouble filling out the brief forms for Fairfield and Queens, but the application from Wesleyan, a thick bond bearing a big red shield with a fleur-de-lis, immediately threw me. It asked for a five-hundred-word autobiography, which I started over and over. Finally I hit my stride, putting in that I liked to go to Greenwich Village to attend poetry readings; how I enjoyed the paintings of Walter Keane and had a framed reproduction of one of his little girls with big eyes; that I listened to a poetry program on Sunday mornings called "Hyacinths and Biscuits"; that I'd outgrown Murray the K's rock 'n' roll and now tuned to Charles Duvall, a disc jockey with a French accent who played easy-listening music; that I loved New York's great museums, especially Ripley's Believe It or Not Odditorium and Hubert's Freak Museum and Congress of Strange People; that I had broadened my interest in science by listening to Long John Nebel's late-night talk show, where I heard a man who had invented a ruler that measured from the middle, so that imperfections in measurement on the right would be corrected by imperfections on the left.

And I wrote that I had no hobbies, a truth that stunned me into rewriting the essay.

I lied that I had a stamp and a coin collection but that my real hobby was drawing. I tried to make myself into a civic model with an artistic dimension and came up with what I thought was the perfect combination of art and life. With a feeling of triumph, a feeling so truly false I become emotional over inventing it, I wrote that I could draw portraits of all the presidents and my specialty was Thomas Jefferson's profile. I showed it to my mother, who said, "You can't send that, it's not true. But do you think that would be a good project for me?" Linda said simply, "Suppose they ask you to draw one?" The next day she brought home a book called, *How to be Accepted by the College of Your Choice*, and I imitated the tone of the sample essays: cheery yet earnest, modest but self-confident.

I was certain my first sentence was a winner: *Our small family has always been a happy one.*

And I continued in that vein:

I felt that high school was one of the most rewarding experiences of my life. Since our school was not in the vicinity of our home, I was able to make many new friends. Fact: I was rejected by the local Catholic high school and had to travel by subway one hour each way to a lousy neighborhood in Astoria. The trip involved harassment by upperclassmen, including having my book bag tossed onto the tracks.

Academically, I enjoyed English very much. This year I was selected to the advanced English class, where I was one of a small group. This class was a type of seminar in which we discussed literary works, and I enjoyed it immensely. Fact: My English teacher from junior year insisted I be admitted to this class, a clique of all the honor students who had been together the previous three years. The teacher was a brother who gestured wildly with his wrists. An oval medallion of the Blessed Virgin

228

dangled from his watch, making a constant clinking noise I always think of when I hear the words, "honor student."

Throughout school I had a full schedule requiring a good deal of hard work, which was satisfying to me because of the knowledge I gained. Fact: The screwy syntax of this sentence meant to disguise the fact that I'd taken some phrases in it right from the book.

I am now a candidate for the National Honor Society, but I have not, as yet, heard the results. Fact: And just as well, because I would not have been able to associate myself with the society if I had.

The opportunities for extracurricular activities were many, and I was a member of the Yearbook Writing Staff, the Young Christian Students, and the Debating Team. Fact: I wrote four captions for the yearbook; joined the Christian students because a pretty girl member was reported to be a Communist; served only as a timekeeper for the debate team.

This past summer I worked at Paramount Pictures, 1501 Broadway, New York City, full-time. Fact: The word *Broadway* thrilled me, and I hoped it would thrill them too.

My main interest is reading poetry and novels. Fact: The only true line in the essay.

I have written a few poems for my own enjoyment, although in my sophomore year I wrote a poem that was included in a leaflet distributed to the English classes. Fact: Along with everyone else who put pen to paper.

I have chosen Wesleyan University, since I deeply feel it is the one college that will surely help me achieve my goals. Aside from its academic qualities, I am looking forward to participating in the many extracurricular activities which Wesleyan offers. Fact: I hoped they would be impressed by the sound of their own name.

Faking the essay made me want to avoid college; I couldn't keep up that pretension for four years. I envied my friend Cooney, who knew his future: straight to the police academy and then the force. I still dreamed that Fred would call and ask me to live with him. I dreamed Linda moved away and left me alone. I dreamed I married Jeanie and she got small parts in movies and we were very happy. I did nothing but dream, and now I sat before an admissions officer who would spot me as a dreamer as he licked his forefinger and turned the pages of my crazy essay.

He asked what books I'd read recently, and I said, *Lord of the Flies*. "Would you call Golding a determinist?" he asked. I had no idea what a determinist was and thought maybe it meant he was determined to become a novelist. He tried to help, asking, "Do you think he believes in free will?" I recalled the violence on the island as I stared past him, out his window and into the branches.

"On the one hand, you could say he does," I said. "And on the other hand, you could say he doesn't."

He dropped a long blue arm down to his desert boot and brushed at a mar on the suede.

"What did you think of the epilogue?" he asked.

"I didn't read the epilogue," I admitted, "because I borrowed the book from a friend and had to return it."

"The epilogue says the ship saved the boys from the island, but who will save the boys from the ship?" He stood up and held out his hand.

I told Linda about our discussion when we stopped in Bridgeport at a diner called "Shangri-La." She didn't mention Mr. Sadler. Tom was excited by the machines in the men's room and his purchase there. While we sat in the booth, he chased a plastic white scottie around the pepper shaker with a black one, propelled by magnets. Linda said, "That was kind of a kooky place—maybe you should wait a while before taking this big step." She hinted again that she might move to Manhattan and that I was welcome. I was distraught over my answer to the administrator's question, and that I hadn't read the epilogue because I had borrowed Arty Leed's book. But that feeling passed. I was excited simply by having walked on a college campus, and the hamburgers were good in Shangri-La.

I waited all spring to hear from Wesleyan. Fred hadn't called, and I painfully reviewed my conduct in his company: the ill-timed outbreak of hives, my reluctance to meet Roy Eldridge, the failure to impress Madeline, my ignorance of the facts of life. I knew Fred's luck had turned bad and my presence only reminded him of better times. Linda couldn't stand the mention of Fred, since Mr. Sadler hadn't shown up. She didn't even call him to complain. She dumped that broken deal in the same heap with Fred's sick cherry trees, slow watches, and unpaid twenties.

230

The letters from Queens and Wesleyan arrived on a Saturday morning along with *The New Yorker*, the cover a fat goose wearing a pith helmet. Linda sat in the kitchen with my mother, while I took the mail into the dining room. Before opening the envelopes at the table, I looked into the aquarium and guessed I'd be doing homework in front of that teeming tank for another four years, madly creeping downstairs to spy on Linda. I tore open an acceptance from Queens, and I pictured myself on the bus that ran to the nearby Flushing campus, past Flushing hospital, where I was born. *Flushing.* The word itself deadened my heart. *Flushing.* A kind of blushing. The act of violently purging. My mother never tired of repeating the old joke: What are the two greatest feats of man? Flushing Long Island and Wheeling West Virginia.

"Got into Queens," I yelled.

"That's great, Johnny," my mother called, and my aunt said, "Congratulations."

Wesleyan's coat of arms blazed on the watermarked stock, and I had difficulty ripping the envelope. The last sentence read, "Perhaps future events will show our decision to be shortsighted." In the kitchen my aunt said, "Remember, many of the top men at Paramount went to night school. And you're half-Italian, that didn't help." My mother was not upset. She wanted me home. Linda looked at the letter, and I could see she was impressed by the weight of the bond by the way she held it to the light. The letter was signed by Christopher C. Hoy, President. I thought immediately of a nonsense phrase used all the time by Long John Nebel to mean bullshit, and I said it to myself, "Wack-a-Ding-Hoy."

Suddenly Linda became angry. She said, "You didn't have a chance, and we wouldn't have gone through this if it wasn't for your uncle and his big friends. You still haven't heard from Fairfield, and at least you can count on Queens."

My mother said, "You can always stay here and go to Queens."

"There's still the job as a salesman for Tanner and night school," Linda said.

My mother mentioned that I could work with my father, a generous suggestion, since she would lose both of us to the road. "You could see the country," she said. "Dad says the nights out are amusing. He says great entertainers are going unappreciated, playing in every little town." She described different nightclub acts he had told her about, a one-man band; parrots on roller skates; barbershop quartets.

"You have plenty of options," Linda said. "Remember that."

Although Long John had let me down, I couldn't stop recalling the images of the Ivy League he'd painted when we first met: the secret clubs and neckties whose designs had meaning to those in the know.

I pinned all my hopes on Fairfield.

"There's some spaghetti and clams left over from last night," my mother said.

"Thanks," I said. She reheated my favorite dish in the kitchen while she sang, cheerfully and unconsciously, a song from the forties, "Bongo, Bongo, Bongo," about not leaving the Congo.

The discussions every day in my homeroom involved acceptances and rejections, and I still hadn't heard from Fairfield. I went to bed early each night, fatigued, remembering the guidance counselor's description of Fairfield's Japanese gardens. He said, "No graduate has yet distinguished himself, but you could be the one . . . they have a black swan there. I think that's the place, a pond at the foot of a hill. Well, they have swans there, even if the black one is gone."

One evening Linda called my name as I sat in my room tuning to stations below the 540 AM mark, a hobby I'd gotten from a pamphlet called *Secret Frequencies*. It made radio romantic, with a quote on the cover from David Sarnoff that read, "The richest man cannot buy for himself what the poorest man gets free by radio." A southern drawl came through the static, selling flypaper, a deluxe roll with adhesive so strong, the voice said, you could stretch it across a barn floor and catch rats, which the announcer pronounced, "ray-ettes." The pitch was good, and I wanted to send for it, but the long box number of the mailing address faded out. When I went downstairs, Linda stood by the dining-room table wearing her short bathrobe, hair wrapped in a towel. My close listening to the flypaper salesman, ear pressed to the transistor's speaker, had made me miss her running water. She held a tissue in one hand and pointed to the ceiling. "There's a big spider up there," she said. I saw the stool next to my grandmother's armchair. "Hold that steady, and I'll get it." She pretended to be concerned about the bug and looked at the dark beams seriously. I wanted to bend down and stare at Linda again, but I was sick of peeking. I was torn between getting what I wanted and my disappointment with so little of it. I moved quickly to the hall and came back with Tom Peck's long pole with the sponge on the end. I popped it at the ceiling, and the spider stuck. "It's from Tom," I said. "His father invented it."

Linda looked at the crushed speck and said, "I guess it works." She pinched the spider with the Kleenex, her face a confusion of annoyance and relief as I walked upstairs. I returned to my study of secret frequencies, half-concentrating on a description of devices that monitored conversations in police precincts. It was still early, hours away from Nebel. Dreary, sluggish, I dozed off, and when I woke, Linda stood by the side of my bed. She sipped a glass of white wine and placed it on the toy chest filled with underwear. I sat up, and she knelt between my knees, a reversal of our earlier positions. She was drunk and she lurched, grabbing the edge of my mattress to straighten herself. Then she took my hands in hers and brought her knuckles to my face. "Do you believe these?" she asked. "Do you believe these?" She began to sob, her chin pressing against her breastbone.

"Don't cry," I said. "Why are you crying?"

"You know why," she said, and picked up her glass and left. I heard her managing the stairs very slowly. I did know. I was tired of my lust for her, even as it raged. She felt I had spurned her as the only other man in her life, Mac, had spurned her. She felt rejected as well as guilty.

I decided to clean my room and piled my books and magazines into neat stacks. I placed my key, subway pass, and wallet in a straight line on the toy chest. Then I realized it looked like the top of my father's dresser. At the foot of the closet I found an old shoe box. I had left an apple there months back, an apple my mother brought me when I was packing Christmas lights to bring to the cellar, making the room livable. I had forgotten to eat it, leaving it in the shoebox of rabbit's feet, magnets, and marbles. I was surprised at how shriveled and fragrant it had become.

A few days later my mother sat in the living room, where she had set up two TV trays. Merv Griffin showed a clip of W. C. Fields describing his new girlfriend. He said, "She's half-elf and half-hummingbird. And so sensitive, she can eat only the white of an egg beaten up in a spoonful of cream with some grated sponge cake." My mother went to the kitchen, bringing back a box of chocolate snaps and glasses of milk along with the mail.

She handed me a big envelope from Fairfield, and the letter inside welcomed me to the incoming class, the masthead a huge profile of the college mascot, The Stag, with the school's full name circling its rack of antlers: Fairfield University of St. Robert Bellarmine. I ran down to borrow Linda's *Complete Lives of the Saints*. The book opened automatically to the well-worn chapters describing the penitent practices of St. Thomas à Kempis and Ignatius Loyola. Kempis and Loyola flagellated themselves regularly, and Linda had regularly turned to these pages. When I found Bellarmine, I was surprised that the university would have named itself after the chief persecutor of Galileo.

"Congratulations," my mother said. "I think you'll be happier there than at Wesleyan, with those characters Linda told me about."

My mother walked to the kitchen. I heard the oven opening and closing. When she returned, she said, "You're missing the chance with Tanner, but maybe it'll come again." She slapped a potholder near the aquarium, so that a school of tiger barbs flashed away, scared. "To think they live their whole lives in this tank," she said.

The night before I left for Fairfield, I lay in bed listening to Nebel from midnight till dawn, adjusting the tiny transistor, which I'd wrapped in wire from my train set and fastened to the radiator with an alligator clip. This homemade antenna boosted the signal just a bit. I was resigned to finagling with it, because I never bought the Trans-Oceanic. One Sunday I did go downtown to Nathan's for the big shortwave, but when I got there, I couldn't bring myself to part with the money. Instead, on my mother's advice, I put it into a Christmas Club at the Jamaica Savings Bank. Fred cursed when he heard this, as the account paid no interest.

Nebel's guests were particularly nutty. The mystic barber spoke in space language, and another guest claimed to have been transported to a world called Lemuria, where he found a crystal skull. When his trip was disparaged by the panelists, he remained unflappable, repeating, "I only know that I remember Lemuria." Nebel's theme song, "Forbidden Planet," signaled the show's end, and I got out of bed and watched light take over the room. I clicked the childish nautical lamp on my dresser. The little drawstring chain was attached to a ship's steering wheel, the shade an etching of the *Yankee Clipper* rolling over whitecaps. A few days before, my mother had talked about redoing the room. She smoothed her hand along the brown wallpaper, the pattern displaying my old friend, the rooster, peering over a fence, and she said, "I might get something a little less masculine."

In the morning I loaded Tom Peck's Chevelle with clothes, jars of bouillon cubes, blankets, a hot pot, and a box of sheets and towels from Linda's dowry. Everyone who walked by shook my hand, and a crowd of children watched. Tom leaned over the car's hood, studying the map printed on the inside of the Fairfield catalog. He wore a fresh tan Con Edison uniform, his name scripted over the breast pocket. He had thoughtfully parked right in front of our house, saving the space the day before with two huge official cones marked BUG, for Brooklyn Union Gas. My mother dressed in an outfit she had made from her own pattern. Blue and white, almost nautical, it made her look like she was the one starting a voyage. She held a handkerchief to her face and cried, while one of the women on the block, a fellow member of Monsignor Little's thespian club, tried to cheer her with imitations of Jack Benny and Rochester. Two little boys standing on the curb giggled and demanded, "Do Lambchop! Do Lambchop!" Tom lowered the map and turned to them, puzzled.

"I will," our neighbor said, looking over and trying to include him. "But first I have to tell Tom who he is."

Tom's head snapped back and his dim eyes widened as if he were about to learn something of tremendous significance. He leaned toward the woman and asked, "Who *am* I?"

She said, "Oh, you!" and began playing the parts of Shari Lewis and the cast. My mother started to cry again and said, "I love you, Johnny."

"I love you too, Mom," I said, and kissed her good-bye.

Linda pulled me away, and we stood together on the sidewalk under a big maple. She handed me a large package wrapped in brown paper. "This arrived today. From Fred," she said, and she gave me a long hug. "I'm glad you're getting those linens," she said. Then she whispered, "I'm glad you'll be the one using my things, instead of a man like Mac." As we looked at the crowd she talked incessantly, about the people on the block, Tom's polished car, my mother's outfit, filling in any lull in the conversation, as if we might vanish if she stopped. And then she stopped. And then I vanished.

Everyone waved as we pulled away, and Tom asked, looking into the rearview mirror, "Are you ever coming back?"

"Oh, yeah, I'll be home for the holidays," I said, but his question felt big, especially against the heartfelt noise of the tiny crowd's farewell. We cut through the marshy parts of Queens to the Grand Central Parkway near Shea Stadium. Mufflers, exhaust pipes, coils, and other gizmos filled the lanes, shaken loose by the frame-rattling craters and heaves. Abandoned cars lined the shoulders, more fossils than automobiles. When the Chevelle lurched, the pen Tom kept on the dash rolled to the floor. He groped around the gas pedal, putting it in exactly the same place, where it fell again and again.

As we approached the Whitestone Bridge, Tom talked about seeing Bob Hope movies where the college students wore raccoon coats and cheered through megaphones. I looked at him as he spoke, touched by his effort and by his taking the time to drive me. Slowly he began to frown, his mouth turning down, his eyes squinting at the road, and I spun my head toward the windshield, seeing, just as we were upon it, the carcass of a big dead dog, a German shepherd. Tom glanced left and right, but the cars on both sides made it impossible for him to swerve. We hit it dead on, the impact instantly converted to a rubbing sound as we dragged the body. Tom couldn't shake it loose no matter how hard he fishtailed and, after half a mile, he pulled over. The stiff legs were impaled into the exhaust system, as if trying to lift us from the ground, and we couldn't pry the paws free. The big dog's eyes were open and glazed like a statue's. I was afraid of missing the first orientation meeting. When the tow truck came, it hoisted us high and the driver yanked the dog down, cursing as he held the sides of its putrid chest. Kicking his way past a pile of oil filters, he said, "This boy's been dead a long time." He tossed the carcass off the shoulder, where it landed on an old box spring. As we got back onto 95, Tom said, "In those movies, they take something like that, a dead dog, and put it in a professor's office."

"I'm not ready for that yet," I said.

"I wouldn't want that in my trunk anyway," Tom said. "It might have a BM."

The stagnant black ruts along the Grand Central changed in Westport into ponds of clear blue water, and mallards replaced the worn tires that crowded the edges of the city's muck.

Students from the orientation committee met me at Loyola Dorm, wearing white sweatshirts with FU stitched in red on the front. They

236

quickly unpacked the car and took my bags and boxes to my room. Tom Peck stood by the Chevelle, eyeing the other freshmen, bluff boys in blazers toting golf bags and skis. Several of them stared at Tom's neatly pressed uniform. He ran two fingers down the sleeve of his starched shirt, smoothing the crease. I thanked him and we shook hands. He said he'd tell my mother and aunt that I arrived safely.

Fred's package contained two gifts. The first was a sweater, a soft blue angora. The second was an original painting by the black artist, the "kook" who painted in the bar. A still life of a long vase, a cup and saucer. But there was something else right in the middle of the canvas, just as Fred described it, hanging in the air—a big orange bowl. Floating. The paint was thick, the colors garish, almost rude. I pegged it as a cross between Keane and Pollock.

That first night, as I lay in bed after meetings and events where we wore freshman beanies and played egg-tossing games with taunting but good-natured upperclassmen, I thought about my mother doing puzzles, waiting for my father. And Linda below her, adding to her library of books and magazines on punishment, punishing herself. I hoped Tom cheered them with a description of the birds and lakes and left out running down the dead dog. Floodlights from the rooftops shone onto our spare cinderblock walls. My roommate from New Jersey, Ray, passed out under his new, rust-colored Indian blanket, which he had first considered hanging on the door, he was so taken with its geometric design. Like most freshmen, he was unable to resist the flowing kegs in the gym after dinner. Since it wasn't a novelty to me, I drank only a few beers and longed for the burnished feeling of stiff whiskey, a longing I didn't know then would become insatiable. I looked toward the closet, at the jacket from Delancey Street, the good shirt with the Brooks Brothers roll, and my suit. I pictured myself in the suit while I recited in class or arrived at mixers. A few minutes later I couldn't see myself on campus at all. I felt the awful confusion I'd once had in geometry class, when I found the trapezoid among a tangle of shapes and raised my hand. By the time the teacher called on me, I looked back at the page, but the shape had disappeared into the complex of lines.

Suddenly war whoops echoed through the corridors, and every door on the hall shook with the hammering fists of uproarious seniors commanding us outside. Ray left quickly, tugged from bed by his friends from Jersey. I decided to wear the luxuriant sweater, perfect for early fall.

An immense bonfire raged in the quadrangle, and we chanted the college rallying cry, *Stags are Tough*, as we faced the flames. I had never seen a fire so high and great, a fire ignited not for heat but to produce an indelible light. I stepped close, inspecting the logs and branches that flared and broke. Nearer, the gnarled stack felt charged, and I pressed my open palm toward its warmth. Then the refined hairs, the long silky strands of angora, curled and shriveled along my sleeves. I looked at my chest and, there too, the fabric dissolved, drifting sky-ward. I stepped back into the chorus of roaring Stags. No one in the sweltering romp noticed my predicament, and I flipped the sweater over my head just in time, as the flames stretched out and snapped Fred's gift into the air.